To the Memory of

Professor Leroy S. Rouner,
Director of the Institute (1975–2003),
in friendship and great appreciation

Deliver Us from Evil

Deliver Us from Evil

Edited by
M. David Eckel
Bradley L. Herling

Boston University Studies in
Philosophy and Religion

continuum

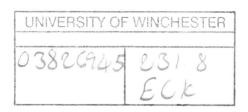
Continuum International Publishing Group

The Tower Building   80 Maiden Lane
11 York Road   Suite 704
London   New York
SE1 7NX   NY 10038

www.continuumbooks.com

British Library Cataloguing-in-Publication Data
A catalogue record for this book is available from the British Library.

ISBN: PB: 978-1-4411-0939-2

Library of Congress Cataloging-in-Publication Data
A catalog record for this book is available from the Library of Congress.

Typeset by Newgen Imaging Systems Pvt Ltd, Chennai, India
Printed and bound in Great Britain by the MPG Books Group

Contents

Preface

This volume in the Boston University Studies in Philosophy and Religion series is a joint project of the Boston University Institute for Philosophy and Religion and Continuum International Publishing Group. The essays collected here are the edited versions of lectures that were presented as part of a three-year study of the concept of "Evil" within the Institute. They represent the Institute's commitment to a lively, interdisciplinary exploration of central problems in society and human experience.

The Boston University Institute for Philosophy and Religion was begun informally in 1970 under the leadership of Professor Peter Bertocci of the Department of Philosophy, with the cooperation of Dean Walter Muelder of the School of Theology, Professor James Purvis of the Department of Religion, and Professor Marx Wartofsky, chair of the Department of Philosophy. Professor Bertocci set out to institutionalize one of the most creative features of "Boston Personalism," its interdisciplinary approach to fundamental issues of human life. When Professor Leroy S. Rouner became director in 1975, and the Institute became a formal part of the Boston University Graduate School, every effort was made to continue that vision of an ecumenical and interdisciplinary forum. After Professor Rouner retired in 2003, all of us in the community of the Institute have attempted to honor that legacy. This remarkable volume on "Evil" is one of the results.

By bridging many different disciplines in the university, the Institute is committed to an open interchange on fundamental human questions that transcend the narrow specializations of academic curricula. We seek to counter the trends in higher education that emphasize technical expertise and transform undergraduate liberal arts education into pre-professional training. At a time when too much academic writing is incomprehensible, irrelevant, or both, our goal is to present readable essays by acknowledged authorities on critical human issues.

As is true in all interdisciplinary, cooperative efforts, there are many individuals and institutions to thank for the final completion of this project. First and foremost, this volume would not have been possible without the authors themselves. We are grateful not only for their efforts to provide us with thoughtful and engaging essays, but also for their remarkable patience as this multi-year project wound slowly to its conclusion.

I am grateful to David Nichols and Shawn Arthur, whose assistance made the lecture series possible. Professor Bradley Herling deserves thanks not only for helping to organize the final year of the lecture series, during his appointment as Assistant Director of the Institute, but also for his editorial skill in melding the lectures and essays together into a lively and cogent volume. During the editorial process, it has been a great pleasure to work with Rebecca Vaughan-Williams at Continuum and P. Muralidharan at Newgen Imaging Systems. We are grateful that the Institute series has found such a welcome home.

Finally, we would like to express our thanks to the Graduate School of Arts and Sciences, the Humanities Foundation, the School of Theology, and the Core Curriculum at Boston University for the financial support that made this series possible. They have been generous patrons indeed.

Malcolm David Eckel
Director
Institute for Philosophy and Religion
Boston University

Introduction

Deliver Us from Evil

M. David Eckel
Boston University

and

Bradley L. Herling
Marymount Manhattan College

Romeo Dallaire, the commander of the United Nations peacekeeping force in Rwanda during the 1994 genocide, tells a harrowing tale about his meeting with leaders of the Interahamwe, the Hutu militia that did much of the killing. The genocide was underway, and Dallaire was not allowed to intervene militarily, so he decided to engage in the only tactic that remained: negotiation with the perpetrators. A meeting was arranged, and it began with handshakes. Dallaire noticed bloodstains on the hands of the militia leaders. The thought occurred to him: how many innocent people had these hands hacked to death? At that moment, Dallaire reports, something terrifying happened: "I was not talking with humans, I literally was talking with evil, personified. . . . I was totally overcome by the evil. These three guys just brought it into reality, brought evil into reality. . . . I was facing something that had to be destroyed."[1]

Dallaire's experience shows how difficult it is to face the worst of the worst. How do we put a name on the unspeakable miseries that befall us and our fellow human beings, sometimes at the hands of perpetrators we can identify and sometimes as a result of seemingly impersonal forces? Dallaire chose to use the word "evil." But what does it mean to call someone "evil" or to face an evil that has been "brought . . . into reality"?

Questions like this have only intensified since September 11, 2001. The intimacy of Dallaire's handshake contrasts markedly with the sheer spectacle that was 9/11, and yet, for many, the horror of that day evoked the same palpable sense of evil. In his comments after the fall of the twin towers, for example, President George W. Bush often expressed this sentiment: Evil exists, and we have seen it. As for the terrorists, they're flat out evil. They are instruments of evil, evil-doers. We will hunt them down and bring them to justice.[2]

Bush extended the rhetoric by referring to hostile regimes as an "axis of evil," recalling both the "Axis powers" of World War II and Ronald Reagan's characterization of the Soviet Union as an "evil empire."

Bush's references, like much public discourse that erupted after the events of 9/11, suggest that "evil" is a transparent concept. Even as 2001 begins to recede somewhat from the forefront of our cultural memory, "evil" remains the term we often reach for first when there is a need to lament unwarranted suffering and condemn those who perpetrate it. Its appeal is undeniable: in a world full of ambiguities, the forthrightness of calling something or someone "evil" can be intensely gratifying because of the sense of moral clarity that often accompanies it. But when we look more closely at what we mean, the concept no longer seems so clear. The concept of "evil" has a long and varied history; it has been used for many social, political, philosophical, and psychological purposes; and it is associated with many deep and perplexing issues in the realm of ethics and in the comparative study of religion. An idea that initially seems so unambiguous quickly becomes an invitation for rigorous intellectual investigation.

In fall 2004, the Boston University Institute for Philosophy of Religion responded to this challenge by launching a three-year project to explore "evil" in all of its complexity. In keeping with the Institute's identity as a meeting place for scholars from all fields of the humanities and from many of the schools and colleges of the university, the program was designed to be both capacious and interdisciplinary. Prominent philosophers, scholars of religion, and theologians played a major role in the series, but other voices, from political theory, the natural sciences, journalism, literary criticism, film studies, and psychology, also took part in the discussion. And the project was not only interdisciplinary; it was also cross-cultural, incorporating the work of scholars whose expertise led them to explore "evil" (or cognate notions) in non-Western settings. The cross-cultural dimension of this larger project was on vivid display during a special two-day symposium in April, 2005 on "Theodicy Revisited: Evil as an Aspect of the Divine." This symposium brought together scholars of Eastern Orthodox Christianity, Zoroastrianism, Hinduism, Buddhism, and Islam for a wide-ranging discussion of the relationship between evil and the nature of divinity.

In the final year of the project, the lectures were brought together under the title "Deliver Us From Evil." We had no illusion that we had exhausted the topic or, for that matter, had made the problem go away: it was as present at the end of the series as it had been at the beginning. But many of our contributors proposed that the very process of exploring the problem and grappling with it bestows a measure of "deliverance." Not all would agree with William James that the world is richer for having the devil in it, but James may have had a point in observing that the closest we can get to *overcoming* evil is to keep our foot on the devil's neck: we can never eliminate evil or explain it away, but we can continue to apply intellectual pressure, and in that very act, some redemption is found.[3]

This book gathers together essays that were originally presented as lectures in all three years of our series. Each contributor has a unique voice and a distinct perspective, but the essays also speak to each other across the boundaries of philosophical systems, religious traditions, and academic disciplines. The result is a rich, textured, and cohesive collection of essays on a problem that is of crucial importance within the academy—and for all thoughtful people.

The first section in the volume focuses on the representations of evil in different religious traditions, with special attention to mythology, literature, and film. The first contribution, "Bottom of the Universe: Dante and Evil" by Peter Hawkins, was presented as the inaugural lecture in the series in the Fall of 2004. Hawkins begins his essay by dramatizing the visceral reality behind the intellectual problem of evil; then he carries out a close reading of the famous Ugolino episode from Canto 32 of *Inferno*, exploring the story of the Pisan traitor who was imprisoned with his young sons. In Dante's rendering of this episode, the four boys die of starvation, one after another, while Ugolino watches their suffering. Eventually Ugolino also dies, but not before he seems to engage in an act of desperate cannibalism to prolong his own life. Hawkins' analysis of this tale leaves us with a disturbing question: does evil rub off on us, when we, like Dante, play the role of observers and "connoisseurs" of evil?

In contrast to Dante's image of Lucifer impotently trapped in the pit of hell, the Muslim tradition gives us an intensely active picture of Satan, as Eric Ormsby's essay, "The Three Faces of Satan in Islam," makes clear. This figure tempts and defiles human beings, but in some circles can also be conceived as an ally and fellow sufferer. Among the Sufis, the story of Iblīs's refusal to bow down to Adam took on a distinctive meaning: Satan became the ultimate exemplar of devotion to God. The celebration of this myth, according to Ormsby, signaled the arrival of a clearly defined conception of devotional love for God in Islam. It also reveals a hidden "sympathy for the devil" within certain strands of the Muslim tradition.

In "Evil, Motherhood, and the Hindu Goddess Kālī," Rachel Fell McDermott shows that evil and devotion can be just as proximate, if not more so, in the Hindu tradition. On the face of it, this goddess seems to represent the evil or ruthless aspect of the divine, yet her devotees call out for her mercy and even protest when they do not receive it. McDermott helps us understand the distinctive quality of the theodicy that surrounds the goddess Kālī—a theodicy that presents a vivid challenge to other forms of theistic commitment. Seemingly unwarranted suffering is an ever-present reality and might easily be blamed on the figure of a destructive goddess, yet her followers generally do not blame Kālī; instead they emphasize her maternal, protective side, while also acknowledging her power and predilection for violence.

Georges Dreyfus explores the significance of another divine figure who seems to cross the line from good to evil in "The Predicament of Evil: The Case of Dorje Shukden." Dreyfus explains that the normative view of evil in the

Buddhist tradition treats it as a form of illusion. This does not prevent many practitioners of Tibetan Buddhism, however, from acting as if there were a sinister realm of destructive power to be both feared and channeled for human purposes. The deity Dorje Shukden, for example, is considered a "dharma protector" who employs violence to protect his allies and devotees. His activities therefore present a normative problem for a tradition that *prohibits* violence. The solution, Dreyfus explains, is to emphasize the good intentions of deities like Shukden and thereby explain, if not excuse, their sometimes unsavory work.

The interplay between avoidance of evil and attraction to it, a theme that runs throughout the essays in this opening section, is punctuated by David Frankfurter's contribution, "Awakening to Satanic Conspiracy: *Rosemary's Baby* and the Cult Next Door." Frankfurter draws upon the classic 1968 Roman Polanski film to identify important elements of the American "Satanic cult panic" of the 1980s and 1990s, which the film anticipates. In the wake of the 1960s, Frankfurter suggests, many Americans began to imagine that a secret Satanic plot somehow accounted for their experience of social chaos. *Rosemary's Baby* reached into a deep well of images to depict this threat, while it also played on the voyeuristic curiosity of its viewers. This essay leaves us with a deep sense of respect for the durability and persistence of "cult scares": in the face of difference and otherness, human beings tend to be repelled, then to demonize, and finally to purge.

Alan Olson's contribution, "Ricoeur on Evil and Fault," provides a bridge from religious images of evil, which are often framed by narrative and myth, to philosophical analysis. Focusing on Paul Ricoeur's *The Symbolism of Evil*, Olson examines "the phenomenology of the experience of evil," identifying three aspects of its primordial conceptualization: stain, sin, and guilt. Olson's analysis reminds us that these elements are not long-forgotten stages: they are still with us today. Olson concludes his essay by interpreting 9/11 as a "stain" or "defilement," the "most primordial and immediate schema" of evil. Like a disease, the "stain" makes us recoil in dread and impels us to destroy its cause.

Richard Bernstein continues the analysis of contemporary discourse in his essay "The Abuse of Evil." Bernstein begins with the contention that evil has most often been a *spur* to thinking in the Western intellectual tradition. In the wake of 9/11, however, Bernstein claims that the concept of evil has become shrouded in a thoughtless demonization of the enemy. As an antidote to this view, Bernstein draws upon the political thought of Hannah Arendt and John Dewey and advocates what he calls a "pragmatic fallibilism." Bernstein also argues that the current abuse of the concept of evil compromises religion, because it prevents an acknowledgement of the complexity of one's own religious tradition, while also hindering efforts to understand the tradition of another.

Edwin Delattre's essay, "Evil, Reciprocity, and Rights," turns from a broad, geo-political conceptualizations of evil to "everyday" criminal perpetrators of murder and abuse. Three categories provide the structure for the analysis: diabolical evil, radical evil, and thoughtlessness. Drawing upon his expertise in moral philosophy and social policy, Delattre offers a provocative critique of the first two categories, which are derived from Kant, and in the end argues that Hannah Arendt was right to add "thoughtlessness" to the modern portrait of evil. Often it is sheer heedlessness that leads to the worst kinds of crimes.

Manfred Kuehn's essay, "How Banal Is Evil?" provides a strong rejoinder to Delattre's espousal of Arendt's theory. Kuehn argues that Arendt disassociated evil actions from evil motives in her classic work, *Eichmann in Jerusalem.* By subtracting evil motives from the analysis of evil actions, it is easy to see them as resulting from heedlessness and lack of reflection. Kuehn also inverts Arendt's analysis and asks whether "thinking" can actually serve as an antidote to evil. As the well-known case of Martin Heidegger's complicity with the Nazi regime illustrates, even the greatest "thinkers" can involve themselves in inexcusable crimes. Kuehn argues that Arendt's reduction of evil (a moral state) to "thoughtlessness" (a psychological state) risks reducing the problem of evil to a matter for naturalistic explanation. But a return to the moral analysis of motivation is not necessarily the answer either. When it comes to evil, Kuehn suggests, it may be necessary to be content with judgments about the significance of evil *acts*, without attempting to identify their motivation or source.

In "Evil as Privation: Seeing Darkness, Hearing Silence," Mark Larrimore turns to Augustine, who famously argued that evil is a privation of good. While this view has often been criticized, Larrimore attempts to rehabilitate it, arguing that Augustine's position "disaggregates" *the* problem of evil and focuses our attention on individual, separable goods that are vulnerable and must be fought for. While defining the good remains a constant challenge, Larrimore's essay proposes that this issue should be closer to the top of the philosophical agenda.

Larrimore's call for reflection on the good sets the stage for the essays in last section of the volume, which are devoted to the constructive task of delivering us from evil. Francis X. Clooney's "For Your Own Good: Suffering and Evil in God's Plan According to One Hindu Theologian" exemplifies this approach. Clooney focuses on Vedānta Deśika, a fourteenth century Vaiṣṇava thinker who deliberated extensively on the classic problem of evil: why do bad things happen even to those who have taken refuge in God and follow his rules? Vedānta Deśika responds by saying that God is acting in people's lives for a higher, nobler purpose; thus having faith in the overarching goodness of divine intention "makes it possible that evils can be revalued as goods." Such faith in the overarching goodness of the divine, Clooney argues, is not unlike the vision put forth by Aquinas. To this extent, the two thinkers are "allies sharing the same goal of putting evil back in its subordinate place."

The ultimate goodness of God's plan is also highlighted in "Can Evil Be Redeemed? Unorthodox Tensions in Eastern Orthodox Theology," by Kimberley

C. Patton. Patton begins by connecting traditional forms of theodicy in the West with *The Lord of the Rings* trilogy. This narrative, Patton suggests, echoes a standard theological vision of the struggle between good and evil, wherein evil is eventually overcome but remains eternally unredeemed. As Patton illustrates, the Eastern Orthodox tradition generally agrees with this scheme, but her essay focuses on a minority view that imagines a "universal salvation" at the eschaton—even for evil. In the Biblical sources evil seems indeed to be part of the divine plan and, as such, cannot be set aside in a realm that is inaccessible to God's redemptive power.

In "Desire: Between Good and Evil," Richard Kearney also highlights the idea that evil, *qua* desire, can be redeemed. Kearney identifies a dichotomy in Western thought: one strand of inquiry takes desire as essentially evil, leading to a "hermeneutics of prohibition"; the other is more celebratory of desire, resulting in a "hermeneutics of affirmation." Kearney takes up the "hermeneutics of prohibition" first by analyzing its foundations in the West, both in the Biblical tradition and among the Greeks. On the affirmative side, Kearney considers the *Song of Songs* and argues that its affirmation of desire is not simply opposed to the "hermeneutics of prohibition"; rather, the poetics of the text disrupts the dichotomy itself. The surplus of desire's affirmation in the text shows us, Kearney concludes, "(1) how humans desire God, (2) how God desires humans, and (3) how humans, in this light, desire each other."

The final essay in the volume, "Evil: Reflections of a Psychoanalyst" by Ana-María Rizzuto, provides a fascinating juxtaposition with Kearney's discussion of desire and returns us to the fundamental, experiential challenge of evil. Rizzuto begins with Freud's version of the "hermeneutics of prohibition": he regularly described desire as "evil" and blamed it for many of the ills that befall us. Rizzuto then moves to a classic Freudian case study, recalling her therapeutic encounter with "Mr. T," a man who took pleasure in the psychological abuse of others, especially women (including his therapist). Mr. T could only turn around, according to Rizzuto, when his desires were transformed (through therapy) into respect for himself, which provided the basis for "genuine loving exchanges" with others. Here the victimizer and those whom he would have victimized were "delivered from evil," along with the healer who so compassionately presided over his case.

Taken as a whole, these essays dramatize the tension with which we began: on the face of it, the concept of "evil" seems transparent, but when it is examined, it dissolves into a series of theoretical problems and moral perplexities. One response to the vulnerability of the concept is to give in to skepticism and abandon it altogether. But, as Lance Morrow has argued, this is a mistake: "When people become frustrated in their effort to [understand evil], they are inclined to say that because they do not understand evil, it does not exist—a somewhat self-important fallacy based on the thought that what I do not understand cannot be real."[4] While maintaining their analytical rigor, the authors in

this volume never commit this fallacy. It's not that the word "evil" has no reference; rather, our understanding of it needs to be clarified, especially when it is
so easily distorted and abused. "Evil" needs to be put in perspective and its gran-
diosities deflated, so we can use the term in a thoughtful and sensible way.

The essays in this volume also show that any intellectual reconstruction of the
concept should come with a series of warnings. Printing the word "EVIL" in big
letters at the top of a lecture program has the tendency to suggest that there is
a single topic or problem that all of the lectures address. Even to say that one is
discussing *the* concept of evil suggests that it functions as an abstract universal,
or even a universal substance. Our contributors help us respond to this danger
by maintaining focus on the particular characteristics of concrete cases, such
that the analysis is grounded in a plurality of evils. As Nabokov wrote, "Is sorrow
not . . . the only thing in the world people really possess?"[5] When suffering happens, and when intellectuals attempt to grapple with it, recognizing the sorrow
it produces in all its concreteness and specificity is a crucial premise in doing it
justice.

In this volume particular evils speak with great force, continually renewing
the challenge at hand: 330 people (mostly children) held hostage and then
killed in a school in Beslan, Russia; narratives of child abuse from the pages of
Dostoevsky; Ramakrishna's painful death as a result of throat cancer; the future
Buddha's murder of a ship captain who is himself about to slaughter his hundreds of passengers; the bizarre (imagined) rites of Satanists, and the purges
meant to destroy them; 9/11—that day, and the aftermath; Eric Harris and
Dylan Klebold, the shooters at Columbine High School; the crack addicted
mother whose sons are murdered—and her only concern is how she will continue to get drugs without them; the Holocaust; the sadist who proclaims to his
therapist, "I always hurt the one I love—and I like it." And so on. As unpleasant
as it may be, our authors assert that remaining aware of the visceral reality of
particular evils restrains the flight into speculative abstraction, or the descent
into arid analysis of propositions. In either of these directions, the intellectual
enterprise risks superfluity by losing touch with the lamentable instances that
provoked it in the first place.

At the same time, another danger lurks in these particulars, one that dictates
some distance. In taking up this topic, in immersing oneself in the concrete
particulars that populate it, a kind of melancholic gravity—or even a perverse
attraction—can take hold. Becoming absorbed by evil, becoming a "connoisseur" of it, as one of our authors has written, runs the risk of turning melancholy
into wholesale absorption by the very phenomenon we wish to understand
better, in a more nuanced way. For some "connoisseurs of evil," our book warns,
lamentation has the potential to turn into inveterate anger and reprimand.[6]

As several of our authors note, there is also a hidden attraction to evil, especially in public discourse and pop culture. "Sympathy for the devil" is widespread:
should we go so far as to allow that evil is "sexy" or "cool"? Should we be

concerned that serial killers, for example, are often treated like rock stars in the mass media? The hidden attraction to evil in religious and theological discourses is a crucial part of interrogating the concept, but it would be naïve to think that academics and intellectuals are immune to broader forces that position their inquiries into this topic as "cool" or "fun"—drawing them, in their reception at least, towards simplicity and banality.

The contributors to this collection assist us in charting the best course out of the mire of melancholy—and the slough of superficiality—by means of their careful, measured scholarship, and even more profoundly, through their deep reflections not only on evil, but also on the good. Of course, this turn characterizes the work that intellectuals have done for centuries in grappling with a venerable set of questions: If one happens to believe in a divine being who is good (that is, interested in our well-being), all-powerful, and all-knowing, then how can we account for seemingly unwarranted human suffering? In an even broader sense, why do horrible things happen when every instinct tells us that they should not?[7] And is there any way to conceive of or cope with them, such that our sense of meaning gets stitched together once again?[8]

It seems that for any theodicy (in the broad sense of that term) to be persuasive, it must include, for the theologian, philosopher, or layperson alike, a robust sense of some good: some overriding benefit or overarching goal that makes suffering "sufferable," to use Clifford Geertz's term.[9] As the essays in this volume show, this logic transcends the boundaries of culture, and yet it is always subject to critique. One of its biggest challenges, we come to realize, is facing up to the particular suffering, the particular sorrow that is possessed by the victim. Is it ever adequate to argue, for example, that the death of an innocent has served some greater purpose? Will that explanation ever satisfy the ones who are left to mourn the loss? At the same time, we are also left to consider the role of the perpetrators: Does the logic of most standard theodicies ultimately transform them into agents for "good"? Doesn't that rob us of the ability to make the judgments we so desperately need to make?

These questions continue to resonate, and as one of our authors suggests, perhaps the right response to them is to "disaggregate" evil, to defuse *the* problem of evil as some universal quandary, and instead to think about how individual evils are parasitic on the goods we value. In other words, as we have suggested above, being "delivered from evil" is not an all-or-nothing proposition, a problem to solve or not. Instead, incremental measures of redemption come from grappling with this issue, with the sufferings that we lament, and with the judgments we make—while all the time reminding ourselves that evil absorbs us because it threatens the things we value most. Those things, in the end, should perhaps be the focus as we continue to make our intellectual stand in a difficult world.

Notes

1 For the full interview, see www.pbs.org/wgbh/pages/frontline/shows/ghosts/interviews/dallaire.html. Also see Dallaire's powerful memoir, *Shake Hands with the Devil: The Failure of Humanity in Rwanda* (New York: Carroll & Graf Publishers, 2004).

2 See the compendium of President Bush's use of the term "evil" in responding to 9/11 at www.irregulartimes.com/evilwar.html.

3 William James, *The Varieties of Religious Experience: A Study in Human Nature* (New York: Penguin, 1987), 50.

4 Lance Morrow, *Evil: An Investigation* (New York: Basic Books), 4.

5 Vladimir Nabokov, *Pnin* (New York: Vintage, 1985), 52.

6 Analysis of evil in terms of lamentation and reprimand can be found in Paul Ricoeur, *Evil: A Challenge to Philosophy and Theology*, trans. John Bowden (London and New York: Continuum, 2007), 35–36.

7 In the wake of the Holocaust, Hannah Arendt articulated this reformulation of the traditional problem of evil in the Western philosophical tradition; Susan Neiman highlights it in *Evil in Modern Thought: An Alternative History of Philosophy* (Princeton and Oxford: Princeton University Press, 2002), 5.

8 The association between the problem of evil and the challenge of maintaining meaning can be traced to Weber: "Behind [beliefs about redemption] always lies a stand towards something in the actual world which is experienced as specifically 'senseless'. Thus, the demand has been implied: that the world order in its totality is, could, and should somehow be a meaningful 'cosmos'." Max Weber, *From Max Weber: Essays in Sociology*, trans. H. H. Gerth and C. Wright Mills (New York: Oxford University Press, 1958), 281. Clifford Geertz continued this Weberian line of analysis, with an emphasis on coping with suffering—finding a way to suffer through—which is not an intellectualist quest for the answer or an avoidance of the problem altogether, but a question of symbolic ordering of the world and proper disposition towards it. See Clifford Geertz, *The Interpretation of Cultures* (New York: Basic Books, 1973), 104–8.

9 Geertz, *The Interpretation of Cultures*, 104.

Part One

Evil and the Religious Imagination

Bottom of the Universe: Dante and Evil

Peter S. Hawkins
Boston University

> *Evil is not a problem to be solved but a mystery to be endured.*
>
> Flannery O'Connor

Dictionary definitions of "evil" give little help in fathoming its reality: all they essentially do is offer a list of synonyms no less vague and generic than the word in question. How far do we advance in our understanding of evil by turning to wickedness, depravity, iniquity, unrighteousness, corruption, baseness? And how exactly are we meant to follow the dictionary's admonition to "See bad?" Google "evil" and you will discover over 18,600,000 hits on the web—too much of a bad thing. Consult Bartleby.com and read through 839 relevant quotations, many of them brilliant, and yet all in some way too lapidary, too confident in their take on the malignant.

A better way to approach evil is through story—and especially through stories about the harm done to children. Such narratives take us out of the realm of mitigating circumstances and adult accountability; they locate us in a very short-lived world called "innocence." Whatever St. Augustine may have said about original sin and the consequent evil even of infants, we presume them to be above suspicion, as well as vulnerable and defenseless. Therefore cruelty to children posits a kind of limit case of what "pure" evil might look like. Remember the distinction Ivan Karamazov makes in Dostoevsky's novel: grown-ups might well expect retribution for their acts, for "they ate the apple, and knew good and evil, and became 'as gods'. And they still go on eating it. But little children have not eaten anything and are not yet guilty of anything."[1] Remember, too, the stories Ivan tells Alyosha in order to explain why he refuses to accept the notion of forgiveness, or of redemptive suffering, or of some ultimate and eternal harmony beyond what we can know now; stories that explain why he is "returning the ticket" to God. Dostoevsky found these accounts in Russian newspapers before they entered the *Brothers Karamazov*. What especially caught his eye were articles about people of class and breeding who seemed to love torturing children. (Alas, these items are by no means foreign to our *Boston Globe* or *New York Times*: "The boy's injuries were approaching the number of weeks he had been alive: some 60 bruises to the head, torso, and limbs, according to an autopsy; along with three recent rib fractures, a broken leg, a crushing blow to the liver, and a bruised duodenum—the first section of his small intestine. He would have turned 2 in three weeks."[2])

Educated parents of a 5-year-old girl, Ivan tells Alyosha, "beat her, flogged her, kicked her, not knowing why themselves, until her whole body was nothing but bruises; finally they attained the height of finesse: in the freezing cold, they locked her all night in the outhouse, because she wouldn't ask to get up and go in the middle of the night . . . —for that they smeared her face with excrement and made her eat the excrement, and it was her mother, her mother that made her" (242).

Ivan finally rests his case with the account of a particular retired general, a wealthy landowner. A peasant child at play on his estate throws a stone that hurts the paw of the general's favorite hound. In revenge, and to make an example for his serfs, the man rounds up his entire estate including the boy's mother:

> The boy is led out of the lockup. [It is] a gloomy, cold, misty autumn day, a great day for hunting. The general orders them to undress the boy; the child is stripped naked, he shivers, he's crazy with fear, he doesn't dare make a peep . . . 'Drive him!' the general commands. The huntsmen shout, 'Run, run!' The boy runs . . . 'Sic him!' screams the general and looses the whole pack of wolfhounds on him. He hunted [the boy] down before his mother's eyes, and the dogs tore the child to pieces. (243)

Whereas definitions only offer us pale ghosts of reality, narratives like these place us inside evil, give it a local habitation and a name; they also force us to be witnesses who are compelled to watch and, presumably, to take a stand on what we see. How would any of us as bystanders respond to such a scene?

Pictures may be even more powerful than words in this regard. Think of the GI snapshots of skeletal children in Auschwitz and Bergen-Belsen, or the 1972 Nick Ut photograph of a naked Vietnamese girl fleeing her napalmed village. To bring horror up to date, recall the video-taped images taken at Middle School No. 1 in Beslan, Russia in 2004. At least 1,200 people were crammed into the school's gymnasium on what was to have been the celebratory first day of classes. Temperatures soon became stifling, and grown ups, parents and teachers alike, stripped down in the oppressive heat and tore up textbooks to use as fans. Some students were so hungry that they took to eating the wilted bouquets of flowers they had brought for their teachers. Thirst was even more severe. The captors took discarded clothes, already wet with the children's urine, and soaked them again in water; then they threw the clothing to the desperate crowd, with people clutching them and wringing them dry above their open mouths. The captors also teased and tormented the children, shot runaways in the back. One boy said he was hoping for a bomb to go off, so that the crisis might end. More than 330 people are known to have died in this assault, with more than half of them children.

It should come as no surprise that the same questions Ivan poses to Alyosha in *The Brothers Karamazov* also hover beneath the lethal network of bombs strung from the Beslan gymnasium ceiling. "Why did my child have to sit there for three days, hungry and thirsty, and go to heaven hungry and thirsty?" one grieving mother said. "What did he do wrong? He's just a child."[3] Another mother searched the morgue every day for a son long missing: "I've become like a dog. . . . After all these days I don't feel anything. My heart is like a stone."[4]

Humans somehow tolerate the atrocities of war. As we know from the aftermath of Abu Ghraib, it is possible, and without embarrassment, to reduce the evidence of torture to nothing worse than a fraternity hazing. Such toleration does not extend, however, to incidents that take place away from a war zone—on an astonishingly beautiful morning at the Twin Towers, for instance, or in a Moscow theater, or on the courtly opening day of school when parents bring children to greet their teachers and teachers accept bouquets of flowers from their new students.

Some people believe in evil empires or in an axis of evil—the Third Reich comes to mind—but often such attributions of depravity can be exchanged, depending on where one stands: insurgents become freedom fighters, and the America that God is meant to bless is the arrogant Great Satan meant to be brought low. Nonetheless, in the stories that Ivan tells Alyosha, or that we can read about in the *Globe* or *Times*—stories about tortured children—we find ourselves confronting a horror that cannot be excused, that can barely be understood. We may try to do so: the parents of the 5-year-old girl who lock her up overnight in a frozen outhouse must have been brutalized by their own parents; the wealthy retired general who turned a little boy into an animal to be hunted down may well have been insane; and the terrorists who wreaked havoc in Beslan, together with the "black widows" wearing bombs around their waists, might ultimately have had in mind the liberation of their people as well as retribution for the prolonged devastation of Chechnya. Yet mitigating factors, whether psychological or political, do nothing to mitigate the sense that terrible evil has occurred. Explanation, even if there is one, offers no exoneration.

One of the ways humankind has found to portray evil as well as to contain it—to articulate the unspeakable and yet in some paradoxical sense to silence it—is through the notion of Hell. It is evil's final recompense. Alan E. Bernstein's *The Formation of Hell* gives an excellent account, showing its roots in the ancient world and malignant flowering in the Christian Middle Ages.[5] On the basis of scattered verses in both biblical testaments, as well as influences coming from the pagan world, Christians constructed a place where evil could be drawn and quartered. Justice may be slow to work in the present age, but it is inevitable and unerring in the afterlife. Bernstein moves from the vivid depiction of the mid-second century CE *Apocalypse of St. Peter* to the less grisly but more influential consideration of St. Augustine in the early fifth-century *City of God* (Bk. 21). It is thanks to the eventual triumph of Augustine over his theological rivals that we owe the notion of Hell as a place of eternal punishment and of the sufferings of the damned as constituting one of the joys of the blessed. One might well speculate that the invention of such a Hell is itself an instance of evil.

In her *Visions of Heaven and Hell before Dante*, Eileen Gardner shows what happened to the ruminations of patristic and medieval theologians when they became the stuff of the popular religious imagination.[6] At the end of this line, as her title suggests, comes Dante Alighieri, whose early fourteenth century *Inferno* takes an antiquated genre, the afterlife vision, and revitalizes it according to "moderno uso." Dante joins the theological subtlety of an Augustine or an Aquinas to the representational power of an extraordinary visual artist and dramatist. For better or worse, his *Inferno* becomes evil's gold standard, and the first installment of his journey among the dead is the readiest way for us to "see bad"—as in a statement this summer by the chief prosecutor in a UN-sponsored Court who, in commenting on ten years of intractable civil war in Sierra Leone, said, "This is a tale of horrors [that moves] beyond the Gothic and into the realm of Dante's *Inferno*."[7]

I want to focus on the very bottom of Dante's infernal universe, where the poet invites us to encounter evil in its most undiluted form. But first it is necessary to establish some preliminaries, such as the "back story" to the formation of Hell and the principles that govern its ways.[8] In the final canto of the *Inferno*, Dante the journey-taker beholds the gigantic (not to mention repellent) figure of Lucifer, the angel of light who through pride became darkness invisible. Dante stresses not only his enormity but the extent to which he is a travesty: his six bat-like wings show the hideous transformation of a seraph; his gross flesh is a "take off" on the Incarnation; the three faces on his head are a grotesque of the Trinity; his ceaseless chewing of three of the damned an inversion of Christ's Eucharist self-offering ("Take, eat, this is my body given for you").[9]

What the poet conveys in this extended parody is a notion he inherited from the theological tradition of Augustine and Aquinas, namely that evil has no positive nature but is only the loss or privation of good: "mali enim nulla natura est: sed amissio boni, mali nomen accepit" (*Confessions* 11.9). When Lucifer, in the poet's words, "lifted his brow against his Maker" ("contra 'l suo fattore alzò le ciglia," *Inf.* 34.35)—or when, according to Augustine, he preferred to love himself rather than God—he lost his being. He devolved into a bad joke, a perverse imitation, a parody of the One he aspired to surpass.

If the notion of evil as the privation of the good inspired Dante to imagine Lucifer/Satan as a composite negation, it also controlled his construction of the *Inferno* as a whole. When Satan was expelled from Heaven and embedded at the center of the earth, we're told in *Inf.* 34, the earth shrank from his presence, forming around him a funnel-shaped cavity of gradually smaller rings. Like the "emperor of the sorrowful kingdom" himself, Hell's nine concentric

circles are also perverse imitation of the nine celestial spheres that spin about
the divine still point. Instead of moving upward, as Dante does both in *Purgatorio*
and *Paradiso*, he moves steadily downward, and in the direction of the sinister
left. Instead of discovering "the great sea of being" ("lo gran mar de l'essere,"
Par. 1.113), he takes step after step toward nothingness, descending into the
spiritual version of a black hole.

The *Commedia* will culminate in the City of God, whose only boundaries are
light and love (*Par.* 28.54), but in his first canticle the poet gives us an urban
sink. It is constructed, so to speak, out of allusions to the wrongdoings of Siena,
Pisa, Genova, and (most of all) Florence, whose nefarious former citizens crowd
Hell's open tombs and burning sands. What the *Inferno* presents is our world
without grace, our cities without love, and our *libido dominandi* without mercy.
Here the self is sovereign, cut off, frozen in obsessive monomania, always alone
no matter how dense the crowd. The journey through *Inferno* engages Dante's
empathy from time to time by reminding him how often evil is a flawed good, a
corrupted virtue. Yet by the time he comes to the frozen lake at the nadir of the
universe, Hell has been exposed for what it is—a world where the atrocities of
earth rage for eternity. Here, however, horror is turned against those who once
perpetuated the suffering and the victimizers become victims of their own evil.
As if to bring home this point, Dante tells us that the rivers which collectively
torment the damned have a common source on the earth: they all begin as the
lacrimae rerum, the tears of violated humanity. In the spirit of retributive justice,
what has gone around comes around again—and lasts forever.

The journey through Hell travels down the proverbially slippery slope as
bad leads to worse. Sins of the appetite are encountered first, and through
them the corruption of the flesh. Once inside the City of Dis, Dante comes to
know the corruption of a higher human faculty, the will, as it turns in various
ways toward violence. Another descent deposits him in Malebolgia, where fraud
provides examples of intelligence and ingenuity—*ingegno*, or genius—when it
has been brought into the service of evil. Finally, Dante is lowered to the "fondo
a tutto l'universo" (32.8), to the bottom of the entire universe, where he finds
permutations of treachery that vitiate every human connection, whether to kin,
to those joined by covenant, to guests, or a superior—in Satan's case, God.
Cocytus is the *Commedia*'s place of pure evil, and for this reason the poet shows
it to be a realm not of fire but of ice.

It is here that I want to bring you, to "lo mezzo/ al quale ogne gravezza
si rauna" (32.73–74), to the center toward which every weight collects (in Robert
Durling's translation) or, to be more literal, to the center toward which every
weight "reunites itself" or "makes itself one again." Any true notion of *e pluribus
unum*, of one out of many, is antithetical to the spirit of Hell, which finally is
all about the relentless private ego and the absolute refusal of partnership.
Nonetheless, the reflexive "si rauna," with its suggestion of union, ironically sets

the stage for what to my mind is Dante's most disturbing exposure of the heart of darkness.[10] Our passage begins toward the end of canto 32:

> I saw two frozen
> in one hole so that one head was a hat to the other;
>
> and as bread is eaten by the starving, so the one
> above put his teeth to the other, there where the
> brain joins the nape:
>
> not otherwise did Tydaeus gnaw Menalippus's
> temples in his rage, than this one did the skull and
> the other things.
>
> "O you who show by such a bestial sign your
> hatred over him you are eating, tell me why," I said,
> "with this pact,
>
> that if you justly complain of him, when I know
> who you are and what his sin, in the world above I
> shall repay you for it,
>
> if that with which I speak does not dry up."

The poet starts off with a shocking visual effect: in a grotesque rendering of a back-to-front embrace—the "spoon" position—one man gnaws the skull of another. The precision of this description is gruesome: the two skulls are so close that "l'un capo a l'altro era cappello" (v. 126), one head was a hat to the other; the placement of teeth on bone is exactly "là 've 'l cervel s'aggiunge con la nuca" (v. 129), there where the brain joins the nape; and if you want to know the ferocity with which this attack is being prosecuted, you have only to imagine a starving man confronting food or remember the inveterate enemies from Statius's epic, *The Thebaid*: Tydaeus "soaked with gore from the shattered brain, defiled his mouth with [Menalippus's] living blood" (8.760–761).[11] It may take several readings of these lines to get beyond the blood and gore, to see, for instance, that Dante is playing, hideously, with notions of unity: two figures are frozen in one hole; one man's head is the other's hat; one man's teeth are fused with another man's skull ("and the other things"). This vision of dog eat dog is also the perversion of a meal, with flesh becoming bread. It is also a sign of hatred so deep that only cannibalism will suggest its bestiality.

Because Dante wants to understand who these figures are and what motivates such disfiguring rage, he promises to share what he learns with the living, if indeed "quella con ch'io parlo non si secca" (v. 139), if his tongue does not dry up on the spot. With that possibility in mind, the next canto opens with another visual shock:

> That sinner lifted up his mouth from his savage
> meal, wiping it on the hairs of the head he had
> wasted from behind.

Then he began: "You wish me to renew desperate
grief that already presses my heart merely thinking,
even before I speak of it.

But if my words will be seed to bear the fruit of
infamy for the traitor I gnaw, you will see me speak
and weep together."

In the Italian, the initial word of the opening line is "La bocca," the mouth: it both gnaws *and* speaks, both eats this savage meal *and* delivers the words, the bestial signs, of the narrative to follow. With these details the poet places the speaker outside the sphere of the human: he "wastes" the head in front of him and then wipes the filth from his mouth with his victim's hair. But Dante also presents the speaker as a figure of sensibility looking for pity, someone whose memory is grief, and whose heart contracts "pur pensando," merely thinking about the past. Above all, the one who gnaws and speaks has a mission: his words are to be seeds, his narrative to bear "the fruit of infamy," and his object to destroy whatever remains on earth of the "traditor ch'i rodo," the traitor I chew on. So be it: Cocytus is the region of treachery, and therefore the masticated *traditor* is where he belongs.

But given Hell's unerring sentence, so too the speaker, who is allowed to participate in the punishment of his "companion," is nonetheless frozen in the same hole, imprisoned in the same nether region as the sinner he ravages. He plays the part of avenging angel, but that role turns out to be an aspect of his own damnation: he can never hate enough, never entirely consume his enemy.

I know not who you are nor in what manner you
have come down here; but truly, you seem to me
a Florentine when I hear you.

You are to know that I was Count Ugolino and
this is the Archbishop Ruggieri: now I will tell you
why I am such a neighbor to him.

That by effect of his evil thoughts, trusting him,
I was taken and killed, there is no need to say;

but what you could not have heard, that is, how
cruel my death was, you shall hear, and you shall
know if he has injured me.

As happens elsewhere in the *Commedia*, Dante is recognized by his *bocca*, that is, by the way he speaks: his words give him away as a native of Florence. As also happens frequently, he finds himself among Italian compatriots, in this case two traitors from the neighboring city of Pisa. The one who speaks is Count

Ugolino, the one spoken about, Archbishop Ruggieri. As *conte* and *arcivescovo* respectively, they are high representatives of Pisan state and church. No authority on earth seems to be free of treachery.

The fate Ugolino goes on to describe was surely familiar to Dante. The poet was 23 when the event took place; he was also a friend of Ugolino's grandson, Nino Visconti, against whom both Ugolino and Ruggieri conspired in order to wrest control of the city into their own hands. To gain power in Pisa, the count was not only willing to change his long-standing party affiliation from Ghibelline to Guelf, but then to switch back to the Ghibellines once they were restored. It was after this last switch of allegiance that he allied himself with Ruggieri to overthrow his grandson. Lured back to Florence by his fellow conspirator, Ugolino was then arrested by the double-crossing Archbishop and imprisoned along with two sons and two grandsons. This took place in July 1288; he died 8 months later.

It is interesting to note what Ugolino avoids mentioning, when we meet him in Antenora, the subdivision of Cocytus where traitors to party are punished, and where the count just happens to be located. (It is almost as if he hunted down his enemy and then decided to stay!) We hear nothing of his going back and forth between Ghibelline and Guelf factions, and certainly nothing about treachery against a godson. Of these things, says Ugolino, "dir non è mestieri," it is not necessary to speak. Trusting Ruggieri, he was taken by surprise and then killed; he was acted upon, made a victim: and that was that. If you want to understand why he has become so savage a "neighbor" ("tal vicino"), he says, you need only to hear "how cruel *my* death was," learn how much "he has injured *me*." Note the extent to which it is all about him. Ugolino then builds his case:

> A small aperture within that molting tower
> (which because of me has the name of Hunger, and where
> others must still be shut)

> had shown me through its opening several moons
> already, when I dreamed the evil dream that rent the veil
> of the future for me.

> This man appeared to me master and lord,
> hunting the wolf and his little cubs on the mountain
> for which the Pisans cannot see Lucca.

> With lean, eager, alert hunting dogs, he had put
> the Gualandi family with the Sismondi and Lanfranchi
> in the lead.

> In brief course the father and his sons seemed
> To tire, and I seemed to see the sharp fangs of the dogs
> tearing their flanks.

> When I awoke before the dawn, I heard my sons,
> who were with me, crying in their sleep and asking
> for bread.
>
> You are surely cruel if you do not already grieve,
> thinking what my heart was announcing to me; and
> if you are not weeping, about what do you usually
> weep?

In this recounting Ugolino describes a world within a world, a story within a story. First, he takes us back to Pisa and places us in the Tower called Hunger. We are told that it took on this name because of the fate that befell *him* within its walls ("per me ha 'l titol de la fame") although this may be less a fact than an aspect of the constant self-referencing that characterizes his overall speech. In any event, it is not only *his* prison house but one "where others still must be shut"—a Pisan Hell-on-earth that will go on to swallow up others, and therefore a terrifying image of what the earthly city can become. Nothing about the *torre* is specified except a single detail: there is a "breve pertugio," a small opening, which admits some ray of moon- or sun-light into the darkness. In the pitch black of a particular night, he says, "I dreamed the evil dream that rent the veil of the future for me." With this recollection he takes us from the nightmare of the tower to a just-before-dawn dream that was commonly understood to be true and prophetic: it tears away the veil from events soon to take place. In it, Ugolino and his sons are wolf and cubs; pursuing them are "Lord" Ruggieri, his Ghibelline cohorts, and a pack of hunting dogs. Ugolino wakes suddenly when he "sees" the sharp fangs of the dogs tearing into the wolves' exhausted flesh. With a start, he realizes that his sons, lying close to him, are all weeping in their sleep—weeping and crying out for bread.

The story is spellbinding. My guess is that only a very alert reader notices that Ugolino likens himself to a wolf, the traditional enemy of humankind and, within the *Commedia*, indeed from the opening canto, a figure of treachery. Perhaps the historian also wonders how two sons and two grandsons became four boys of the same youthful generation. Is Ugolino heightening the pathos of the situation or is it the poet who does so? Most likely, however, the reader's response to these words is simply pity: you are surely cruel if you are not weeping as you hear this narrative; and if you are not, whatever is it that gets you to cry? Yet Dante reveals no feeling at all, unlike those earlier occasions in the *Inferno* that touch him deeply. The text gives us no prompts about what to think or feel: we are simply on our own as Ugolino continues his narrative:

> They were already awake, and the hour was
> drawing near when our food used to be brought to
> us, and each was afraid because of his dream;

and I heard them nailing up the door at the base
of the horrible tower, hence I looked into the faces
of my sons without a word.

I was not weeping; I so turned to stone within:
they were weeping; and my Anselmuccio said:
"You have such a look, father! what is it?"

Therefore I did not shed tears, nor did I reply all
that day or the night after, until the next sun came
forth into the world.

When a little ray had entered into our dolorous prison,
and I perceived on four faces my own appearance,

both my hands I bit for rage; and they, thinking
that I must be doing it out of a desire to eat,
suddenly stood up

and said: "Father, it will be much less pain for
us if you eat of us: you clothed us with this wretched
flesh, so do you now divest us of it."

I quieted myself then, so as not to make them
sadder; that day and the next we were all mute: ah,
hard earth, why did you not open?

After we had reached the fourth day, Gaddo
threw himself stretched out at my feet, saying,
"My father, why do you not help me?"

There he died; and as you see me, I saw the three
fall one by one between the fifth day and the sixth;
and I,

already blind, took to groping over each of them, and
for two days I called them, after they were dead.
Then fasting had more power than grief."

When he had said that, with eyes askance he took
the wretched skull in his teeth again, which were
strong against the bone, like a dog's.

With these last lines we realize that this entire interaction has taken place
between mouthfuls. Vengeance momentarily takes the form of words, and then
falls back into the inarticulate gnawing of teeth on bone. Ugolino begins his
speech by lifting his mouth to wipe it clean on the hairs of the head "he had
wasted from behind"; he ends with a furious return to his "savage meal." This is

what blind hatred looks like, and indeed there is abundant cause for hatred. A betrayed man and his sons are starved to death; helpless, he is forced to witness their suffering, which quadruples his own. He lets us know what this experience does to him: how he turns to stone, is unable to speak, bites his own flesh in a sign of frustration over his impotence and in rage at Ruggieri, his former colleague, who engineered this evil. At the very end of his words, as he tells us that he groped the corpses of his sons, we are told that "fasting had more power than grief." Either he too drops from starvation or he is driven by desperation to eat the flesh of his children—the text allows for both interpretations.

In either case, it would seem that the Tower of Hunger, with its door nailed shut at precisely the time when food used to come, gives us a foretaste of Hell. The membrane between Pisa and Inferno seems porous, the difference between our cities and Satan's at times difficult to discern. What is more, there is no *deus ex machina* to snatch us out of the nightmare: no divine intervention, no ram in the thicket to substitute for the human sacrifice, no rescue from the lion's den, and no exit. If there were any occasion on which one might, following Ivan Karamazov's example, return the ticket to God, this is it.

For Ugolino, "già cieco," already blind, there is nothing more than this darkness. Without a thought for the God who is apparently not there, he takes his hatred for Ruggieri into eternity and continues to gnaw on it, world without end. And yet, his narrative reveals (to us if not to him) that there was more available in that Tower than darkness. It was not, after all, pitch black. There was "un poco di raggio," a little light, coming in through one "breve pertugio," small aperture. Although it is the *tiny* size of this opening, and the *brief* glimpses of sun- and moon-light, that are emphasized, light is there nonetheless.

But then there is also another kind of illumination that Ugolino cannot recognize in the words he himself speaks: the uncanny echo of Christ's Passion that his sons unwittingly provided for him when they in effect bring Good Friday into the Tower of Hunger. In some sense, it is as if he had four versions of Christ gathered around him, and through them recollections of Gesthemane and Golgotha: the sense of abandonment, the nails driven, the curtain rent, and the cry of "Padre!" "Father!" resounding three times in quick succession (vv. 51, 61, 69).

Unlike Ugolino who turns in upon himself and can make no overture, can say not a single word to his boys, Anselmuccio (the diminutive of the name "Anselmo" is almost unbearable in this context) turns to him in genuine concern: "Tu guardi sì, padre! Che hai?" "You have such a look, father! What is it?" Seeing him bite both of his hands in rage, the boys offer themselves as bread ("Father, it will be much less pain for us if you eat of us") recalling the Last Supper on the night Christ was betrayed, as well as the words he spoke at table: "This is my body given for you." Finally, Gaddo throws himself at Ugolino's feet and cries out to him something very like *Eli, eli, lama sabbachtani*: "Padre mio, ché non m'aiuti?" "My father, why do you not help me?"

Ugolino can make nothing of this Gospel resonance, which, had he been able to acknowledge it, might have enabled him to discover the Cross in the horror of his own situation, in his children's suffering. He might have perceived the sign of the incarnate God's participation in the very depth of the human condition—and therefore had a cause for hope. But because he is deaf as well as blind to the possible divine presence in the Tower of Hunger, he is cut off from those other last words of Christ which, had he been able to appropriate them, might have transformed his mortal ending and therefore his eternal life: "Father, forgive them for they know not what they do"; "Into your hands I commend my spirit." Instead of this final turning over of the self to God, his last breath burns with hatred. His hunger is for revenge alone.

Revenge is indeed what Ugolino "gets" in the afterlife. Yet, as we can plainly see, it brings him no satisfaction. There is no end to it, no point at which the wasted skull of Ruggieri will be consumed no matter how strong against the bone ("like a dog's") are his teeth. What Dante poet offers instead of revenge is the Christ Story, the little ray of light in the darkness, the bread of heaven rather than the savage meal. The alternative to this refusal of vengeance, the Ugolino episode suggests, is a Tower whose door is nailed again and again, "e che conviene ancor ch'altrui si chiuda" (v. 24), where others must still be shut.

Even as I present these comments, which I believe to represent Dante's theological conviction, I am aware of the lines that follow immediately upon Ugolino's return to the ravaged skull of the Archbishop—lines in which Dante, speaking in his authorial voice, sounds more like Ugolino inveighing against his enemy than he does like Christ from the cross:

> Ah, Pisa, shame of the peoples of the lovely land
> where sì is spoken, since your neighbors are slow to
> punish you,
>
> let Capraia and Gorgona move and make a barrier
> at the mouth of the Arno, so that it may drown every
> person in you!
>
> For if Count Ugolino was reported to have
> betrayed your fortresses, you should not have put his
> sons on such a cross.
>
> Their young age, O new Thebes, made Uguiccione
> and Brigata innocent, and the other two my song
> names above.

I noted above that the character Dante has no reaction to Ugolino's words and never seems to shed a tear. As we see here, however, it is the poet who gives himself away. That Ugolino betrayed his city is not in question: the last minute mention of his handing over Pisan fortresses only augments Antenora's implicit charges against him for treachery. The poet's greater concern, however, is not with Ugolino himself but rather with the innocent suffering of the man's children, who, through no fault of their own, were dragged into the Tower on account of their father. In an immediate sense, of course, it was Archbishop Ruggieri who brought them "a tal croce," to a cross of suffering. Yet is not Ugolino also to be held accountable for their deaths, accountable for the construction of a political world in which revenge is finally no respecter of persons?

Dante seems to make this point by concluding his diatribe not with reference to Ruggieri or Ugolino but to the city the two traitors shared. Dante denounces their Pisa as "novella Tebe," a new Thebes, and therefore to Dante's mind the earthly entity that most approximates the reality of Hell. Pisa is the shame of Italy, a canker in the "bel paese." Since the nearby cities are slow to punish their hateful "*vicino*"—neighbor is Ugolino's term for Ruggieri in 32.15—Dante takes it upon himself to invoke a catastrophe, to call for another lethal Deluge to wipe the place clean by wiping it out. Let two small offshore islands suddenly block the river Arno and so flood the city "ch'elli annieghi in te ogne persona!" (v. 84), that it may drown every person in you!

It was God who called for a flood at the beginning of human history "because [the earth] was corrupt in God's sight" (Gen. 6.11); it was a man, Abraham, who interceded on the behalf of Sodom and Gomorrah by convincing the Lord not to destroy the city if ten just men could be found (Gen. 18.16–33). Dante, however, is not interested in mercy's half measures. He usurps the divine perspective (and the prerogative that goes with it), proposing to revenge the deaths of the Pisan *innocenti* by drowning an entire civic population—one that no doubt would include its fair share of children like Anselmuccio, Brigata, "and the other two [his] song names above."

What do we make of this? On the one hand, Dante uses the Ugolino story to urge an end to violence and revenge. May no one ever again lose his children in the Tower of Hunger, even if he were reported to have betrayed some fortresses. For Christ's sake, tear it down, down to its foundations: let no more babies be dashed against the rocks. On the other hand, the poet calls for a divine vendetta on Pisa, counting on his authority as a "sacred poet" who claims in some sense to be co-authoring a text with God. Let Capraia and Gorgona dam up the Arno—and let the "damnation" of Pisa begin.

I do not know whether an omniscient Dante is staging this moment in order to show, through his own persona as poet, how difficult it is to withstand the impulse toward evil, and perhaps most especially for those who are in the business of righteousness. Or are we rather catching the poet with his guard down—seeing him as an angry man embittered by his personal experience of the political process, who writes this lengthy poem about divine judgment in order to settle accounts precisely as he (and, of course, God) see them? Perhaps this is what happens when you descend to the bottom of the universe in your imagination and describe it so brilliantly: you devour the whole apple; you take on the attributes of that angel of light who, even before Adam and Eve, wanted to be divine; you destroy one group of innocents in order to avenge another. It may be as dangerous to be a connoisseur of evil as to pretend that it does not exist.

Whatever Dante's personal demons may have been, however, he was certainly under no illusions about the existence of evil. But what of us? In what has proved to be a controversial Op-Ed piece in the *New York Times* (September 7, 2004, A: 23), David Brooks wrote:

> When you look at the Western reaction to the Beslan massacres, you see people so quick to divert their attention away from the core horror of this act, as if to say: We don't want to stare into this abyss. We don't want to acknowledge those parts of human nature that were on display in Beslan. Something here, if thought about too deeply, undermines the categories we use to live our lives, undermines our faith in the essential goodness of human beings.

Contrary to the present-day oblivion that Brooks indicts, Dante forces us to stare into the abyss, to acknowledge that we are capable of horrendous acts. In the larger trajectory of the *Commedia*, however, the poet also does a great deal more than that. For his vision of the evil that is at once within ourselves and all around us does not have the last word: *Inferno* opens the door first on the *Purgatorio* and then on the *Paradiso*. After a glimpse of damnation he moves us through the experience of human transformation and into an approximation of beatitude. Over the course of the poem, darkness visible "develops" into "viva luce etterna." Indeed, the innocent deaths we hear about in the penultimate canto of the *Inferno* are recalled in the parallel canto of *Paradiso* after Dante recognizes at the center of the heavenly rose, "li volti e anche . . . le voci puerili" (32.46–47), the faces and also the singing voices of children.

There is something important to be learned from the poet's insistence on the big picture. For what any healthy examination of evil may require (lest a focus on negation get the better of us) is a vivid and compelling sense of the Good from which it deviates. We need a "breve pertugio," a small aperture that lets light into the darkness; and then we need the courage to act on what we see.

Notes

[1] Fyodor Dostoevsky, *The Brothers Karamazov*, trans. Richard Pevear and Larissa Volokhonsky (New York: Knopf, 1992), 242. For the larger passage see 237–38.

[2] *The New York Times*, September 21, 2004, B: 4.

[3] *The New York Times*, September 16, 2004, A: 8.

[4] *The New York Times*, September 17, 2004, A: 3

[5] Robert Bernstein, *The Formation of Hell* (Ithaca, NY: Cornell University Press, 1993).

⁶ Eileen Gardner, *Visions of Heaven and Hell before Dante* (New York: Italica Press, 1989).

⁷ *San Francisco Chronicle*, July 5, 2004, A: 5.

⁸ Citations of *Inferno* are from *The Divine Comedy of Dante Alighieri*, Vol. 1: *Inferno*, ed. and trans. Robert M. Durling (New York and Oxford: Oxford University Press, 1996); those from *Paradiso* come from the translation and commentary of Allen Mandelbaum (New York: Bantam Books, 1984).

⁹ All citations of the Bible are from the New Revised Standard Version.

¹⁰ In addition to Durling's excellent excursus on the Ugolino episode (578–80), the following works are helpful: Giorgio Bàrberi-Squarotti, "L'orazione del conte Ugolino," *Lettere italiane* 22 (1971): 3–28; Umberto Bosco and Giovanni Reggio, *Dante Alighieri, La Divina Comedia, Inferno* (Florence: Le Monnier, 1988), 482–87; John Freccero, "Bestial Sign and Bread of Angels," in *Dante: Poetics of Conversion*, ed. Rachel Jacoff (Cambridge, MA: Harvard University Press, 1986), 152–66; Ronald B. Herzman, "Cannibalism and Communion in Inferno XXXIII," *Dante Studies* 98 (1980): 53–78; and Rachel Jacoff, "The Hermeneutics of Hunger," in *Speaking Images: Essays in Honor of V. A. Kolve* (Asheville, NC: Pegasus Press, 2001), 95–110.

¹¹ Statius, *Thebaid*, trans. J. H. Mozley, 2 vols. (Cambridge, MA: Harvard University Press, 1967).

The Three Faces of Satan in Islam

Eric Ormsby
McGill University

We don't usually think of Satan as a family man, but in at least one legend from the Islamic tradition, we find him saddled with the chief problem of a single parent: child care. (Of Mrs. Satan we know nothing.) Satan had a young son, a mere toddler, whose name was Khannās.[1] The devil has always been a busy fellow and so was often in need of babysitters. One morning he stopped by Adam and Eve's home when Adam was out and asked, "Would you please watch my little boy for a few hours?" The kind-hearted mother of mankind agreed. When Adam returned he found the devil's child sitting in his own house and was furious. He seized Khannās and chopped him into little pieces, which he then scattered over a field. When Satan returned, he called out to his child, and all the chopped-up pieces instantly reassembled. A few days later, Satan again asked Eve to babysit. Despite her fear of Adam's disapproval, she agreed once again. Adam came home, fell into a rage at Eve, grabbed Khannās, and burned him to ashes, which he then sprinkled to the winds. Satan appeared and called his son by name, and the ashes recomposed themselves into the child. On another day, Satan appeared for a third time and again asked Eve to mind the child. Against her better judgement, Eve consented. When Adam discovered the child a third time in his home, he was beside himself. He butchered Khannās and roasted him in the oven, then he and Eve ate him for supper. Satan returned. He called his child. Khannās answered him from inside the bodies of Adam and Eve. And Satan exclaimed, "It worked! This is just what I wanted!"[2] And from that day to this man has the devil in his flesh.

This is a preacher's tale with a paraenetic punch. The notion of an urge to wickedness in the very fibres of our flesh, a prompting inseparable from our deepest selves—like the *yetzer ha-ra'* of Jewish tradition—finds warrant in the Qur'ān. In a famous verse from the *sūra* of Joseph, we read: "Man's very soul incites him to evil."[3] And yet, part of the force of the tale is that this is an ingested evil, a propensity to wickedness that has come into mankind from outside.

Satan has at least three faces in the Islamic tradition. Two of these—Satan the defiler and Satan the tempter—will be familiar. The third face, that of Satan as not only our most intimate enemy but our secret ally, may be less so. In describing this final face of our ancient adversary, I will propose, as nothing more than a sort of working hypothesis, that this ultimate visage takes its shape concurrent with a renewed emphasis by Muslim mystics on the love of God. If I use rather broad strokes to depict this triple-visaged devil—somewhat in the manner of a police artist constructing a composite portrait of a malefactor—I nevertheless hope to convey something of the paradox and subtlety of the "Great Satan" in the Islamic tradition.

There would seem to be nothing either paradoxical or particularly subtle about the "Great Satan"—the *shayṭān-i buzūrg*—of furious mobs in Tehran or, more recently, in Beirut, who howl "Death to America!" as their rallying cry. For them, we Americans collectively are incarnations of the satanic. This, of course, is the devil as an irremediable other, an entity intrinsically repugnant and malignant, a source of evil that is absolutely outside of ourselves, a resolutely external wickedness that stands in violent opposition, and in contradiction, to the values and beliefs of the members of the chosen community and which is hated and feared in equal measure—hated, because it appears as the antithesis of belief; feared, because it has the malign power of a contagion.

This outer, and alien, Satan is the same devil whom Muslim pilgrims stone during the annual *ḥajj* or pilgrimage. The ritual, which takes place at Mina, nine miles from the plain of ʿArafāt, and which lasts 3 days, dates from pagan times. The "stoning of Satan," accompanied by shouts of "God is most great!" is believed to commemorate the action of Adam himself, the first prophet of Islam, who drove the devil away with stones. Each pilgrim flings seven pebbles at each of the three standing stones, the largest of which represents the devil, or Iblīs, himself. This is the same Satan from whom Muslims flee when they recite the formula "I take refuge with God from the accursed Satan" (*aʿūdhu billāhi min ash-shayṭāni r-rajīm*). It is the Satan the ninth-century Sufi master Yaḥyā ibn Muʿādh invokes when he exclaims to an opponent, "Your morals are pharaonic, your faces satanic!"[4]

The "accursed" (literally, "stoned") Satan is a primitive but potent embodiment of evil. He forms part of that eerie horde of supernatural beings Islam inherited from its Arabian pre-history, not only various voracious female deities, such as ʿIzzat and Lāt (identified with the sun), but the mysterious beings known as the *jinn* and assorted forms of ghoul. The *jinn* represent a separate category of being; they are creatures of "pure fire" and are often mentioned in the Qurʾān. In Sūra 55, for example, we read that God "created mankind out of dried clay, like pottery, the *jinn* out of smokeless fire" (55.14–15). In Sūra 72, entitled "The Jinn," we learn that these beings eavesdropped on recitations of the Qurʾān and were converted, even though, as it is written there, "men have sought refuge with the *jinn* in the past, but they only misguided them further." And yet the *jinn* are not necessarily evil; in the same passage they proclaim, "Some of us are righteous and others less so: we follow different paths" (72.11).

The *jinn* are tricky; sometimes they do good, at others they deceive, dazzle, and mislead. The common Arabic word for "crazy" (*majnūn*) reflects their power over humans; to be insane is to be possessed by a *jinn*. And in several passages of the Qur'ān it is explicitly denied that Muḥammad is insane, i.e., *jinn*-possessed (e.g., 34.46).

Of other supernatural desert-dwelling beings the ghoul is probably the most horrific (our English word comes from Arabic *ghūl*). Ghouls are predatory, and deception is their hallmark. Taking the appearance of beautiful women, they loiter by the roadside to entice unwary men. If a man approaches them, they reveal their true shapes, leap upon his back, and rape him. Men raped by ghouls often conceive and bring forth little ghouls.

The ninth-century writer al-Jāḥiz in his *Book of Animals* cites an anonymous verse to show that ghouls even occasionally trick men into marrying them (as do the *jinn*): "In my youth I married a ghoul/who resembled a gazelle, the dowry an old wine-skin" (of course, this may say more about marital discontent in the desert than about ghouls).[5] And the eighth-century poet al-Farazdaq could describe a terrifying landscape as being "like the vulva of a ghoul" (*ka-farj al-ghūl*).[6]

The *jinn*, ghouls and other monsters, have in common the practice of deceit. Satan is deceitful too, but his brand of falsehood is not merely a matter of outward appearance or of disguise. Satan's mendacity is subtler, and it is also more dangerous, because his wiles collude with our own innermost propensities.

In the Qur'ān, especially in the earlier-revealed Meccan portions, Satan appears as a whispering insinuator. Mischievous or malicious whispering—conveyed in Arabic by the wonderful word *waswās*—stands in stark contrast to the full-throated, clarion utterances of God and His Prophet. The final chapter of the Qur'ān (*sūra* 114) conveys this with supreme succinctness: "I seek refuge with the Lord of people, the Master of people, the God of people, against the evil of the slinking whisperer (*khannās*)—who whispers into the hearts of people—whether they be *jinn* or people." (From this we see that the *jinn* too can be led astray by malicious promptings!) This face of Satan is ringed in such early *sūras* of the Qur'ān with an aura of darkness, of spells and sly whispers, with the witches "who blow on knots" (113.4), with all that is uncanny, menacing, spooky, and sinister. But it is not the final face of Satan as he appears in the holy text. That face is more complex and even somewhat contradictory. And the enigma of that compound visage engendered a rich tradition over the centuries in Islam, especially among those mystics known as Sufis.

In several passages of the Qur'ān we encounter Satan, the rebel who refuses to bow down to man, under both his principal names: Shayṭān and Iblīs (e.g., 2.30–37, 7.10–19, 18.50, 38.71–85). The name Shayṭān is, of course, from a Semitic root; in Hebrew, *ha-Saṭan* is "the adversary" or "opponent," as he appears, for example, in the Book of Job. By contrast, Iblīs is an arabicized version of the Greek word *diabolos*, "devil." In these passages (which I here conflate),

God informs His angels that he intends to create a vice-regent (literally, a *khalīfa*) on earth. The angels object; mankind, they say, will wreak havoc and cause bloodshed. God says simply, "I know things you do not." He then proceeds to teach Adam the names of all things. He brings Adam to the angelic assembly and challenges the angels to tell Him the names of things. When they cannot, God asks Adam to say the names. He does so and God commands the angels, "Bow down before Adam."

Here our devil makes his appearance. All the angels bowed except for "Iblīs, who refused and was arrogant; he was one of the *kāfirs*" (2.34 and 7.11). When God questions him about his refusal to bow, Satan replies, "I am better than him; You created me from fire and him from clay" (7.12, 38.76). This refusal marks Satan's disgrace before God and lies at the root of his enmity with all mankind; he goes so far as to declare to God, "Because you have put me in the wrong, I will lie in wait for them all on Your straight path: I will come at them— from their front and back, from their right and their left" (7.16–17). In the Arabic text of 2.34 it reads that Iblīs "refused and was arrogant" (*abā wa'stakbara*); hence, he is termed "one of the unbelievers" (*min al-kāfirīn*). To be arrogant here means to consider or proclaim oneself great, a prerogative reserved for God alone; the Arabic word is double-edged, meaning "great" or "mighty" when applied to God but "swaggering" and "arrogant" when applied to man.[7] Arrogance is the sin of Pharaoh who exclaimed, "I am your Lord most high!"[8] Whether or not this bifurcation of names has significance—and I suspect that it does—when the devil refuses to bow down, the name Iblīs is used; when he has Adam and Eve banished from paradise, the name Shayṭān is used.

It seems odd to call Satan a *kāfir*, the word commonly translated as "unbeliever." But the Arabic word so translated possesses a span of meanings quite different from our equivalents. *Kufr* has connotations of hiding something and hence of ingratitude; a *kāfir* hides what benefits he has received and doesn't express thanks.[9] More generally, a *kāfir* may be defined as someone who stands excluded from the Islamic community of belief, and by belief I mean not merely subscribing to a creed but acting in belief. Where, then, does Satan's *kufr* lie? Not solely in outright defiance of God, but also in repudiation of His creation in human form. It is in his rejection of man that his "disbelief" resides.

This small distinction would have large consequences, for just as Satan/Iblīs will be transformed by radical mystics into a figure to emulate, so too, even the term *kufr*, one of the most abhorrent in the creedal lexicon, will become, for some, the most extreme expression of its opposite: pure untrammelled belief.[10]

The notion of Satan as a sly and whispering seducer of humankind takes on force as it develops because it coincides with a deepening understanding within Islam of the psychic construction of the human agent. We might say that from being a purely external agency of temptation, Satan turns inward and begins to collude with human flesh; even so, he is never entirely *le diable au corps*—a purely internalized personification of evil—however intimate a collaborator with our most unruly impulses he proves to be. In a cautionary tale reported by the twelfth century Ḥanbalite theologian Ibn al-Jawzī, in his aptly entitled work "The Machinations of Iblīs" (*Talbīs Iblīs*), Satan is still the seducer from outside, the "inciter" or "baiter" (*muḥarriḍ*) who urges man to excess. Thus, a pious monk, who has been entrusted by her three brothers with the care of their virgin sister while they are on a military expedition, irresistibly falls prey to Satan's sly blandishments. At first he keeps her in an adjacent house under lock and key, neither looking at her nor speaking with her, and only leaving her food on the stoop for her to fetch after he has hidden himself safely away in his cell. But Satan "courteously cajoles him" (*talaṭṭafa la-hu*), day-by-day and hour-by-hour, with patient insinuation, until soon enough the ascetic is not only sharing meals and chatting with the girl but manages to get her pregnant. Satan then persuades him to kill the girl and her child and bury them under "a large rock" to escape the righteous fury of her brothers. At each stage of the story, the ascetic's temptations are rigorously externalized, coming never from within himself but always from the outside agitations of Satan.[11]

Of course, Satan himself—in Islam as in Judaism—is circumscribed severely in his power. The conception of an entity somehow in a position to challenge God was unthinkable for Muslims from the earliest period, and the figure of Satan is never invoked to explain, for instance, the persistence of evil or the fall of man. Rather, Satan is a kind of unofficial servant—a Sabbath goy, if you will—called in for shady or difficult cases, such as putting Job to the test. We're familiar with this aspect of Satan, not only from the Hebrew Bible but from literature. In Goethe's *Faust*, to cite but the most prominent case, Mephistopheles presents himself as ". . . .ein Teil von jener Kraft,/Die stets das Böse will und stets das Gute schafft."[12]

The Islamic Satan may not turn bad to good but what power, or surrogate power, he possesses derives, with God's permission, from the weakness of human will. Human beings are endowed with a kind of life-force or "soul" called *nafs* (an Arabic word derived from the same root as "breath," *nafas*, and cognate with Hebrew *nefesh*). There is no single English word that conveys the range of connotations of *nafs*. We see it rendered as "soul" or "carnal soul," sometimes too as "self" or "lower self." Sometimes it seems to represent what a Freudian would call the "id." In essence, it is that blind, craving, voracious component of the person that both gives us vitality and energy and also leads to a slavish dependence on the appetites. (When I try to explain this notion to students, I tell them that if they want to meet their own *nafs*, they need only to quit smoking, give up beer, or go on a diet. I guarantee that the *nafs* will make an appearance in about 15 minutes.)

The greedy self offers Satan a breach of our defences. Indeed, according to the early ascetic and Sufi al-Ḥārith ibn Asad al-Muḥāsibī, who died around the year 857 CE in the city of Basra, this self is not only sly and seductive but also invariably obstructs a man on the way to God; indeed, it "seduces more than Satan" for "in it all is deception."[13] Even so, the self is not intrinsically evil; rather, it is a retarding element that holds a person back and causes him to cling to habit. The *nafs* is our "deep sensual layer," whereas the heart or mind— the Arabic word *qalb* denotes both—represents our "deep spiritual layer." Of course, a heart may also be good or bad; as the *nafs* prompts the actions of the limbs and organs, the heart undergoes its own inner actions, for good or for evil. The heart is the seat of faith, but it may become the seat of doubt, or of hypocrisy, as well.[14]

Given our inner and outer natures we are vulnerable to the whisperings of Satan who knows our weakness. How may we combat this? Al-Muḥāsibī developed a method which had wide influence on pious practice and which, almost incidentally, contributed decisively to the development of a mystical psychology in Islam.

The name "Muḥāsibī" derives from the verbal noun *muḥāsaba* which denotes an accounting or reckoning. In the case of al-Muḥāsibī himself, his cultivation of a form of moral accounting led to the moniker he was to bear forever after. This moral accounting is similar to what we might call the "examination of conscience." For a ninth-century Sufi, it betokened standing in judgement upon oneself just as God will do at the Last Judgment. Al-Muḥāsibī elaborates what this entails in the following passage:

> [The Sufi] comes to know his sins by recalling the hours of the day just past; only thus can he know them. He recalls how he comported himself in these past hours of his life; how he handled the duties that he neglected, or the trespasses that he committed. He reviews the days of his life that have passed, how he behaved during these days; what he did and what he did not do, and what his inner disposition was when he so acted. He recalls how he behaved when he was angry or when things went well for him; how he loved and how he hated, acquired and expended and retained; how he remitted what he owed and how he accepted what others owed to him, whether honestly or not. He recalls how he spoke, looked, and listened, how he placed his feet when he walked, and how he took hold of things with his hand. He calls to mind the annoyances he suffered unjustly when people brought claims against him with regard to their property or their honor, as well as the duties he has to his relatives and to others to whom he is obligated. He practices recollection as one does who is determined to be pure before he stands before the face of God.[15]

Elsewhere he introduces an analogy, comparing such a man to one who finds a basket full of bottles by the road, all of which are sealed with stoppers. Though most people pass by without noticing, he pauses and removes the stoppers. Out of certain bottles pleasant odors arise, such as musk, amber or saffron and jasmine; out of others, however, foul stenches climb—naphtha, tar and pitch. In this way he learns his own good and bad qualities.[16]

We should not infer from this that al-Muḥāsibī regards man as the sole source of evil. The devil still plays his role. In fact, Satan has a supreme advantage over humans and this abets his seductions. Though he cannot see the future, Satan has a long past and a good memory. Our adversary knows the human heart and soul from time immemorial. He plays the human soul as a practised musician manipulates a lute. Our defences, by contrast, are meagre. All our stratagems avail us little. After all, even our virtues nourish our vanity, and it is adepts in particular, those who think to have routed Satan, who are most in danger. We must examine the self—that equipoise of heart and soul—in order not only to cleanse and scour it but to dispense with it entirely. One way alone promises escape from the whispering lures of Satan. That is complete absorption in God. The precondition for such immersion is vigilance. Nothing but incessant watchfulness over body and soul can combat the supreme fault of *ghafla*, or complacent heedlessness.

But watchfulness was concerned not exclusively with tracking down and exterminating evil impulses. These, after all, originated in the human self; they were obstructions and bore witness to our frailty. More interesting by far were other, profounder workings of the psyche, and as Sufism developed in sophistication and depth, these "signs" became apparent as well. If the human being is a kind of hypostasis of heart and soul, mind and self, in incessant tension, as one early ascetic put it—if man is a being of sundered extremes,[17] in another Islamic formulation reminiscent of Pascal's definition of man as midway between a beast and an angel—then he is also a creature fashioned by the hand of God. And God's wonders, the marvels of His artistry, are evident as well in man. "Man is the most amazing of beings," writes a later mystic, "and yet, he does not seize himself with awe."[18]

Needless to say, we are far here from the worlds of the theologian and philosopher. For the theologians ("dialecticians," or *mutakallimūn* in Arabic), good and evil are ethical values, defined as *ḥusn* for "goodness" or *qubḥ* for "badness." The words also denote what is pleasing or beautiful and what is repellent or ugly (like their counterparts in Greek). Indeed, later, for "mainstream" theologians of the Ashʿarite "school" (which came to prevail in Sunni Islam), evil lost all meaning as an independent ethical quality. For it is God Himself who creates both good and evil. Whatever happens must be good because it would not have happened if God had not willed it. God's actions define value, not vice-versa.

For the philosophers (or *falāsifa*, a word taken over from Greek) such as al-Fārābī or Ibn Sīnā (Avicenna), the issue becomes even more abstract. Following Plato, Aristotle, and Plotinus, the ancient masters whose thought they continued and elaborated, evil is sheer lack of good (the στέρησις of Plato and Aristotle or the Scholastic *privatio boni*).[19] Goodness exists in the fullness of being; evil in its diminishment. There were other notions, to be sure. One, which has a long history of its own, holds that evil—here conveyed by the Arabic word *zulm*, denoting "tyranny" or "injustice"—results from displacement. Things—persons as well as acts—have a rightful and proper God-given place in existence; evil occurs when they are put in a wrong or improper place. The tyrant who usurps the place of a rightful ruler is a favourite example of such "displacement."[20] Nevertheless, in none of these more refined discussions does the devil make an appearance.

Returning to the Sufis, the exercise in self-knowledge which I have sketched would lead eventually in the Islamic mystical tradition to a pronounced deepening of the relationship between God and His human creatures. From the outset, even in the early highly ascetic period of Sufism, when the fear of God, assiduously cultivated, led to painstaking concentration on the actions of the heart and the body, there were glimmerings of an awareness of the possibility, if not the full reality, of a love of God.

Belief in the love of God, so prominent in the Christian tradition, is conspicuous by its absence in the major canonical works of Islamic theology and ritual practice. No dogmatic theologian discusses it. In fact, it is precluded, both logically and theologically, by the early treatises. Logically, because a relationship can exist only between members of the same genus and species, and God transcends both. Theologically, because, even if the Qur'ān does affirm that "He loves them and they love Him" (5.54), love is not a divine attribute, as power, knowledge, will, and the others are. Divine love is present throughout the Qur'ān, to be sure, but it takes the form of supreme compassion, of mercifulness, rather than that love which depends upon some affinity and reciprocity between persons.

Certain early Sufis, such as the famous woman mystic Rābiʿa al-ʿAdawīya (who died ca. 801 CE) and especially Abū al-Ḥasan al-Nūrī (who died a century later, in 907 CE), did reportedly teach a doctrine of God's love. Al-Nūrī, however, suffered for his views: he and some 75 other proponents of divine love were put on trial in Baghdad at the instigation of Ghulām Khalīl, a strict old-fashioned ascetic mystic, abetted by the chief *qāḍī* of Baghdad.[21] Because he had used the word *ʿishq*, an Arabic term that signifies intense, usually erotic love, to describe the feelings he had for God, he was charged with heresy.[22] Al-Nūrī was acquitted in the end, but the scandal remained, to be carried to its furthest consequences by the slightly later mystic, Ḥusayn ibn Manṣūr al-Ḥallāj, who was executed horribly in 922 CE. The accusations against him were various but the most damaging charge held that he had exclaimed, "I am the Truth" (i.e., "I am God," *anā al-Ḥaqq*) in a Baghdad mosque.[23]

These crucial early figures, and the tendencies and "schools" they engendered, have been studied intensively for some time now by such great scholars as Louis Massignon, Hellmut Ritter, Josef van Ess and others, and I will refrain from recapitulating their findings. My hypothesis builds on a somewhat different foundation. Briefly put, it is this: the doctrine of the love of God coincides with the transformation of Satan in the Islamic mystical tradition in a way that suggests that the two are linked.

Historically, the decisive impetus for a new emphasis on God's love comes from a somewhat unlikely source: the jurist, theologian and philosopher, and Sufi author Abū Ḥāmid al-Ghazālī, who died in 1111 CE, and who composed in Arabic the most thorough and systematic treatise on divine love. Among Sufis, to be sure, love of God had been an important theme from the earliest period, and the subject has a long history; however, none of these early works attempted either to systematize—I am tempted to say "schematize"—a doctrine of divine love, or to articulate its implications for the uninitiated, as al-Ghazālī's work did.[24] The transformation of Satan begins to take shape only slightly later in the work of al-Ghazālī's younger brother, Aḥmad al-Ghazālī, who died in 1126 CE and wrote mostly in Persian, the mother tongue of both brothers.

The two brothers could not have been more different, at least in outward expression. Abū Ḥāmid, the elder and more famous, even today, was a medieval polymath of dazzling virtuosity whose massive, and most famous, work, "The Revival of the Sciences of Religion" (*Iḥyā' 'ulūm al-dīn*), is still read and revered by Muslims, Sunni as well as Shi'i. Younger brother Aḥmad, though perhaps equally learned, must have been quite dissimilar. He was a preacher, a homilist, a master of the telling anecdote. Moreover, because he wrote almost exclusively in Persian and was a gifted stylist in that language, he created a lexicon of love and a set of tropes that were to dominate Persian poetry for centuries to come. His influence permeates the lyrics of Ḥāfiz, the subtlest and most melodious of all Persian mystical poets.

It is Aḥmad who elaborates a new transformative theology of Satan. This is not entirely his own; he owes a debt to earlier masters, and especially to al-Ḥallāj. The latter, after all, had been bold enough to declare: "There was no monotheist like Iblis among the inhabitants of the heavens. When the essence revealed itself to him in stunning glory, he renounced even a glance at it and worshipped God in ascetic isolation . . . God said to him, 'Bow!' he replied, 'To no other!' He said to him, 'Even if My curse be upon you?' He cried out, 'To no other!'"[25]

Despite Aḥmad's own innovative treatment of Satan, it was the elder al-Ghazālī, I would argue, who, by establishing the plausibility of a relationship of love between God and man, and by doing so cogently, methodically and irrefutably (an endeavour, incidentally, that would not have been possible had he not made the Avicennian world-system so intensely his own),[26] set the stage for the reappearance of Satan in transmogrified guise.

Though the figure of Satan was always quite ambiguous, his transformation into God's ultimate lover could not have occurred until the possibility of a relationship of love between God and the creature had been convincingly enunciated. Once that had been done, as it was in fact done in the elder al-Ghazālī's *magnum opus*, it was only a matter of time before someone—in this case, his own brother—would bring the two possibilities into fruitful conjunction. I say it was only a matter of time; perhaps it would be more correct to say that it was inevitable given the peculiar inner dynamic of a certain strain of Sufism, a dynamic that thrives on paradox coupled with an intense penchant for extremes (of which al-Ḥallāj is the obvious representative). For such Sufis, only the way of paradox could do justice to a truth that was endlessly multifoliate and imbricated beyond all possibility of human unravelling. It is no accident in this respect that while both the brothers Ghazālī insist on the primacy of love between God and man, the sober and circumspect Abū Ḥāmid posits some ultimate intimacy with God, while his younger brother, more daringly, asserts that separation and perpetual yearning, not union, characterize that relationship at its most profound.

What more fitting exemplar for the farthest extreme of love at its most paradoxical than Satan himself? For Satan is in one sense the ultimate lover of God. He loves God even though God curses and casts him out; indeed, he loves God because God does banish him. To be singled out by God in such a way is, perversely, to assume the badge—perhaps "scar" would be the better word—of a radical distinction. To love God against God is to love God for His own sole sake. No reward for such love may be expected. And with the removal of reward, love is based purely upon itself.

One early Sufi who exemplified this attitude has left a beautiful prayer, which the elder al-Ghazālī quotes approvingly in his treatise on divine love. The prayer is worth citing here, if only to counter the excessively austere impression "orthodox" Islam sometimes makes on those approaching it. The author is the same Yaḥyā ibn Muʿādh (d. 871 CE), whose denunciation I quoted earlier, here praising God in his old age, as though he were a bee drunk on the divine pollen:

God, I stand in Your courtyard, riven with praise of You. You took me to You when I was young. You clothed me in Your knowledge. You gave me strength through Your favour. You turned me this way, then that, in my deeds through concealment and repentance, renunciation and longing, contentment and love. You gave me to drink from Your cisterns. You let me wander freely in Your gardens. I clung to Your commandments, I remained in love with Your word, even after my mustache sprouted and the harbinger of my destiny appeared. Now I am grown but how can I depart from You? I became used to Your ways when I was young. Now there remains for me nothing but buzzing, and in entreating you nothing but humming, for I am a lover and every lover is rapt in his beloved and cares for nothing but what he loves.[27]

Satan's refusal to bow down with all the other angels before God's creation in human form signifies that Satan alone manifests the purest devotion to God's oneness. He will not compromise his adherence to this monotheistic ideal even if God Himself commands him to. Satan the disobedient thus becomes the improbable champion of *tawḥīd*, the unwavering conviction that God is eternally and essentially one and alone to be worshipped. Hellmut Ritter has summarized the crux of the matter well: "The demand to bow down in worship before a created being, someone other than God, is in fact a direct slap in the face to the most sacred command of mystical monotheism. Strictly speaking, the refusal to prostrate oneself before a being other than God must have seemed to them [Sufis] an act of genuine monotheistic adoration of God. In this way Satan now becomes, so to speak, more monotheistic than God Himself."[28]

The belief in God's oneness is both the central theme and the central crux of Islamic theology. It seems utterly simple: To state "God is one," whether with the *Shma' Yisroel, Adonay elohenu, Adonay echad* or the *shahāda* of Islam, would seem unproblematic. To proclaim "there is no God but God and Muḥammad is the emissary of God" is the indispensable prerequisite of becoming a Muslim. But in fact no tenet is so vexed in the long history of Islamic thought.

Beyond such external threats to monotheism as Christianity and Manichaeism, there lies the fatal fact, embedded in our very natures, that we are creatures given to idolatry. Our very selves, in their insatiable avidity, conspire in this. Sensual pleasures are obvious idols. But there are also intellectual and spiritual idols as well; the ruler idolizes power, the scholar idolizes his books and learning itself, the warrior his skill at arms, etc. Our hearts and minds collude continually in this hidden idolatry.

Pious practices—fasting and prayer, alms-giving, pilgrimage—assist us, but ultimately only a kind of excision of the self will serve. This self-extirpation, which the Sufis call *fanā'*, is no mystical swoon. Rather, it entails a meticulous, dogged, gradual and unrelenting diminution of the individual identity, a willed erosion of the stubborn nugget of the self.

Satan becomes for certain mystics the exemplar of this single-minded devotion to the oneness of God. From devotion to a principle to love of its chief subject is but a small step, and it is this that occurs in the transformation of Satan from disobedient rebel to stubborn monotheist to afflicted lover of the very God who casts him out. For Satan's devotion and love are all the more admirable in that they go unrewarded and indeed, unacknowledged. In a Sacred Tradition, a man said to the Prophet, "O Emissary of God, I love you," and Muḥammad replied, "Prepare for destitution." The man then said, "I love God." The Prophet replied, "Prepare for misery." Affliction, whether in the form of ostracism, poverty, loathsome disease, or social disgrace, can be a mark of God's attention. And Satan is the most afflicted of all.

In another tradition, Jesus (counted a prophet in Islam) encounters three groups. The first group have wasted bodies and pallid faces. These are the believers who worship God out of fear of hell. The second group are even more emaciated; these have grown thin out of longing for paradise. The third group are utterly skeletal but their faces glow like "mirrors of light." These are the lovers of God who are beyond either fear of hell or hope of heaven. And Jesus exclaims to them three times, "You are those brought near to God!"

To love God without fear or hope: that is the ultimate Sufi ideal. It dates back to the times of Rabi'a and Abū Yazīd al-Bisṭāmī but comes to full and fervent elaboration only in later centuries. To love Him purely for Himself. To love Him even if He damns you; indeed, to love Him especially if He damns you because in hell your praise and adoration of Him will be selfless. This is what distinguishes the Sufi Satan.

One of the more outrageous Sufis, Abū Bakr al-Shiblī (who spent much time in a lunatic asylum before his death in 945 C.E.), meets Satan while on pilgrimage to Mecca. Astonished, he asks Satan what he hopes to achieve by performing the *ḥajj*. Satan answers:

> I worshipped God for 100,000 years between fear and hope. I showed the angels the way to His presence. I opened the door for every person who had lost his way to God. My heart was filled with His sublimity. I professed His Oneness. If He sent me away from His door for no reason despite all these acts of obedience . . . then He can also accept me again without any reason. Since there is no 'how' and 'why' in God's acts, one should never abandon hope in Him. His harshness rejected me but His kindness may call me back.[29]

The same al-Shiblī was also heard to exclaim on his death-bed, "I am jealous of Satan on whom God bestowed His curse!" To show how far this jealous passion for God might go, al-Shiblī also declared, "True love consists in your being too jealous regarding the Beloved to let someone like yourself love Him" (*Ḥaqīqat al-maḥabbati an taghāra 'alā 'al-maḥbūbi an yuḥibbahū mithluka*).[30]

For Aḥmad al-Ghazālī, the kid brother of the renowned Imam (the "Proof of Islam," Abū Ḥāmid), Satan becomes a model figure. Satan is the "black light."[31] What does it mean to be such a light? First, the black light stands in relation to the "light of Muḥammad," the *nūr Muḥammadīya*, not as its negation but as its correlative. A light that radiates darkness: could there be any greater contrast than with God Himself, the "light of the heavens and the earth" and "light upon light," as the famous verses have it?[32] Second, Aḥmad goes on to claim that this "black light is higher than the unpointed word."[33] (The "unpointed word" refers to the Muslim proclamation of faith, "There is no God but God and Muḥammad is His Emissary," which in Arabic script possesses no "points" or diacritical marks: *lā ilāha illā llāh* . . .). To say the formula is only too easy; to realize its import in one's very flesh is to be a true *muwaḥḥid*, or monotheist. And for this reason, Satan the black light is a better believer than an ordinary believer who utters the sacred formula with his tongue, even if from the depths of his heart.

For Aḥmad, Satan is a tragic lover of God. He defends him by saying, "The poor guy didn't know that the claws of Providence draw blood when they scratch and that the arrows of Predestination kill quickly when they fly."[34] I believe that this unexpected transformation of Satan may not be unconnected with the renewal and gradual elaboration of the doctrine of the love of God that spread among Muslim mystics and was to become one of the defining characteristics of Persian and Indian Sufism in later centuries. And I think it is no exaggeration to see the brothers Ghazālī as having been crucial to this development. The older brother, with that remarkable sanitizing touch he possessed, made it acceptable, if not immediately respectable, to speak of God in amorous terms to a non-Sufi audience; he would do the same, by the way, for Aristotelian logic which, after his intervention, would eventually become incorporated into works of unimpeachable orthodoxy. The younger brother drew out all the implications of the doctrine, sometimes alarmingly so, and it was his influence, not his more prudent older brother's, that would transform Sufism. Put another way, we might say that Abū Ḥāmid had to make the possibility of love between God and man respectable so that Aḥmad might make it fruitfully disrespectable; for him, as for his later followers, to love God is to love not comfortably but in a kind of anguish of rapture.

Accordingly, Sufi writing on the love of God draws for its vocabulary and tropes on the conventional erotic poetry of Arabic and, later, Persian literature. The lover—the *muḥibb*—sighs, yearns, tosses and turns, utters rending sobs and heartbroken groans. He is tormented by longing (*shawq* in Arabic), burns for intimacy (*uns*) with the beloved, whose coquettish mockery and prevarications he must endure. Sometimes he even dies for love, especially when he overhears a line of poetry or a melody that reminds him of his beloved. The protocols of amorous intrigue have been transposed to the transcendent realm.

The most authentic such love is that which is chaste, unrequited and rejected. The purest lover is he who can hope for nothing and yet, continues to burn in the fiery passion that consumes him. In this respect, Satan, who has loved God without hope for countless millennia, appears as the truest lover as well as the truest monotheist.

These two themes—love and God's oneness—coalesce in the mystic's experience. To love God is to know Him, and to know Him is to recognize that everything in creation, "from the scratching of a black ant on a dark stone at night" to the motions of the celestial spheres, moves only through His will and command. Such love leads the mystic to recognize that what we habitually think of as agency or causality is a fiction. Causality is God's custom, His usual way of running the world, but it is not intrinsically necessary or even finally demonstrable. Rather, everything at every instant of time is created afresh by God by "the specifying action of His will," and so everything, from the discrete quanta of time itself to all the possible objects of creation—from the physical world to the inner mental world and even "the stray thoughts in the mind"—originate in the divine volition. This is a theological way of putting it; in fact, it is the way in which the elder al-Ghazālī expressed it in his youth when he was still committed to theology, before he realized that the truth could only be "tasted," not merely conceptualized.[35]

The theologian proclaims this; the Sufi lives it. To grasp this perception is one thing; to grasp it and to love God because of it, quite another. The millennial hopelessness of the devil in Islam, but also his darkly radiant grandeur, is to be such a knowing lover of the very God who has banished him. God of course may relent; He is supremely free to do so. But Iblīs does not love Him out of hope of forgiveness. He loves Him purely, without hope or fear. The Islamic Satan is still, and perennially, the wily corrupter of souls, the whispering seducer and yet, is he not at the same time, even against God, fulfilling God's secret will? "God writes straight by crooked lines," runs a Portuguese proverb, and is not Iblīs, tempter as well as unswerving monotheist, in some way His unacknowledged scribe? For the Sufis, and especially those more audacious mystics among them for whom all dualities are dissolved in a vision of ecstatic oneness, Satan has assumed still another face, mythic and tragic at once, where they see their own most extreme aspirations reflected in an effulgence of shadow.

Notes

[1] The word denotes "slinking, drawing back"; see Qur. 114.4 (the "slinking whisperer"), in *The Qur'an*, trans. Muhammad A. S. Abdel Haleem (Oxford and New York: Oxford University Press, 2004). Quotations from the Qur'ān are from this translation in what follows.

[2] For the tale, see Hellmut Ritter, *Das Meer der Seele* (Leiden: Brill, 1955), 536–37; *Idem, The Ocean of the Soul*, trans. John O'Kane (Leiden: Brill, 2003), 553–54. The Persian original, attributed to the Sufi master Ḥakīm al-Tirmidhī (d. *c.* 932 CE), may be found in the work of the thirteenth-century mystic and poet Farīd al-Dīn ʿAṭṭār, *Ilāhī-nāmah* ed. H. Ritter (Leipzig and Istanbul: F. A. Brockhaus and Maʿarif, 1940), 127–28.

[3] Qur. 12.53 (*inna nafsa la-ammāratun bi-l-sūʾi*).

[4] ʿAṭṭār, *Ilāhī-nāmah*: 98.

[5] *Kitāb al-hayawān*, ed. Abd al-Salam Hārūn, vol. 6 (Cairo: n.p., 1967), 158. According to the same author, ghouls are adept at transformation but cannot disguise their feet (220); sometimes a swindled husband will discover his wife's ghoul-nature by catching a glimpse of them.

[6] al-Farazdaq, *Dīwān al-Farazdaq*, vol. 2 (Beirut: Dār Ṣādir, n.d.), 331.

[7] See *Wörterbuch der klassischen arabischen Sprache*, ed. Manfred Ullmann, vol. 1 (Wiesbaden: Harassowitz, 1970), 23.

[8] Qur. 79.24.

[9] *Wörterbuch der klassischen arabischen Sprache*, vol. 1, 261 ff.

[10] See al-Tahānawī, *Kashshāf iṣṭilāḥāt al-funūn*, ed. A. Sprenger, vol. 2, 1252.

[11] Ibn al-Jawzī, *Talbīs Iblīs* (Beirut: Dār al-Kutub al-ʿIlmīya, n.d.), 27–28.

[12] "A portion of that power,/That ever wills the bad but always does the good" (*Faust* I, scene 3).

[13] See Margaret Smith, *An Early Mystic of Baghdad: A Study of the Life and Teaching of Ḥārith b. Asad al-Muḥāsibī A.D. 781–857* (London: Sheldon Press, 1977), 90.

[14] For the discussion of both *nafs* and *qalb* here I am indebted to Josef van Ess, *Die Gedankenwelt des Ḥārit al-Muḥāsibī* (Bonn: Selbstverlag des Orientalischen Seminars der Universität Bonn, 1961), 32–35.

[15] Al-Muḥāsibī, *al-Riʿāya li-ḥuqūq Allāh*, ed. Margaret Smith (London: n.p., 1940), 31 ff.; see also van Ess, *Die Gedankenwelt des Ḥārit al-Muḥāsibī*, 141 f.

[16] van Ess, *ibid.*, 142.

[17] So the Andalusian theologian and jurist Ibn Ḥazm (d. 1064 CE); see my article "Ibn Ḥazm," in *The Cambridge History of Arabic Literature: The Literature of Al-Andalus*, ed. María Rosa Menocal, Raymond P. Scheindlin, and Michael Sells (Cambridge: Cambridge University Press, 2000), 237–51, esp. 241.

[18] Abū Ḥāmid al-Ghazālī, *Iḥyā ʾ ʿulūm al-dīn*, vol. 4 (Cairo: n.p., 1916), 376.

[19] See, among many possible sources, Plotinus, *Enneads* I.8.3 and III.2.5; also, St. Augustine: "Evil is not a positive substance: the loss of good has been given the name of 'evil'," in *Concerning the City of God against the Pagans* (Harmondsworth: Penguin, 1972), 440. For the notion in Stoic thought, see Max Pohlenz, *Die Stoa*, vol. 2 (Göttingen: Vandenhoeck & Ruprecht, 1970), 57.

[20] See the discussion in my *Theodicy in Islamic Thought* (Princeton: Princeton University Press, 1984), 227–28.

[21] See Alexander Knysh, *Islamic Mysticism: A Short History* (Leiden: Brill, 1999), 61–62.

[22] For a discussion, see the work of the eleventh-century Sufi Abū al-Ḥasan ʿAlī b. Mohammad al-Daylamī, translated as *A Treatise on Mystical Love* by Joseph Norment Bell and Hassan Mahmood Abdul Latif Al Shafie (Edinburgh: Edinburgh University Press, 2005), 24 ff; the translators render ʿishq throughout as "eros."

[23] The standard study is, of course, that of Louis Massignon, *La passion de Husayn Ibn Mansûr Hallâj. Martyr mystique de l'Islam exécuté à Bagdad le 26 mars 922*, 2nd edition (Paris: Gallimard, 1975).

[24] A pioneering history was first provided by Ignaz Goldziher in his still valuable article, "Die Gottesliebe in der islamischen Theologie," *Der Islam* 9 (1919): 144–58; for a more recent overview, see Binyamin Abrahamov, *Divine Love in Islamic Mysticism: The Teachings of al-Ghazālī and al-Dabbāgh* (London: Routledge, 2003).

[25] Cited in Peter Awn, *Satan's Tragedy and Redemption: Iblis in Sufi Psychology* (Leiden: Brill, 1993), 124.

[26] For a discussion of the primacy of love in the Avicennian system, see Louis Gardet, *La Pensée Religieuse d'Avicenne* (Paris: Vrin, 1951), 167–74.

[27] Abū Ḥāmid Al-Ghazālī, *Iḥyā ʾ ʿulūm al-dīn* (*Kitāb al-mahabba*), as given in Murtaḍā al-Zabīdī, *Itḥāf al-sādat al-muttaqīn*, vol. 9 (Cairo: n.p., 1894), 550.

[28] Farīd al-Dīn ʿAṭṭār, *Ilāhī-nāmah*, 555.

[29] ʿAṭṭār, *Ilāhī-nāmah*, 272; as Ritter notes, Satan is probably basing his hope on Qur. 12.87: "Do not despair of God's mercy—only disbelievers despair of God's mercy!"

[30] ʿAṭṭār, *Ilāhī-nāmah*, ed. Ritter, 544.

[31] Aḥmad al-Ghazālī, *Savāniḥ*, ed. Pourjavadi, 20; trans. Pourjavadi, 39 and 99–100 (commentary). In many respects, the thought can be understood only with reference to the writings of Aḥmad al-Ghazālī's great follower ʿAyn al-Quḍāt al-Hamadhānī (executed 1131 CE); for a discussion, see Awn, *Satan*, 134 ff.

[32] Qur. 24.35: "God is the light of the heavens and earth. His Light is like this: there is a niche, and in it a lamp, the lamp inside a glass, a glass like a glittering star, fuelled from a blessed olive tree from neither east nor west, whose oil almost gives light even when no fire touches it—light upon light."

[33] "Vān nūr-i siyah z lā nuqaṭ bartar dān/Zān nīz guzashtīm nah īn mānad u-nah ān" in al-Ghazālī, *Savāniḥ*, *loc. cit.*

[34] The remark is reported by Ibn al-Jawzī and cited in ʿAṭṭār, *Ilāhī-nāmah*, 557; the statement reminds me of a remark supposedly made by the nineteenth century French novelist Joris-Karl Huysmans, who moved from Satanism to devout Catholicism: "With his hooked paw the devil drew me to God." Here, of course, it is the devil who is "pawed."

[35] The phrases in quotations come from al-Ghazālī's early dogmatic treatise *al-Iqtiṣād fīal-Iʿtiqād ("The Just Balance in Belief")*; see, for example, p. 101 of the Ankara (1962) edition. For the notion of "taste" (*dhawq*), which al-Ghazālī derives from Ibn Sīnā, see my "The Taste of Truth: The Literary Structure of the *Munqidh min al-ḍalāl*," in *Islamic Studies Presented to Charles J. Adams*, ed. Wael B. Hallaq and Donald P. Little (Leiden: Brill, 1991), 129–48.

Evil, Motherhood, and the Hindu Goddess Kālī

Rachel Fell McDermott
Barnard College

Whether because of her popular iconographic form, her New Age press, or two centuries of antagonistic Christian missionary preaching, Kālī is often thought of as an "evil" Hindu goddess, or, at the least, a goddess who can embody or mete out a good bit of evil. Indeed, fierce Indian goddesses like Kālī, and also Durgā, Cāmuṇḍā, Śītalā, and Chinnamastā, look horrific, with their battles against demons, their often ugly bodies shining with dripping blood, and their ability to send disease. Their myths also portray them as potent, easily angered, and dangerous, and where there are developed theological reflections concerning their significance, these goddesses are said to push devotees to new consciousness through forced confrontation with their dread characteristics. For people interested in theodicy, therefore, Kālī would seem to be a prime example of a deity whose devotees do not shy away from accepting evil in divinity—and hence she makes a good foil for much of current Western thinking about evil and God.

But the "problem" of evil, at least in its classic Western formulations, makes sense only in two contexts: first, that of belief, and second, that of a perceived contradiction between theological claims about God and experienced reality. If one is not a devotee of Kālī, then her nature in relation to the world is of no significant interest, and if one does not cherish ideas about her that are challenged by suffering and pain, then one is not in the realm of theodicy. If Kālī were simply evil, one would not need to debate why she allows this or that evil in the world. I know of no classical treatment of the "problem of evil" in the Kālī-centered literature; her hymns, myths, ritual texts, devotional poems, and devotees' testimonies are more concerned to announce her power, harness it for human ends, and plead for mercy.[1] And yet theodical questions **are** present in her tradition; her devotees **do** agonize about the perceived disjunction between her celebrated mercy and the realities of their lives. In what follows I chart some of these Hindu ruminations, some more explicit than others, by examining her Bengali iconographic tradition; Sanskrit myths and hymns; rituals, mantras, and philosophical claims as contained in the class of Sanskrit texts called the Tantras; Bengali devotional poetry; and biography and personal testimony. In parallel with many Western treatments of this topic, I proceed from a discussion of natural to moral evil, and conclude with what is unique, in terms of the theodicy debates, to this Goddess tradition. Throughout, I am interested in how, practically, devotees Eastern and Western have handled their pain, given the theological faith claims and resources available to them in their Kālī-focused heritage.

"When, and to whom, have you ever been kind?"[2] The Goddess and natural evil

Natural evil is that evil, from whatever non-human source, that comes from the outside and impinges upon our lives. It can include natural disasters like devastation from earthquakes or floods, the desolation of disease, and accidents that seem to have no human explanation. There are several perspectives, proceeding from the abstract to the more personal, from which Kālī can be said to be responsible for such evil. In very general terms, she is the Śākta equivalent of the Advaitic Brahman: as the supreme Śakti she is the All, the mistress of life and death in whom opposites are manifested and ultimately transcended. A slightly more personalized version of this explanation for evil envisions the Goddess as the self-absorbed player, the magician's daughter,[3] and the spinner of *māyā*, whose seemingly arbitrary play (*līlā*) is beyond our comprehension and yet must be accepted. According to both formulations, happiness and pain, ease and discomfort, health and sickness, and life and death, are all ultimately a part of her purview. This is expressed pictorially in Kālī's most famous iconographic pose, with two of her four hands showing boon-bestowing and fearlessness-granting gestures and the other two holding a scimitar and a sliced off head. Her visage is said to be horrible and off-putting, as well as charming, with a radiant smile. Opposites stand out on her body.

Her most famous myths also make the same claim. The sixth-century Sanskrit *Devī-Māhātmya*, a collection of three stories about the power of the Goddess in her various forms, is full of statements concerning her inherently paradoxical character: she is both deluder and liberator of the world (1.42–44); she creates, preserves and destroys, the last in her form as "the great night, the terrible night of delusion" (I.56–57, 59); she is fortune, or Lakṣmī, in the homes of those who do good, and misfortune, or Alakṣmī, in the abodes of those whose souls are wicked (4.4, 12.37); and she is said to be extremely charming and yet able to strike fear into her enemies (4.21, 25; 5.11).[4] Her devotional poetry tradition, begun in Bengal at the end of the eighteenth century and continuing up to today, makes similar assertions: in a famous song by Kamalākānta Bhaṭṭācārya (*c*. 1769–1820), Kālī is chided for cutting down—and hence rendering illegitimate the distinction between—evil **and** good.[5]

This set of claims about Kālī's embodiment of, supremacy over, and transcendence of the pairs of opposites may seem rather abstract and not terribly helpful to people suffering pain. But for those with a philosophical frame of mind, those used to meditating on the Goddess as the equivalent of Brahman,[6] it can be comforting. The Bengali saint Ramakrishna (1836–1886), perhaps the most famous of all recent Kālī-*bhaktas*, died slowly and extremely painfully of throat cancer in the last two years of his life. His experience of cancer was not docetic; it was agonizing, and he admitted it. "It was revealed to me in a vision that during my last days I should have to live on pudding. During my present illness my wife was one day feeding me with pudding. I burst into tears and said, 'Is this my living on pudding near the end, and so painfully?'"[7] And yet, when asked by the future Swami Vivekananda to pray to the Goddess for his own recovery, Ramakrishna reported, "I said to her, 'Mother, I cannot swallow food because of my pain. Make it possible for me to eat a little.' She pointed you all out to me and said, 'What? You are eating through all those mouths. Isn't that so?' I was ashamed and could not utter another word."[8] He saw that Kālī was all, a view consistent with the Śāktādvaita philosophy that underpins Kālī's Bengali tradition. During the rest of his illness he repeatedly spoke of his cancerous body, and the healthy bodies of his disciples, as pervaded by the same Śakti.

Non-Indian Kālī devotees have also found this aspect of the Goddess powerfully comforting. The German artist and writer Alice Bonner (1889–1981), who lived much of her adult life in Banaras, wrote during the World War II about the power of the Goddess Kālī "stalking the earth. I gave myself up to her universal embrace. There was a sweetness in this resignation of all will and effort—to put what is left of life into her hands and to let her mould it at her will, to become completely indifferent to the future, to life and death, and to accept anything at her hands, anything, either life with further realization or death and reabsorption into divine creation . . . ."[9] The painting of Kālī that Bonner slaved over for years aims to convey exactly this sense of the comfort of Kālī's duality as both destroyer and mother: Kālī's raised *abhaya mudrā* "in the black tragedy of life . . . is the hope and the assurance that the divine essence will finally prevail."[10] Rowan Hagen, a more recent devotee now living in Australia, describes a brush with pain that only Kālī could heal:

> In the mid '80s and early '90s, I underwent periods of intense experience and harsh insight that could not be contained, explained, or healed by the liturgy and practices of Paganism. Its world-view seemed too Utopian and superficial to bear under my emotional and existential crises. Only Kali-Ma was able to accompany and guide me though these waste-lands. Through her presence I was able to begin to understand and accept all the confusion, pain, and anger without any denial or contradiction of the capacity for clarity, compassion, and transcendence that also exists within us all.[11]

Hagen's friend and the founder of a group called "Mystics of Kali," Colin Robinson, shares this experience: "Like the king and the merchant in the *Devi Mahatmya*, I discovered the goddess in a period of frustration, loss, and confusion.

And the Goddess I discovered was not simply a comforter: at times she was a terrible, shattering presence . . . . Having encountered that side of her, I did not expect to live. But I . . . went on to discover the healing side of my Goddess."[12]

As the voices of these varied devotees attest, this conception of Kālī as embodying the play of opposites **can** be comforting, especially if one has trained oneself, through familiarity with Kālī's iconography, myths, hymns, and philosophical traditions, to expect her to be a union of polarities.[13] At its most abstract, this is equivalent to the tapestry and aesthetic solutions to the problem of evil in the West. At a more personal level, it echoes Isaiah 45, where God is said to send weal and create woe.[14]

Kālī is not simply an abstraction. She is also a mother, with a personality, a recognized form, and a set of myths. Swami Vivekananda (1863–1902), Ramakrishna's most famous disciple, had a special, even hidden relationship with Kālī, and he wrote two poems often quoted for their theodical content: "Kālī the Mother" and "And Let Shyama Dance There."[15] In both he alludes to the Goddess's stance among the corpses on the burning grounds, utilizing the image to make a spiritual point: learn to accept, even love, Kālī for her dread, terror-inspiring nature; only this method of facing fear will dissipate it. He

who dares misery love
and hug the form of death,
dance in destruction's dance,
to him the Mother comes.

Some devotees, lacking this type of temerity, see the dread side of Kālī less for its character-building potential than for its punitive value. For the Goddess's myths also imply that natural evil is the result of her active, anthropomorphically conceived will: she is disciplining, punishing, or testing her disciples. This rather more aggressive side to her character is affirmed in the *Devī-Māhātmya*, where she is dangerous, both to her foes and even to her followers,[16] and it is enunciated poetically in the *bhakti* tradition, where her devotees sometimes express their trepidation of the Mother.[17] Several contemporary Kālī-*bhaktas* in Calcutta over the past 15 years have admitted to me that they fear the Goddess, particularly for her retributive power.[18] The devotional poetry tradition provides an outlet for protesting against such willed "acts of God," especially if they are thought to be unjust. Here is an example from Rāmprasād Sen (ca. 1718–1775):

I'll die of this mental anguish.
My story is unbelievable;
what will people say
when they hear it?

The son of the World-Mother
is dying of hunger pangs!

The one You keep in happiness,
is he Your favorite child?

Am I so guilty
that I can't even get a little salt
with my spinach?

You called and called me,
took me on Your lap,
and then dashed my heart
on the ground!

Mother,
You have acted like a true mother;
people will praise You.[19]

In spite of the resource available in such poems—and sarcasm drips from the last stanza—interviews among Bengali and Western Kālī-devotees indicate that very few are willing to take this rather pugnacious approach to the Goddess; praying "along with" the *bhakti* poets in order to voice one's reproaches is apparently not, like the Jewish and Christian usage of the Psalms, a typical part of Kālī-devotionalism.[20] It is perhaps easier to attribute suffering to an abstract conception of the Goddess than, with a Vivekananda or a Rāmprasād, to square willed pain with a merciful Divine Mother.

The Mother can, however, help one in situations of distress, even if one is unwilling to attribute their cause to her intention. What we would in the West call the "faith" or "mystery solution" is very appealing the world over: one trusts in the ability of the Lord to save, and does not think too deeply about divine responsibility. Among her devotees, Kālī is universally invoked for help; here her iconography and mythology are an asset, as she is renowned for killing demons, whether Caṇḍa, Muṇḍa, and Raktabīja in the *Devī-Māhātmya*,[21] or generic demons in our lives. Precisely **because** she is fear-inspiring and grue-some, she is potent. Many of the 108 Names of Kālī and several of her various mantras, for instance, contain epithets describing her salvific potential: although she is terrible (*bhīmā*), with a frightful laugh (*aṭṭahāsyā*) and a horrible face (*karālavadanā*), she destroys sins (*pāpahāriṇī*), grants *mokṣa* (*mokṣadāyinī*), takes away the fear of death (*kālabhayavināśinī*), kills demons (*danuja-dalanī*), works for our benefit (*maṅgalakāriṇī*), awards yogic powers (*siddhapradāyinī*), and removes suffering (*duḥkha-hārā*).[22] This stance toward the Goddess is beautifully summed up in a signature line to a *bhakti* poem by the early nine-teenth-century Bengali poet, Raghunāth Rāy. Speaking of Kālī's form, he says,

"This is a frightful sight; it can make you fear./ But for a devotee/ She's a blessing who takes away fear."[23] David Kinsley, who popularized Kālī to a Western academic audience from the mid-1970s on, found comfort in this vision of the goddess. He nick-named the radiation machine that was battling his lung cancer Durgā, because of her ability to slay the cancer-cell demons, and before he died he told me that he took great solace in thinking of himself as returning to Kālī, the earth mother from which all things arise.

"I'm drowning in waters I made myself"[24]: Understanding moral evil

The law of karma, which is perhaps the most widely known answer to the problem of evil in the Hindu religious tradition,[25] is, of course, important to Śāktas as well. While karma falls within the realm of **moral** evil, since it is the result of actions we willingly and freely undertake, karma is also frequently blamed for **natural** evil, since, like fate, destiny, or the Goddess's inscrutable will, it is an abstraction that explains in general terms why something bad has happened. The Bengali devotional poetry is full of petitions to Kālī to rescue aspirants from the net of their own sins, and the poets often berate themselves for their pig-headedness in persisting in sinful behavior, when they know it to produce bad karma. The Tantras, when they do discuss suffering, usually do so in the context of desire and ignorance, which cause pain. For example, in the *Mahānirvāṇa Tantra*, suffering and sin are related, and are addressed under "expiatory acts," in chapter 11.[26] Too, the whole text of the *Kulārṇava Tantra* is framed by a conversation between Śiva and Devī (1.1-121), in which Śiva lectures the Goddess on the suffering and evil that arise from human attachment (v. 55).[27] Many Kālī-devotees use sacrificial ritual as a way to appease the Goddess's potential wrath against their sinful ways; in the famed *Kālikā Purāṇa*, the *locus classicus* for discussions of vegetable and animal sacrifice, goat sacrifice is said to please the Goddess, guarantee prosperity (59.29), destroy the misfortune of the giver (55.7b–11a), and cause the death of one's enemies (sometimes understood as sins), which are being impersonated by the live animals (67.151).[28]

In a sense, karma is the most satisfying theodicy theory, vis-à-vis God, because it allows one to blame oneself and to protect the divine from any hint of malfeasance. From a philosophical point of view, of course, this is a weak protection; one still might want to know why, if every soul began the same way, my karma has become worse than my neighbor's. Such a doubt is expressed poetically by Kamalākānta Bhaṭṭācārya, who taunts Kālī, saying: "Kind to some,/ harmful to others,/ You cover Your own fault/ by shifting the blame to others."[29] Swami Vivekananda, in a poem composed for his Western disciple Sister Nivedita (1867–1911), anticipated this objection. In the first stanza of

"The Cup," Nivedita's life path is blamed on her karma, in the second God tells her that the divine will controls her life, and in the third she is told to take comfort in letting go entirely of her intellective faculty. Trust is ultimately the best answer to suffering.[30]

> This is your cup—the cup assigned
> to you from the beginning.
>
> Nay, My child, I know how much
> of that dark drink is your own brew
> Of fault and passion, ages long ago,
> In the deep years of yesterday, I know.
>
> This is your road—a painful road and drear,
> I made the stones that never give you rest.
>
> I set your friend in pleasant ways and clear,
> And he shall come like you, unto My breast.
>
> But you, My child, must travel here.
> This is your task. It has no joy nor grace,
> But it is not meant for any other hand,
> And in My universe hath measured place,
> Take it. I do not bid you understand.
>
> I bid you close your eyes to see My face.

Conclusion: "There is mercy behind the Karalavadana"

In this last section, I discuss two topics: the ways in which the Kālī-centered religious tradition of Bengal seems to approach theodical thinking in a unique way, different from what we find in the West; and the several components of the "problem of evil" that are familiar to us in a Western context but appear to be missing here.

First, what is unique, or at least different in emphasis. In addition to their adoption of the karma theory of human suffering, we have seen among Kālī's devotees an explicit willingness to admit **both** the dangerous and awe-inspiring **and** the playful and seemingly arbitrary sides of divinity—although neither of these is evil, *per se*. Indeed, Kālī's personality is defined by the type of mother she is perceived to be: she is fiercely protective, like a mother, and, like all mothers, she may be occasionally angry and seemingly neglectful. However, her motherhood is quite unlike that of many other Hindu goddesses, also called Mā. Although she is described as beautiful, with uplifted breasts and a thin waist, such body parts are also said to be adorned with necklaces and skirts of cut heads and arms, and her torso is splashed with the blood of her victims. We do not encounter here the milk-oozing breasts of a loving Umā or Lakṣmī.[31] The ability to hold both the fierce and the merciful aspects of the Goddess together, and, with a Śāktādvaitic perspective, to insist that they are one, is movingly brought home to me by my friend and Śākta mentor, Minati Kar. In 2004 she suffered not only through a disfiguring operation to remove a third of her jaw, rotted with cancer, but also through the sudden death of her husband, in the middle of her radiation ordeal. In a letter to me about her experiences as a Kālī-devotee, she wrote, "there is mercy behind the Karala-vadana (or Terrible-faced One). Never for a second have I thought of Kali's evil nature that caused me so much of suffering. I think there is something beyond. When I was going through this turmoil I felt so many people loved me, so many people were concerned about me. This is also a gain. I pray and pray to keep alive in my heart the Karalavadana who is ever compassionate to a crying soul."[32]

If the karma theory and a place for the terrible in God are aspects of the solution to the problem of evil specific to Bengali Śāktism, there are other elements one might expect that are absent. For example, there is nothing in this tradition that is akin to the idea of a suffering God, a God who experiences what we do and hence models for us how to handle it. Unlike Jesus, there are no myths in which Kālī is a victim of moral or natural evil, although insofar as she is the All she shares in every experience of her embodied creation. Indeed, there are very few myths at all from which one might draw. For, in comparison with gods like Śiva and Viṣṇu, Kālī has few stories in her repertoire. The *Devī-Māhātmya* contains the most, but even this is not a great resource, as she appears only in the third story, and then only in the context of killing demons. The reason, I think, that a large narrative tradition has not grown up around Kālī is that she became, by the medieval period in eastern India, primarily a Tantric goddess. Her standard iconographic form is derived from the Tantric *dhyānas*, or prescribed visualization techniques for meditation, and although Kālī's stance upon Śiva on the cremation grounds has gained a popular story about her embarrassment at indecently stepping on the body of her husband, this interpretation is not derived from any text, and post-dates the earlier Tantric function of the icon, which was not to tell a story but to invite visual concentration. In Tantric meditation, one is supposed to focus on the Goddess's fierce might over the forbidding and the forbidden, and to understand the inherent complementarity between Śiva and Śakti, shown by her capacity to keep Śiva ever aroused.

As an aside, the closest in related myths that we get to a divine sufferer is Śiva, in his grief over the death of his wife, Satī. From a modern psychological vantage point, the Purāṇic description of his pain is very realistic: Śiva swoons, rolls on the ground, embraces her dead body, cries bitterly, and calls out her name.

Brahmā tries to console Śiva by talking him out of his sorrow, reminding him of his immutable nature. When this does not work, he promises Śiva that Satī will become his wife again, and eventually, simply sits with him by the shores of a secluded lake, where Śiva's mind begins to be soothed. Later, when Viṣṇu cuts off Satī's body parts bit by bit, Śiva loses contact with Satī's physicality and is at last calmed.[33] Whether Hindus grieving over the death of a loved one take comfort in this myth I do not know, but Śiva is not Kālī, and he is not the one whose tradition we are examining here.

Perhaps Ramakrishna, understood as an incarnation sometimes of Viṣṇu and sometimes of Kālī, serves better. Ramakrishna's disciples tried to cast his agony from throat cancer in a Christian light, wondering whether his pain was, like the crucifixion, accepted on behalf of the world, and many Kālī-devotees take comfort from his model of how to handle suffering. Note that the theological ruminations of Ramakrishna's Westernized disciples notwithstanding, there is little hint in Śākta literature or biography of anything resembling the Christian conception of atonement. Śāktas agree with Saint Paul that expiation can only be granted by God, through the mystery of divine grace; there is nothing automatic about human sacrificial and expiatory action. However, in Śāktism there is no intermediary figure, whether divine or human, who effects a propitiation, and no sense that someone cheats the devil out of his due, pays a ransom to God, or undergoes for us the punishment that God would inflict upon us. There is no parallel to Jesus the "lamb of God," who, as a sacrificial offering, paves the way for divine–human reconciliation. Kālī **is** occasionally homologized with the goat being offered to her, but only by anti-sacrifice advocates, who try to convince by means of special, illustrated posters that one should **not** offer animals to the Goddess, since that would amount to striking and decapitating her.

Another interesting lacuna in the theodical tool box of the Kālī tradition is the lack of an explicit recourse to the afterlife as a means of mollifying the suffering victim. There is no "Kālī's heaven" like the Vaiṣṇava Vaikuṇṭha or the various *bodhisattva* heavens of the Mahāyāna Buddhists, where pious souls will be rewarded or recompensed for their travails on earth. In the Christian tradition, the "afterlife solution" to the problem of evil is one way of excusing God for inequities, for all will be made clear later, after this life. Theologians refer to such explanations as contributing to a concept of "weak" evil: there is ultimately nothing that will not be redeemed, from a later perspective, and hence no evil remains evil, in the minds of the sufferer, forever. Only relatively recently, since the 1960s among post-Holocaust Jewish theologians, has there been any serious challenge to the concept of weak evil. Writers like Richard Rubenstein have argued famously that to deny "strong evil"—i.e., that evil that will never, ever be explained away—is to rob Holocaust victims of their dignity and to excuse an inexcusable God for the enormity of genocidal violence.[34]

As far as I can see, there is no concept of strong evil in the Śākta tradition, for this would militate against the bedrock assertion of Kālī's devotees that, in spite of her outward manifestation, she is a merciful Mother who is the ultimate essence of all, beyond the opposites of good and evil. Even the demons she kills are blessed by her touch and sent to heaven.[35] In her oscillating see–saw play, neither good nor evil gains the upper hand forever.

In sum, Bengali Śāktism presents us with a number of ways to approach theodicy. What we see, overall, is a tradition with the resources in it to blame the divine for suffering and evil. That few do so is merely evidence that Śāktas, like the rest of us, are human and find it easier not to blame God. But this, it seems to me, is not a drawback, for, as Elie Wiesel beautifully comments, "if you want difficulties, choose to live *with* God. . . . The real tragedy, the real drama, is the drama of the believer"[36]—and, I would add, the believer who must harmonize personal tragedy with a compassionate Mother of legendary, if rarely intellectually harnessed, fierceness.

Notes

[1] Nor are all Kālī-centered texts devotional in nature. Her Tantric ritual manuals are quite explicit in enunciating the super-human powers that her worship confers. For example, the Karpūrādi Stotra promises, "O Kālikā, O auspicious Kālikā with disheveled hair, from the corners of whose mouth two streams of blood trickle, they who recite . . . [your bīja mantras] destroy all their enemies, and bring under subjection the three worlds" (v. 3). Again, he who meditates on you and recites your mantra "has every pleasure that he wills upon the earth, and holds all great powers in the grasp of his lotus-like hands" (v. 11). See Sir John Woodroffe, *Hymns to the Goddess and Hymn to Kali* (Wilmot, WI: Lotus Light Publications, 1981), 290 and 310.

[2] This is the refrain to a Bengali devotional poem by Anthony Saheb castigating the Goddess for her unfair treatment. See Rachel Fell McDermott, *Singing to the Goddess: Poems to Kālī and Umā from Bengal* (New York: Oxford University Press, 2001), 56–58.

[3] One finds a number of references to the magician's daughter in the Bengali poetry. See, for example, McDermott, *Singing to the Goddess*, 48.

[4] See the translation by Thomas B. Coburn, *Encountering the Goddess: A Translation of the Devī-Māhātmya and a Study of Its Interpretation* (Albany, NY: State University of New York Press, 1991), 35, 37, 48, 50, 51, 53, and 82.

[5] Sadānandamayī Kālī; see McDermott, *Singing to the Goddess*, 49.

[6] Ramakrishna Paramahamsa was famous for his explicit equation of Brahman with Kālī. See, for example, M, *The Gospel of Sri Ramakrishna*, trans. Swami Nikhilananda, abridged edition (New York: Ramakrishna-Vivekananda Center, 1970), 378.

[7] *The Gospel of Sri Ramakrishna*, 473, in the diary entry for Wednesday, December 23, 1884.

8   *Ibid.*, "Introduction," 110. M also reports that Ramakrishna told him that his illness "is the will of the Divine Mother. This is how she is sporting through his body." *Ibid.*, 515; diary entry for Thursday, April 22, 1886.

9   Alice Bonner, *Diaries: India, 1934–1967*, ed. Georgette Bonner, Luitgard Soni, and Jayandra Soni (Delhi: Motilal Banarsidass, 1993), 99; entry for October 23, 1941, Banaras. Bonner also experienced the paradoxical nature of Kālī in a personal manner: "I felt [the touch of Kali] in Manali, Kulu Valley . . . Kali's destroying power is full of love, destroying all inanities and vacuities in which our life is so hopelessly enmeshed, and redeeming us for living Truth—opening the way to life eternal through sacrifice and death. . . . When it comes in the form of an experience there are hardly any words to be found for it. She came to me in an outburst of love which immediately broke down all the accumulated vanity of intellectual endeavor." *Ibid.*, 103–104; entry for July 23, 1942.

10 *Ibid.*, 199; entry for November 14, 1955, Banaras.

11 Rowan Hagen, "My life's journey has been different," *Ferment* (July 1999): 4.

12 Colin Robinson, "Discovering the divine in the depths of confusion," *Ferment* (April 1998): 7.

13 This point is also made by Edward C. Dimock, Jr., in reference to the disease goddess Śītalā, whose origin stories, or Maṅgalakāvyas, emphasize her polarities. Dimock asserts that reading and thinking about these polarities may help one later, when in trouble, for the texts demonstrate that only spiritually blind people find Śītalā to be malevolent. "By hearing of suffering, by realizing the extent of human frailty, one with eyes to see may be spared the necessity of more particular pain." However, not all devotees find such explanations helpful. It is hard to see grace in affliction. See Edward C. Dimock, Jr., "A Theology of the Repulsive: The Myth of the Goddess Śītalā," in *The Sound of Silent Guns and Other Essays* (Delhi: Oxford University Press, 1989), 131–32, 137, and 142.

14 Is. 45.6–7.

15 Swami Vivekananda, *The Complete Works of Swami Vivekananda*, vol. 4, 11th ed. (Mayavati: Advaita Ashrama, 1978), 384 and 506–10.

16 "Enraged, you (can) destroy (whole) families in a trice" (4.13). "When delighted, you destroy all afflictions, but when angered, you destroy all longed for desires" (11.28). See Coburn, *Encountering the Goddess*, 49 and 76.

17 Rāmprasād Sen, in one of his signature lines, states, "Shield your slave who cries out in utter horror!" (see McDermott, *Singing to the Goddess*, 26–27); Dāśarathi Rāy (d. 1857) characterizes Kālī, killing and laughing, as his enemy, (*ibid.*, 29–30); and Dīnrām (contemporary) complains, "I took shelter with you, I craved fearlessness, but I am dying of fear" (*ibid.*, 62).

18 Sadaycānd Mahārājādhirāj Māhtāb Bāhādur, former scion of the Burdwan Raj House, told me that because of the curse Kālī's poet-saint Kamalākānta placed on his house in the nineteenth century, he was "afraid to voice any complaint" to her (interview, October 13, 1991), and several heads of Śākta families in Calcutta whose tradition it is to sacrifice goats to the Goddess expressed a fear of stopping the tradition lest they upset her and cause her to punish them through some misfortune.

19 Rāmprasād Sen; see McDermott, *Singing to the Goddess*, 52–53. Other poems of this ilk can be found on 53–54, 54, 59–60, and 79. This tradition of critiquing the

Goddess for her behavior is not unique to the Bengali poetry; see the Sanskrit Tantric Karpūrādi Stotra, where she is told that it is not befitting her to be angry toward her ignorant creatures (v. 9). Woodroffe, *Hymns to the Goddess and Hymn to Kali*, 306.

[20] Minati Kar and Sanjukta Gupta, both Bengali Śākta theologians and adepts, told me that this practice is common only to select devotees of an unusually strong frame of mind (personal communications, March 17, 2005, and February 12, 2005, respectively). Colin Robinson, of the Mystics of Kali, reiterated the point: no one in his group or whom he knows cavils against her injustices (e-mail communication, March 12, 2005).

[21] Durgā (also called Ambikā and Caṇḍikā) and Kālī are primarily protectors and avengers in the *Devī-Māhātmya*. At the conclusion of the text, Durgā promises that anyone in any danger, from forest fires, villains, death sentences, prison, shipwreck, or personal affliction, will be released by listening to the *Māhātmya* stories (12.23–29). See Coburn, *Encountering the Goddess*, 81.

[22] See *Śrī Śrī Kālīr Aṣṭottar-śatanām*, ed. Śrī Kāliprasānna Vidyāratna (Calcutta: Aksay Library, n.d.).

[23] See McDermott, *Singing to the Goddess*, 24–25.

[24] Line 1b of a song by Dāśarathi Rāy; see McDermott, *Singing to the Goddess*, 72.

[25] Max Weber famously opined, "The most complete formal solution to the problem of theodicy is the special achievement of the Indian doctrine of karma, the so-called belief in the transmigration of souls." *The Sociology of Religion*, trans. Ephraim Fischoff, 4th ed. (Boston: Beacon Press, 1963), 145.

[26] See *Tantra of the Great Liberation (Mahānirvāṇa Tantra)*, trans. Arthur Avalon (New York: Dover Books, 1972), 262–80.

[27] See Sir John Woodroffe and M. P. Pandit, *Kulārṇava Tantra* (Delhi: Motilal Banarsidass, 1965), 5–6 and 132–43.

[28] *Kālikā Purāṇa*, trans. Biswanarayan Shastri, 3 vols. (Delhi: Nag Publishers, 1991), vol. 2, 771–72, and 849; vol. 3, 1025.

[29] McDermott, *Singing to the Goddess*, 60.

[30] Swami Vivekananda, "The Cup," in *The Complete Works of Swami Vivekananda*, vol. 5, 10th ed. (Mayavati: Advaita Ashrama, 1978), 177. I am grateful to Swami Tapasananda for drawing this poem to my attention. E-mail correspondence April 8, 2005.

[31] Compare, for example, the descriptions of two Hindu goddesses as found in Francis X. Clooney's book, *Divine Mother, Blessed Mother: Hindu Goddesses and the Virgin Mary* (New York: Oxford University Press, 2005). From the Sanskrit *Saundarya Laharī*, a hymn to Devī, v. 80: "O Goddess,/Your breasts perspire and rub against Your armpits,/then suddenly burst the garment covering them on each side;/to save Your threefold waist from breaking/the slender one binds it three times over,/quite enough,/as if with lavalī creepers" (63); and from the Tamil *Apirāmi Antāti*, a hymn to a South Indian form of Devī, v. 42: "Adorned with pearls/Your firm yet tender breasts grown as large as hills,/make the Lord's strong heart dance;/Your vagina is a fine cobra's head,/the Veda's cooling words are Your anklet bells,/O excellent lady" (76). It is interesting in this regard that when Bengali Kālī-bhaktas attempt to sweeten and soften the edges of their divine Mother, one of the ways they do so is to change her iconographic

depiction such that her body is more rounded, pleasant, and anthropomorphized; her weapons and trophies of victory more diminutive; and the expression on her face more compassionate.

[32] Minati Kar, personal communication, March 17, 2005.

[33] *Kālikā Purāṇa*, vol. 1, 187–223.

[34] The most succinct statement of this position is by Richard Rubenstein, *After Auschwitz: Radical Theology and Contemporary Judaism*, 2nd ed. (1966; Baltimore: Johns Hopkins University Press, 1992). See also Eliezer Berkovits, *Faith After the Holocaust* (New York: KTAV Publishing House, 1973), and Emil Fackenheim, *God's Presence in History: Jewish Affirmations and Philosophical Reflections* (New York: Harper and Row, 1972).

[35] In the *Devī-Māhātmya*, Caṇḍikā is credited with wanting her foes to go to heaven; that is why she slays them (4.17). Coburn, *Encountering the Goddess*, 50. In chapter 60 of the *Kālikā Purāṇa* we read of a future demon named Mahiṣa, who has a premonition of being killed by Durgā. He accepts this as part of his immutable destiny, but goes to her, extracting a boon that he will always lie at her feet and be blessed, even in death. *Kālikā Purāṇa*, vol. 2, 874–79.

[36] Elie Wiesel, "Richard L. Rubenstein and Elie Wiesel: An Exchange," in *Holocaust: Religious and Philosophical Implications*, eds. Michael Berenbaum and John Roth (New York: Paragon, 1989), 367.

The Predicament of Evil: The Case of Dorje Shukden

Georges Dreyfus
Williams College

Weak and strong concepts of evil

In dealing with the problem of evil in Tibetan Buddhism and its relation to the controversial deity Gyelchen Dorje Shukden (*rgyal chen rdo rje shugs ldan*), it may be helpful to start by gaining a minimum of clarity about what is meant here by *evil*. There is a way in which the term *evil* can be used as an equivalent of *bad* to characterize a morally reprehensible action. In Tibetan Buddhist terms, such an action is described as non-virtuous (*mi dge ba*), a moral fault (*sdig pa*)[1] and a bad action (*bya ba ngan pa*). Such an action is evil in what we could call the weak sense of the term.[2] But there is also a much stronger sense in which the term is used, for, more often than not, this word does not just describe an action or even express a qualified moral judgment, but rather gives voice to the much stronger condemnation of an action as representing a radical threat, an otherness that is too utterly frightening to be dealt with in usual ways. In this stronger sense, the more banal moral failings such as lying, cheating or insulting others do not qualify as evil. Only actions that are thought especially loathsome, particularly those that are taken to be threatening to the self, do. Few people in this country would hesitate in characterizing the 9/11 attack in this way, though many would not show the same readiness when discussing the killing of tens of thousands of civilians through aerial bombardments.[3]

It is clear that this distinction between weak and strong concepts of evil is artificial. It is not the case that there are two distinct notions whose use can be marked apart. Nevertheless, it becomes possible to make analytic distinctions among various uses of these terms when we stop thinking about good and evil as intrinsic properties of actions and consider them as polar opposites that we deploy when faced with particularly problematic events. In such circumstances, we use these evaluative categories to form judgments about events and decide about a course of action. But in doing so, we also create new problems. For when we use these categories, we are easily tempted into holding tightly to them, reifying them and putting a great deal of explanatory weight on them. We make a radical separation between good and bad, reifying evil into some kind of

autonomous external force bent on bringing harm. In this perspective, extraordinary harmful events such as diseases, catastrophes and premature deaths
are not the result of natural processes but come to be seen as the works of dark
forces.

It is in this strong, reified and polarized sense that I will use this term here
and ask the question of the place of evil in the Tibetan Buddhist universe and
its relation to a particular deity. It is often assumed that the use of a highly reified concept of external evil is alien to the spirit of Buddhism, a tradition based
on the rejection of such overly dualistic and polarized notions. David Loy
expresses well this normative view when he says, "For Buddhism, evil, like everything else, has no essence or substance of its own; it is a product of impermanent
causes and conditions. Buddhism places less emphasis on the *concept* of evil
than on its roots: three causes of evil, also known as the three poisons—greed,
ill-will and delusion."[4] For Loy, and for many other Buddhist thinkers, the use
of the concept of evil as referring to an external realm of dark forces opposed
to the good is deeply problematic. Buddhism emphasizes the fact that what
makes an action bad is not the intrinsic nature of its author but his or her lack
of understanding. In this perspective, bad actions arise from ignorance, greed
and ill-will, not from the deeper nature of individuals, who are seen as remaining uncorrupted in their nature and hence as having the possibility of freeing
themselves entirely from these defilements.[5] Thus, bad actions, however morally regrettable they may be, do not qualify as evil in the radical sense of the
term. Rather, they are mistakes that will lead their authors to temporary, though
profound, sufferings, and the agents who commit such deeds are to be seen
with compassion rather than castigated as fallen or corrupted.[6]

This normative view of evil is well enshrined in the tradition, going back to
its starting point, the enlightenment of the Buddha and his struggle with the
personification of evil, Māra. It is out of this struggle with the Evil One, the representation of all what is bad and dangerous in the Buddhist universe, that the
Buddha's enlightenment arises. This struggle is well known and does not need
to detain us here. What should be clear, however, is that Māra's story confirms
the normative view sketched above. Māra, who attempts to prevent the Bodhisattva from reaching enlightenment, fails miserably and is presented more as
an object of compassion than a veritably fearsome being. As Ling shows, most
of the relevant passages do not present the struggle between the Bodhisattva
and Māra as a real confrontation but as a dismissal. Māra is recognized for what
it is, deflated and dismissed as powerless and pitiful. Buddhists are further
advised to adopt the same attitude, viewing the difficulties of life less as brought
about by radically negative forces and more as resulting from the internal delu-
sions that cloud our judgment and thus lead us to suffering.[7]

This is not to say that Buddhist traditions deny the reality of external evil
forces. On the contrary, the existence of such forces has broad acceptance
within the classical normative tradition, but the role of these forces is usually

downplayed. It is the internal poisons mentioned above that are the real dangers, not the external beings, however fearsome they may appear at first sight. Māra's story confirms this view, for the power of Māra depends on the failure of the person to recognize temptation for what it is. Once the Bodhisattva recognizes that Māra's three daughters are just the manifestations of the three poisons, Māra fades away, leaving the Bodhisattva triumphant. Hence, at the end of the day, Māra is less an autonomous external force in the universe than the foil whose subjugation reveals the greatness of the Buddha.

This scenario of the taming of evil forces as a means of glorifying the Buddha and emphasizing his power to overcome radical polarities is repeated in a number of later scriptures. Ronald Davidson has depicted the role that the myth of the subjugation of Maheśvara plays in the establishment of the legitimacy of several tantric traditions.[8] For example, the *Tattvasaṃgraha* presents the subjugation of the god Shiva (*maheśvara*) as one of the important actions inaugurating the mandala of the Buddha Vairocana. Shiva is first shown as defiant, asserting his own power and supremacy, but he is quickly tamed by Vajrapāṇi, who shows him what power is really about. Finally, Vairocana takes pity on the god, and, after renaming him, allows him to enter the mandala and receive the consecration that will open his way to enlightenment.[9] Similar stories appear in connection with various tantric deities, particularly in connection to Cakrasaṃvara, which is presented as emanating extremely fierce Herukas to tame Shiva.

And yet, there is much more to say concerning the role of evil in Buddhism in general and Tibetan Buddhism in particular. The tradition that sees evil as being in need of being deconstructed rather than struggled against represents only one take on the question. This normative view has to be seriously modified once one leaves the rarefied doctrinal domain and inspects Tibetan Buddhism on the ground. One then sees that the strong notion of evil is far from being irrelevant, for there are a number of practices and deities that seem to pertain to this notion, both at the elite and the popular levels. In this essay, I focus on one of these deities, the controversial deity Gyelchen Dorje Shukden, and its relation to evil. I argue that the strong notion of evil as being a realm of dark forces persistently opposed to the good is highly relevant to understanding the role of this deity, despite its problematic status in normative terms. I also examine the relation that this deity seems to have with the forces of evil, showing how this deity, which is in charge of protecting its followers from evil, seems to be contaminated by the very forces that it was meant to prevent. This contagion illustrates what I call here *the predicament of evil*. Once one enters the dark realm, that is, once one radically polarizes the situation and invokes the presence of some radically evil other, it becomes hard to extricate oneself from the polarization and avoid being caught by what one is seeking to overcome. Tibetan Buddhist thinkers have not failed to notice this problem. In the last section of this essay I examine the ways in which they have attempted to account for the deity's violence and solve the predicament that this creates. I conclude that

these attempts have unfortunately failed, particularly in the case of the controversy surrounding Dorje Shukden, which continues to agitate the Tibetan
community with little hope of immediate solution.

Evil and the role of dharma protectors

One may first wonder about the relation of Shukden to the notion of evil. This
was in fact my first reaction when I was asked to discuss this topic. Why speak
of evil in relation to Shukden? It is true that some of Shukden followers have
been accused of committing a triple murder in February 1997 in Dharamsala.
The murder was particularly gruesome, being made to resemble a ritual sacrifice.
Its presumed authors, who were designated as such by the CBI (Central Bureau
of Investigation, the Indian equivalent of the FBI) on the basis of strong forensic evidence but who have fled to Tibet, were known to be highly dedicated to
this deity. Hence, it is not unreasonable to assume that this gruesome murder
was committed by some in the name of this deity in order to punish the victim,
the late Lobzang Gyatso, who had been one of its most forceful critics. But even
if this were true, it would not be enough to establish a meaningful connection
between Shukden and a robust notion of evil. Followers of various divinities are
well known for committing all kind of exaction but we usually do not take this
to be sufficient ground to warrant such a connection.

Another possible but equally unsatisfactory way of connecting Shukden
to evil is *via* its gruesome iconographic representation. Shukden is indeed
depicted as a fearsome deity, holding in his right hand a sword dripping with
blood and in his left hand the heart torn out from the chest of its enemies. But
this seems hardly enough to connect our deity to the notion of evil, for many
tantric deities are surrounded by such violent symbols. This was in fact the
mistake of earlier Orientalists, who when confronted with Tibetan Buddhism
in general and its pantheon in particular, concluded that this tradition was
nothing but a form of devil worship. One of the chief exponent of this view
was L. Waddel, who dismisses the Tibetan pantheon, as being "peopled by a
bizarre crowd of aboriginal gods and hydra-headed demons, who are almost
jostled off the stage by their still more numerous Buddhist rivals and counter-
feits."[10] For Waddell, as for many after him, Tibetan Buddhism is a degeneration
of early Buddhism in which rituals played little role. This originally pure tradition
gradually changed, becoming heavily ritualized and loaded with superstitions.
For Waddell, Tibetan Buddhism is the ultimate stage in this degenerative process.
Tibetans have moved so far from the original model that they not only have
incredibly elaborate forms of ritual but even engage in devil worship. Speaking
of Mahākala, an important protective deity whose role will be examined below,
Waddell says, "The demon-kings, however, are the favorite ones. They are repulsive monsters of the type of the Hindu Śiva. These morbid creations of the later

Tāntrism may be considered a sort of fiendish metamorphoses of the supernatural Buddhas. Each of these popular demon-kings . . . has a consort, who is
even more malignant than her spouse."[11] For Waddell, the iconography of many
Tibetan deities reflects an obvious connection with demonology that extends
not only to protective deities but to the entire realm of wrathful tantric deities
(*khro bo*). For him, it is the very nature of tantra as a form of degeneration that
is revealed by the grotesque and frightening features through which these
deities are represented.

It is clear that this view has by now been thoroughly exposed as reflecting
more the Victorian preoccupation of its author rather than the realities of
Tibetan Buddhism.[12] Tantra is not a degenerate form of Buddhism but the
result of an evolution of a complex and multi-faceted tradition. The wrathful
representations of various deities are not the mark of a demonic cult, but, more
often than not, the sign of the Buddha's ability to transcend evil, as in the
story of Māra. Hence, the question remains: what is the connection of Shukden
with evil? To answer we need to pay closer attention to the nature of the deity.
Shukden belongs to an unusual type of deity, that of the dharma protector
(*chos skyong srung ma*). As its name indicates, this type of deity is in charge
of protecting the Buddhist tradition and its followers. But this raises several
questions. How does the deity protect its followers? And, perhaps more importantly, against whom?

The usual answer is that such a deity protects its followers from the obstacles
(*gegs*) that can harm them. These obstacles can be diseases or accidents. For
example, it is not unusual to invoke such a deity during the rituals performed
to cure people from some sickness. Such a deity can also be invoked in case of
more extraordinary events. For example, many older Shukden followers who
escaped from Tibet confided to me that they were convinced that their escape
from Tibet was due to the intervention of the deity. As support they would cite
various close calls and difficult circumstances which they overcame by implor-
ing their protective deity. But this form of assistance is not the only kind of
protection provided by these deities. For the obstacles are often not just tragic
circumstances but can be actual beings, who are thought to be harming the
deity's followers and preventing them from reaching their goals. These beings
can be other human beings, whose actions, magical or not, are taken to harm
the deity's followers, or they can be non-human beings, many of whom are
thought to be particularly prone to harm humans.

Such beliefs are not unusual in the type of peasant society that was pre-
modern Tibet. In such societies, people tend to think that their life, property,
and happiness are threatened by external agents bent on harming them.
These ill-intentioned agents can be humans, jealous neighbors trying to settle
old scores, relatives envious of one's successes, or unrelated people acting out
of pure malice or bent on creating harm out of spite. But these agents can also
be non-humans, ghosts, spirits, ghouls, mountain gods, lake gods, snake-spirits,

rock spirits, etc. that are thought to surround humans and can at times represent a significant danger.

In pre-modern Tibet, the latter type of evil seems to have been more important than the former. Although attacks from sorcerers or sorceresses were not unknown and the envy of neighbors was feared,[13] the most often cited forms of harm seems to have come from the multiplicity of external entities that inhabit the Tibetan landscape.[14] Some of these entities are not necessarily evil but nevertheless represented a significant danger. For example, the snake-spirits (*glu*, identified with the Indian *nāga*), who reside in sources, lakes and trees, are thought to be very possessive and react to the pollution of the natural entities they inhabit. Similarly, the lords of the soil (*sa bdag*), the local spirits who own the place, can get very angry when their domain is tampered with. But there are other entities that are much more malicious, directly corresponding to the polarized and reified notion of evil discussed here. They are the beings who are bent on harming gratuitously humans, even when they are not offended. The devils (*bdud*, that is, *māra*) are negative spirits, which, having opposed during several lifetimes the positive forces of Buddhism, create trouble for its practitioners. There are also the red-spirits (*tsan*), the spirits of monks, who have fallen from their monastic commitments and have died prematurely. Finally, last but not least, there are the king-spirits (*rgyal po*), the spirits of evil kings or important religious teachers who have died after breaking their pledges. They are considered extremely dangerous because they are the spirits of powerful people whose death has disrupted the normal course of events.[15]

Protecting their followers from this kind of harm is one of the main tasks of protective deities, which are described as deities having taken a special oath of protecting Buddhist practitioners against the attacks of human or non-human enemies. Often such an oath is extracted by a tantric adept, who forces the deities to abandon their evil ways, convert them to Buddhism and entrust them the protection of the Buddhist tradition and its followers. Hence, these deities are called *dharma protectors,* i.e., the protector of the Buddhist doctrine. They are in charge of protecting Buddhists against potential enemies, the "obstacles" we mentioned above. These evil agents are also described as the "enemies of Buddhism" (*bstan dgra*) since they attack the followers of Buddhism. They are the other whose attack is greatly feared and against which the self and group define their identity.

The role of protective deities, however, is not simply to provide a reassuring source of comfort or even a focus of identity. They are supposed to take their task very seriously, offering highly effective protections to their followers, who rely on them. The question is then: how can they accomplish this task? This is where the relation between protectors and evil becomes entangled, for protectors are not just beatific figures who dispel evil through their compassion, like the Buddha did with Māra. Such a peaceful approach is commendable and normatively central to the tradition, but it is not necessarily the most immediate and effective way to protect oneself. There are other more immediate ways to do this, and this is precisely what the protectors are meant to provide, an active and effective guard. The protectors do this by dealing offensively with the evil forces, destroying them and forcefully transforming them into beneficial agents.

The stories associated with Mahākala illustrate quite clearly the role of protective deities as violent defenders of the Buddhist tradition. In some stories, Mahākala is presented as protecting Buddhists against the attacks of their Hindu adversaries. In other narratives, the deity is introduced as a manifestation of Cakrasaṃvara as well as a powerful deity born out of the union of the great gods Shiva and his partner, Umā Devī. The deity is sent to eliminate the evil forces that have taken control of the earth. It enters into a frenzy of violence, piercing the devils with the trident that it had stolen from them, decapitating the king of the evil forces and killing many other devils. The deity's victory is finalized by taking the wife of the king of the devils as partner and the other female devils as servants. The deity then revives all the killed devils and makes them take an oath to abandon their harmful ways and protect the Buddhist teaching.[16]

A similar scenario of the conversion of problematic deities into beneficent protective forces is found in one of the foundational myths of Tibet as a Buddhist country, the saga of Padmasambhava.[17] The tantric adept is described as coming to Tibet at the end of the eighth century at the invitation of the emperor Trisong Detsen (*khri srong sde btsan*) to subdue the local gods, who had attempted to prevent the construction of Samye, the first Buddhist monastery in Tibet. Padmasambhava tamed these local gods through his ritual powers, converting them to Buddhism. He also bound them to an oath, putting them in charge of protecting Buddhist practitioners from potential harm. In this way, he enabled the construction of Samye by the emperor, a metaphor for the transformation of Tibet from a land "beyond the pale" (*mtha' 'khob*) into a Buddhist country of high civilization.[18]

The nature and role of protectors are clearly revealed by these narratives. Protectors are violent deities, who are in charge of opposing the forces of evil, the threatening others. In opposing these forces, protectors tend to act like them, using the kind of violent actions that these entities deploy against humans. Thus, the relation of protectors with the forces of evil is not just oppositional, it is also mimetic, and this is not lacking in serious difficulties, as we will see shortly in the case of Shukden. Finally, it is also clear that the practice of protectors presupposes a particular view of the world as permeated by magical forces. This universe is peopled by a multitude of invisible but real entities such as ghosts, local spirits, mountain and lake gods, snake-spirits, etc. The experience of living in such a living universe is a mode of experience of the world that many Tibetans still hold to be self-evident.[19]

The role of Shukden

The problematic nature of this entanglement is in evidence in the case of our deity, Gyelchen Dorje Shukden. Its very name, "Great Magical King Spirit Endowed with the Adamantine Force," shows quite clearly its relation to evil forces, in this case the king-spirits, one of the most dangerous among the various types of malicious spirits mentioned above, as illustrated by the founding myth of the Shukden cult as understood by its followers.

When asked to explain the origin of the practice of Dorje Shukden, its followers point to a rather obscure and bloody episode of Tibetan history, the premature death of Trulku Drakba Gyeltsen (*sprul sku grags pa rgyal mtshan*, 1618–1655). Drakba Gyeltsen was an important Geluk[20] lama who was a rival of the Fifth Dalai-Lama, Ngakwang Losang Gyatso (*ngag dbang blo bzang rgya mtsho*, 1617–1682).[21] The details of this rivalry are rather obscure and do not need to detain us, since I have discussed them elsewhere.[22] But what is clear is that in 1655 Drakba Gyeltsen suddenly died. The exact conditions of his death are controversial and shrouded in legends, but the important point is that his death seems to have been perceived to relate to his rivalry with the Fifth Dalai-Lama. It was also taken to have been violent and hence the kind of death that leads people to take rebirth as dangerous spirits. According to standard Indian and Tibetan cultural assumptions, a person who is killed often becomes a ghost and seeks revenge.[23] Such a spirit is considered all the more dangerous when the person has religious knowledge, which is said to explain the particular power of Drakba Gyeltsen's spirit. This is not just one among many protectors but a particularly dangerous one, the vengeful ghost of a powerful person who died violently and hence prematurely.

According to the Shukden legend, Drakba Gyeltsen manifested himself as a *gyelpo*, i.e., the dangerous king-spirit of a religious figure bent on extracting revenge against those involved in his death. Since he had been a virtuous lama, however, Drakba Gyeltsen turned his anger from a personal revenge to a nobler task, the protection of the Geluk tradition by punishing those who were tempted to detract from its doctrinal purity by mixing it with the teachings of other Tibetan Buddhist traditions, particularly those of the Nyingma school.[24] The first manifestation of this wrathful mission was the destruction of Drakba Gyeltsen's own estate and the haunting of his silver mausoleum, which became animated by a buzzing noise before being thrown away in the waters of the Kyichu. But the real target was the Fifth Dalai-Lama, less because of his connection to Drakba Gyeltsen's death than because of his practice of Nyingma teachings. The Fifth Dalai-Lama began to encounter various difficulties and troubling signs. Frightened by these wrathful manifestations, he decided to pacify this spirit by establishing its cult at Dol where a small temple was built to pacify the deity.[25]

This striking story is less an historical rendering of troubling events than the founding myth of a religious practice.[26] As such, however, it is highly significant, reflecting a number of important political, religious and cultural themes. For our purpose, it will be sufficient to underline Shukden's nature as the king-spirit of a powerful religious figure killed prematurely. This origin marks Shukden as a particularly powerful and effective spirit. This is not a high benevolent and impotent god, but a deity directly involved in the very dark violence that it is supposed to protect its followers from. This power is reinforced by the fact that Shukden is the spirit of a religiously powerful religious figure, somebody who, according to Tibetan standard cultural assumptions, has strong religious powers, particularly in relation to taming the forces of evil mentioned above. This origin marks Shukden as a highly ambivalent figure, born in violence and in charge of using this violence against the enemies of its followers. Shukden's troubling character is well illustrated by some of the other stories surrounding this deity.

Particularly significant are the stories of two prominent Geluk figures who are presented by Shukden's followers as falling prey to the deity's vengeful activity. The Fifth Penchen Lama, Lobzang Palden (*blo bzang dpal ldan chos kyi grags pa*, 1853–1882), is described as incurring Shukden's wrath because he adopts Nyingma practices. Despite the repeated warnings of the protector, Lobzang Palden refuses to mend his ways and persists in his practice. After an unsuccessful ritual self-defense, which backfires, Lobzang Palden dies at the age of twenty-nine. Another equally troubling story is that of the preceding reincarnation of Zigyab Rinboche (*gzigs rgyab rin po che*), a Geluk lama from Trehor, who studies and practices Nyingma teachings. Later he decides to receive one of its central teachings, Jamgön Kongtrul's (*'jam mgon kong sprul,* 1813–1899) *Rin chen gter mdzod.* According to the story, Shukden warns Zigyab against this course of action but the lama refuses to heed the protector's advice. In short order, he falls sick and dies without having been able to listen to the teachings.

The meaning of these stories, which are found in the texts written by some of the prominent followers of the deity,[27] is as clear as it is troubling. Geluk practitioners should not even listen to the teachings of other Tibetan Buddhist traditions. Any attempt to do so will be taken as a betrayal of the tradition and punished accordingly by the deity, whose very nature as a king-spirit guarantees particularly swift retribution. Moreover, Shukden is not just bent on sectarian violence; he is also extremely vengeful, propelling the victims toward a particularly gruesome death. Some of the victims die mad, whereas others perish while their "wealth, accumulated possessions and descendants disappear without leaving any trace."[28] This sectarian violence shows the particular character of Shukden as a protector and its problematic relation to evil.

The deity is in charge of protecting its followers from evil but in doing so, it mimics and reproduces the very evil that it is supposed to protect from. This is why the deity is thought to be effective, but this is also why its actions are at times particularly troubling. For when Shukden enacts its violence to protect the Geluk tradition, it becomes unclear on which side this violence is. Is it a force for the good, or is it a force that is out of control, killing several virtuous religious figures? In the last two stories, the two lamas who are killed by Shukden are not depicted as bad characters who deserve their fate but as renowned practitioners who remain carelessly unmindful of the vengeful nature of the deity. Thus, the point of these two stories is not that Shukden will take care of bad people but that the deity is so dangerous that even virtuous though careless practitioners are at risk. So, if you are a member of the Geluk tradition, watch out and stop being interested in the teachings of other traditions, otherwise we cannot guarantee your safety, however virtuous you may be!

This highly sectarian message has been the source of a sustained and at times violent controversy among Tibetans. The source of this controversy, which I have explored elsewhere,[29] is easy to understand when one considers the troubling character of the deity's actions. For if the deity is in charge of visiting retribution on those interested in the Nyingma tradition, then it is quite likely that those who do so feel threatened. This is precisely what has happened. The Dalai-Lama, who relies on the Nyingma tradition for many of the rituals that he requires (despite his greater affiliation with the Geluk school) has felt targeted by the cult of the deity. After all, who was the deity's first target, according to the founding myth of the Shukden cult, if not the Fifth Dalai-Lama? For various reasons I cannot enter into here, the present Dalai-Lama has tended to take this sectarian message very seriously and has tried to restrict the cult as much as possible among his followers. The controversy, which started in the 1970s, has continued unabated, going through various highly unfortunate episodes such as the triple murder mentioned above.

These developments also illustrate the particularly troubling relation with evil that a protective deity such as Shukden has. These deities are in charge of protecting their followers from evil by using evil. But evil is not so easy to manipulate. It tends to contaminates those who enter into its orbit, even when they are supposed to fight against it. In her famous work, *Les mots, la mort, les sorts,* Jeanne Favret-Saada describes the persistence of sorcery practices among peasants in the West of France in the 1970s.[30] She shows how many peasants are still routinely engaged in acts of sorcery and counter-sorcery, despite the ridicule heaped on these practices by the dominant Enlightenment discourse. The peasants whom Saada examines are keenly aware of this ridicule and hide their involvement. Nevertheless, when they face misfortunes such as the repeated deaths of cattle or the persistence of unexplained diseases, they have recourse to supernatural explanations. In their own terms, they are "caught" by evil, meaning that they fall prey to the magical attacks of some of ill intentioned neighbors. The only way out is to have recourse to another sorcerer, who will deliver them by casting a counter-spell on the first sorcerer. A magical fight may ensue between the two sorcerers and the patient may be cured only when the first sorcerer is defeated and dies or leaves town. Thus entering into the domain of evil is a very serious matter, which concerns not just those caught in the cycle of magical and counter-magical actions, but extends even to those who open themselves to these sorcery narratives. The very fact of listening and giving credence to these stories is a sign that one has been caught, that one has entered in a dark cycle in which evil can only be countered by equally problematic counter-evil, as claimed by Saada's informants.

The same infectious character seems to be at work in the case of our deity. Shukden's violence is not limited to the destruction of evil forces but engulfs deserving though careless practitioners, who are harmed by the deity in its endeavor to protect the Geluk tradition. This harm is not a retribution for bad actions but is the result of the failure on the part of the two lamas to comprehend the problematic nature of the deity. The deity is born from evil, and it uses evil to accomplish its mission, but in the process, its violence tends to get out of control, harming those who are not careful. As Saada's peasants put it, once evil is unleashed, it "catches" people, even if they are animated by the best intentions. This is why many of Saada's informants are so reluctant to talk about the sorcery stories they have heard. They realize that once one enters into the realm of radical polarities, it is hard to get out unscathed.

Mundane and supramundane protectors

The violent nature of Shukden's actions is not, however, without serious normative problems, since it takes place within a tradition in which violence is considered the first and foremost moral evil. Destroying the life of any being, even a demonic spirit bent on harming humans, is considered an extremely grave moral offense. How then can Buddhists reconcile their reliance on protectors, who use violence, with their very real commitment to the moral norms of their tradition?

Responding to such a question is not an easy task and would require a much more rigorous analysis than is possible here. Let us first notice, however, that the richness of Tibetan Buddhism offers considerable resources for answering this question in normative terms. For example, the bodhisattva ideal,[31] which is at the center of the Tibetan tradition, allows a certain use of violence, use that would have been impossible in the earlier tradition. In some of the Mahāyāna Sūtras, the bodhisattva, who is completely devoted to others' welfare, is allowed the use violence since this violence is entirely deployed for the benefit of others. The *locus classicus* of this doctrine is the story of the Buddha, who in a previous birth killed the evil captain of a ship who was about to murder his five hundred passengers. Seeing the dreadful consequences that this would have had for the killer himself, the bodhisattva took upon himself the negative karma and killed the evil captain.[32]

This use of skillful means for the sake of helping others is further amplified in the tantric tradition where the adept is given a large array of ritual means to achieve this goal. These practices are of various types, ranging from the peaceful (*zhi ba*) rituals intended to appease obstacles to the much more problematic violent (*drag po*) rituals that forcefully tackle them.[33] The latter kind is particularly problematic since it seems to violate the basic moral imperative of the tradition. But here again, the bodhisattva ideal and the doctrine of skillful means allow the integration of this type of ritual action within the normative tradition. Violent rituals can be deployed as skillful means by the bodhisattva provided that he or she performs them for the sake of others and not for his or her own benefit. Moreover, the bodhisattva must be able to control the result of the violence ritually unleashed. Within the framework of tantric practice, this means that the he or she uses rituals to kill the person but also that he or she has to be able to revive them, as Mahākala did with the forces of evil, or at least to ensure the victim's favorable rebirth.

It is within this context that the practice of propitiating protectors has to be understood. Practitioners deal with the protector within the context of their tantric practice. This integration is, however, far from smoothing out all the problems and leaves out a number of questions. First, there are questions about the qualities required for such a practice. If only the bodhisattva who is able to control the long term effects of the ritual is able to unleash such violence, then it would seem that very few people would qualify for this kind of practice. After all, who could seriously make the claim of having such abilities outside of a few saintly figures? Second, there are also questions about the nature of the deities involved in these rituals. It is here that a crucial normative distinction has to be made between two types of deity.

Some of the deities involved in ritual violence, particularly some of the protectors, are supra-mundane deities (*'jig rten las 'da pa'i lha*). They are considered as highly realized bodhisattvas or buddhas who have taken the particular task of protecting their followers. This is the case of Mahākala and of the Great Goddess (*dpal ldan lha mo*, belden lhamo, the Tibetan equivalent of *Mahā-devī*), who are considered wrathful manifestations of the very peaceful Avalokiteshvara. Other protectors such as Shukden and Nechung are considered mundane (*'jig rten pa'i lha*).[34] They may be powerful spirits but remain prisoners of the realm of cyclic existence. Hence, they can become dangerous, especially when they feel offended. As worldly entities, these gods are profoundly different from the tantric deities (*yi dam*), who are enlightened and hence freed from the polarities of the world.

This normative distinction between mundane and supra-mundane gods is very important, but is not without several problems. As Buddhists, Tibetans take refuge only in the Triple Gem, namely, the Buddha (the teacher compared to a wise doctor), the Dharma (his teaching compared to the actual medicine), and the Sangha (the community of realized practitioners),[35] and are not supposed to take refuge in any other principle. This does not mean that Buddhists cannot deal with worldly gods but that they cannot worship them. They may propitiate them, asking their help, but cannot entrust their spiritual welfare to them. This distinction is not, however, always easy to make or keep. Propitiation of worldly gods often shades into feelings of reverence and devotion. Buddhist virtuosi are very attentive to mark this difference, but because they are part of Tibetan culture, they feel the pull and power of worldly gods. They also know, however, that as Buddhist practitioners they cannot go too far in their devotion. Ordinary monks and lay people find themselves in an even more difficult position. They know that they cannot take refuge in these gods, but they feel at their mercy, and are, therefore, tempted to be a little more devoted to them than they should be.

There is also the particular problem raised by the reliance on violent deities. Even if we grant that Buddhists can propitiate worldly deities for the sake of acquiring wealth, getting cured, etc., it would seem that it is entirely a different matter to require the violent intervention of such a deity. If these deities are enlightened, one can trust them to act within the norms of the tradition. But what about worldly protectors? They cannot be trusted to act with such restraint, since it is their very nature not to be bound by such norms. Thus, it would seem that ordinary Tibetan Buddhists, who are clearly not able to satisfy the highly ethical standards demanded by the tradition for the use of violence, should find it difficult to request the violent intervention of such worldly protectors and should limit themselves to the help of enlightened deities. But this limitation would greatly diminish the usefulness of the pantheon, raising the usual problem of the high gods, who may be admirable but too elevated to be of much use in situations where less elevated actions are required. In Buddhist terms, the supramundane protectors are too enlightened to be always useful. As enlightened beings, they unleash their violence only when they consider that the threatening others, the enemies of Buddhism, represent a threat according to the ethical norms of the tradition, as the Bodhisattva did when he killed the evil captain. This kind of violence is strictly motivated by compassion and hence it is impartial, aiming at benefiting the beings who are its target. But this kind of violence is not always very useful since it cannot be used for one's personal advantage or even protection. In the story, the Bodhisattva kills the evil captain not just to protect the five hundred passengers but also to prevent the perpetrator from harming himself.

Quite different is the violence of mundane deities, for it involves beings who are not considered equanimous but are thought to have quasi-human emotions. Since these deities experience these emotions, they are seen as partial and can be enrolled in actions performed on behalf of the person or the group who propitiates them. But this usefulness is in obvious tension with the norms of the tradition, which forbids the use of violence for worldly purpose. Hence, there seems to be a tension within the pantheon of protectors that cannot be easily solved. Either the protector is too high (supramundane), and then it is not useful, or the protector is too low (mundane), and then its use is hardly "kosher." Thus the recourse to protectors is far from solving all questions, though it does provide Tibetan Buddhists with various ways to deal with egregious harmful situations. Violence can be used, but only in certain well delimited circumstances. Outside of those, the practitioners may be in danger of breaking fundamental moral norms.

The tradition has been quite aware of this deep-seated tension and has attempted to find ways to mitigate the problem. Some supramundane deities are coupled with worldly deities, which function as their retinue, performing some of the more unseemly actions without compromising the enlightened integrity of the main deity. This is the case of the Great Goddess, which is surrounded by various ferocious female deities (the *ma mo,* the Tibetan equivalents of the Indian *mātrika*). These deities are particularly vicious. They are often held to be responsible for sickness and other sudden calamities, but their wrath can also be used by followers of the Great Goddess. Similarly, Mahākala is surrounded by a retinue of evil forces that have been converted to the protection of Buddhism but remain dangerous. Hence, an appeal to such a deity can be an effective way to deal with some enemies, particularly non-human ones.

The other way to deal with the problem is to elevate a particular worldly protector within the pantheon. This elevation is not, however, free of problems, for if the deity is elevated too much, it may become useless. Hence, the elevation should be mitigated. In the case of Shukden, most of its followers speak of the deity as being enlightened in nature but worldly in appearance.[36] In this way, the worldliness and hence usefulness of the deity is preserved while strengthening its normative status. But this solution is not without its own problems. For what does it mean to say that a deity is enlightened in nature but not in appearance? Does it mean that the deity is enlightened and hence a proper object of refuge? Some of the most extreme followers of Shukden have taken this road, arguing that this deity is a Buddha on par with all the other Buddhas.[37] Others have denounced this departure from the traditional depiction of the deity. How can a deity who is bent on performing the kind of actions that Shukden is well known to perform be enlightened? Is this deity not a king-spirit, as its name and myth of origin indicate?

Finally, the rise within the pantheon of a deity such as Shukden is bound to create trouble in a society where Buddhism plays such a significant role. Protectors are not just individual deities but also concern communities. Each tradition, monastery, local group or family has its own protector to whom members of the group, individually and collectively, can turn for direct help. For example, the monastic seat of Drepung has its own protectors, the Great Goddess and Pehar, which are also the gods propitiated by the Dalai-Lama and his government.[38] Shukden, on the other hand, is the god of another group, those who hold that the Geluk tradition is superior to the other traditions and who insist on maintaining a strict separation. This is the task assigned Shukden, to take care of those who are tempted by other Buddhist traditions such as the Nyingma. But this task cannot but create strong reactions among the groups targeted by Shukden in its zeal to keep the purity of the Geluk tradition. We now understand some of the reasons why the propitiation of a protector such as Shukden can be so troubling, leading to bitter conflicts between groups, which feel threatened in their very existence. Here again, we appreciate the point repeatedly made by Saada's peasants when they claim that it is hard to escape evil once one is caught. And yet, it is difficult for most people, who live in and are caught by the world of polarities, to avoid having to enter in contact with this dark realm, however great the problems that this creates.

Notes

[1] This term is often rendered as sin. Here I have chosen not to use this term to avoid some of its Christian connotations, such as the idea of fallen condition of humans.

[2] This distinction is made by David Parkin in his introduction to *The Anthropology of Evil* (Oxford: Blackwell, 1985), 9–13.

[3] My goal here is not to establish a moral equivalence between these actions but to draw the attention of my readers to the connection between evil and self, a particularly important point within the "Buddhist/structuralist perspective" that I have adopted here. I also want to make it clear that although the particular forms of evil I am exploring here concern mostly people living in pre-modern societies (with some exceptions, as we will see), the predicament created by the excessive polarization involved in the idea of radical evil also concerns those living in a modern industrialized society.

[4] David R. Loy, *The Great Awakening* (Boston: Wisdom, 2003), 106.

[5] For an exposition of such a normative view, see Masao Abe, "The Problem of Evil in Christianity and Buddhism," in Paul O. Ingram and Frederick J. Streng, *Buddhist–Christian Dialogue* (Honolulu: Hawaii University Press, 1986), 139–54.

[6] The only exception is the doctrine of the Icchantika which was held by a few thinkers in India but had no noticeable influence in Tibet. The Icchantikas are beings who are so depraved that they are precluded from any possibility of spiritual progress. See Liu, Ming-Wood, "The Problem of Icchantika in the Mahayana Parinirvana Sutra," *Journal of International Association of Buddhist Studies* 7, no. 1 (1984): 57–81. For a few reflections on the lack of theodicy in the narrow sense of the word in Indian traditions, see Margeret Chattarjee, "Some Indian Strands of Thought Relating to the Problem of Evil," in Purushottama Bilimoria and J. N. Mohanty, *Relativism, Suffering and Beyond* (New Delhi:Oxford University Press, 1997), 319–35.

[7] Trevor O. Ling, *Buddhism and the Mythology of Evil* (London: Allen and Unwin, 1962), 50.

[8] Ronald Davidson, "Reflections on the Maheśvara Subjugation Myth: Indic Materials, Sa-skya-pa Apologetics, and the Birth of Heruka," *Journal of the International Association of Buddhist Studies* 14 (1990): 197–235.

[9] Davidson, "Reflections on the Maheśvara Subjugation Myth," 200–202.

[10] L. A. Waddell, *Tibetan Buddhism* (1895; New York: Dover, 1972), 324.

[11] Waddell, *Tibetan Buddhism*, 362.

[12] For a study of some aspects of the Western approaches to the study of tantras, see Hugh B. Urban, *Tantra: Sex, Secrecy, Politics and Power in the Study of Religion* (Berkeley: University of California Press, 2003). For a discussion of the role of Waddell in the Western reception of Tibetan Buddhism, see Donald S. Lopez, *Prisoners of Shangri La* (Chicago: University of Chicago Press, 1998).

[13] See, for example, Sherry B. Ortner, *Sherpas Through Their Rituals* (Cambridge: Cambridge University Press, 1978).

[14] Tibetans speak of eight classes of gods and spirits (lha srin sde brgyad). See Geoffrey Samuel, *Civilized Shaman* (Washington: Smithsonian, 1993), 161–163.

[15] Phillipe Cornu, *Tibetan Astrology* (Boston: Shambala, 1997), 250–51.

[16] Lelung Zhayba'i Dorje, *Dam can Bstan Srung gi Rnam Thar* (Beijing: People's Press, 2003), 38–41.

[17] Historically, Padmasambhava appears to have been a relatively minor tantric practitioner, who gave some tantric teachings but whose practices provoked the displeasure of the court. See Samten Karmay, *The Great Perfection* (Leiden: Brill, 1988), 6; Anne-Marie Blondeau, "Le lHa-'dre Bka'-thang," in *Etudes Tibétaines Dédiées à la mémoire de Marcelle Lalou* (Paris: Maisonneuve, 1971), 29–126 and "Analyses of the biographies of Padmasambhava according to Tibetan tradition: classification of sources," in *Tibetan Studies in Honour of Hugh Richardson*, ed. Michael Aris and Aung San Suu Kyi (Warminster: Aris & Phillips, 1980), 45–52.

[18] Those are the self-descriptions used by Tibetans to describe their conversion to Buddhism. See Matthew T. Kapstein, "Remarks on the Mani bKa'-'bum and the Cult of Avalokiteśvara in Tibet," in *Tibetan Buddhism; Reason and Revelation*, ed. Steven D. Goodman and Ronald M. Davidson (Albany: State University of New York Press, 1991), 79–94, and Janet Gyatso, "Down with the Demoness," in *Feminine Ground*, ed. Jan Willis (Ithaca: Snow Lion, 1987), 33.

[19] The belief in such a universe is often described as animism in the classical anthropological literature, where it is viewed as an irrational and primitive superstition. Such a view fails to see that our modern way of seeing the world is no more natural than animism. Philippe Descola quite helpfully distinguishes three ways in which the human-nature relation can be conceptualized: animism, totemism, and naturalism. All three modes of relation are not given but constructed. Once they are acquired, presumably early in life, they become deeply ingrained and do not seem to change significantly later. "Constructing Natures," in *Nature and Society*, ed. P. Descola and G. Palsson (London: Routledge, 1996), 82–102, 87–88.

[20] The Geluk (dge lugs) tradition is the latest among the four main schools of Tibetan Buddhism. It was founded at the beginning of the fifteenth century by Tsong Khapa and later became politically and religiously dominant, enthroning its leading figure, the Dalai-Lama, the religious and temporal leader of Tibet.

[21] Pa-bong-ka, "Supplement to the Explanation of the Preliminaries of the Life Entrusting [Ritual] (rgyal chen srog gtad gyi sngon 'gro bshad pa'i mtshams sbyor kha bskong)," in *Collected Works*, vol. 7 (New Delhi: Chopel Legdan, 1973), 520.

[22] Georges Dreyfus, "The Shuk-den Affair: History and Nature of a Quarrel," *Journal of International Association of Buddhist Studies* 21, no. 2 (1999): 227–70.

[23] See Rene De Nebesky-Wojkowitz, *Oracles and Demons of Tibet* (The Hague: Mouton, 1956).

[24] The Nyingma (rnying ma) tradition represents the oldest strata of Buddhist thought and practice in Tibet. It claims to go back to the early empire when Buddhism was brought to Tibet by Padmasambhava and others great teachers.

[25] Pa-bong-ka, "Supplement," 517–32, 520.

[26] For an analysis of the historical events contained in this story, see my essay, "The Shuk-den Affair."

[27] See, for instance, Dzemay Rinboche, *Account of the Protective Deity Dor-je Shuk-den, Chief Guardian of the Ge-luk Sect, and of the Punishments meted out to Religious and Lay Leaders who incurred His Wrath (mthu dan stobs kyis che ba'i bstan bsrung chen po rdo rje shugs ldan rtsal gyi byung ba brjod pa pha rgod bla ma'i xhal gyi bdud rtsi'i chu khur brtsegs zhing 'jigs rung glog zhags 'gyu ba'i sprin nag 'khrugs pa'i nga ro)* (Delhi: n.p., 1973), 6–9. (The English title is given according to Library of Congress catalogue; henceforth referred to as The Yellow Book.) This text consists of a series of stories which the author had heard informally from his teacher Trijang, one of the main Geluk teachers of his generation as well as one of the two tutors of the present Dalai-Lama. For more on this, again see "The Shuk-den Affair."

[28] Pa-bong-ka, "Collection of [Rituals] concerning the Circle of Offerings, The Special Offering of Drinks, [and] the Exhortation to Action of the Powerful Protectors of Buddhism and [the propitiation of] Wealth Gods and Spirit (mthu ldan bstan srung khag gi 'phrin las bskul gser skyems tshogs mchod sogs dang/ gnod sbyin nor lha' skor 'ga' zhig phogs gcig tu bkod pa)," *Collected Works*, vol. 7 (New Delhi: Chopel Legdan, 1973), 469.

[29] See "The Shuk-den Affair."

[30] Jeanne Favret-Saada, *Les Mots, la Mort, les Sorts* (Paris: Gallimard, 1977).

[31] The bodhisattva is the being who seeks to attain the ultimate perfection of buddhahood for the sake of liberating all sentient beings.

[32] Garma C.C. Chang, *A Treasury of Mahāyāna Sūtras* (Delhi: Motilal, 1991), 452–465.

[33] For a discussion of the four types of rituals, see Ferdinand D. Lessing and Alex Wayman, *Introduction to the Buddhist Tantric Systems* (Delhi: Weiser, 1980), 201.

[34] gNas chung, alias Pehar, is the deity appointed by Padmasambhava as the main guardian of Buddhism in Tibet. It is also the protector of the Dalai-Lama and his government, as well as one of the main protectors of the monastery of Drepung.

[35] The monastic order is the Sangha only inasmuch as it is a symbolic representation of the true Sangha.

[36] Trijang Rinpoche, "The Music that Rejoices the Ocean of Pledge Bound, Being an Account of the Amazing Three Secrets [of Body, Speech and Mind] of Great Magical Dharma Spirit Endowed with the Adamantine Force, The Supreme Manifested Deity Protecting the Ge-den Tradition (dge ldan bstan bsrung ba'i lha mchog sprul pa'i chos rgyal chen po rdo rje shugs ldan rtsal gyi gsang gsum

rmad du byung ba'i rtogs pa brjod pa'i gtam du bya ba dam can can rgya mtsho dgyes pa'i rol mo)," in *Collected Works,* vol. 5 (Delhi: Guru Deva, 1978), 8.

[37] Kelsang Gyatso's Western New Kadampa Tradition seems to be unique among Shukden followers in going as far as to claim that this deity is fully enlightened and hence must be considered a proper object of refuge and worshiped as such. See Kelsang Gyatso, *Jewel Heart* (London: Tharpa, 1991).

[38] G. Lodrö, "'Bras spungs chos' byung," in *Geschichte der Kloster Universität Drepung* (Wiesbaden: Franz Steiner, 1974), 332–35.

Awakening to Satanic Conspiracy:
Rosemary's Baby and the Cult Next Door

David Frankfurter
University of New Hampshire

A great horror movie, like a great tale of horror, foregoes the gruesome spectacle for the tense elaboration of the uncanny. In the best literature, like Poe and Shirley Jackson, the uncanny simply grows and never bursts, so that we never know whether the terror comes from the inside or the outside. Ira Levin's 1967 book *Rosemary's Baby*, of course, does offer an explosive dénouement in the spectacle of the demon-baby in the crib. And it is this spectacle that, historically, spawned a series of ever more grotesque demon-child movies over the course of the 1970s and 1980s. Ira Levin and his 1968 film interpreter Roman Polanski had clearly unearthed a horror *topos* far deeper than anything prior: that—in the words of the critic James Twitchell—"the only thing more frightening than the adult brutalizing the cherubic child is that same situation turned inside out"—the *evil* child who preys on the loving parent.[1]

But Levin delays this revelation to the very end. The brilliance of his story lies in the increasingly uncanny air—rational suspicion, innocent curiosity, and fear in equal parts—stemming from an utterly intangible threat. And as evil does begin to materialize behind innocence, as caring elderly neighbors in an apartment building turn out to lead a Satanic cult, we remain still at a loss as to what danger they pose to the pregnant mother to whom they're being so nice. Indeed, in the 1960s, before the "cult" scare, at a time when Christian demonology was still quite marginalized, and set in a city where nobody could expect cultural homogeneity anyway, Rosemary's plight could almost be read as a send-up of the various weird and conflicting encounters pregnant women will have in urban society, just as Levin's *Stepford Wives* spoofed women's anxieties about the suburban life.[2]

By the late 1980s, however, everybody seemed to know what dangers Satanists next door might pose to the innocent and unsuspecting. A cacophony of media revelations, from Geraldo Rivera to the recovered-memory narrative *Michelle Remembers*, from preschool ritual abuse panics to ever-bolder evangelists' speeches on Satan in society, created a mood in which Satanism and Devil-worship became a familiar and modern discourse. Satanism had come to serve, on the one hand, as a "symptom" of a culture in decline, and on the other hand, as a cluster-point for perennial social anxieties, like child-safety, the nature of the family, and the identification of deviance. In this historical context Levin's work, especially his evocation of suspicion and intimate Satanic conspiracy, becomes quite prescient and quite possibly—to a limited degree—causal.[3]

This essay, then, will examine some of the themes in *Rosemary's Baby* that foreshadowed and became realized in the Satanic cult panic of the 1980s and 1990s. That a story conceived so unusually and fictionally could anticipate a cultural panic reflects its sensitivity to current social concerns, of course, like women's control over their maternity and the status of obstetrics in modern culture.[4] But it also points to some deeper cultural patterns in thinking about evil: as something expressed in conspiracy, something ritualistic, and indeed something captured most focally in terms of women's bodies. These patterns may invite comparisons to early modern witch-hunts: the image of the conspiratorial witches' Sabbat with its formal, infanticidal, and orgiastic rites, as well as inquisitors' obsessive interests in women's bodies as vehicles for the demonic. But what is so striking about the Satanic cult panic that followed *Rosemary's Baby* twenty years later is its primary milieu: *not* the religious enclaves we tend to associate with such elaborate demonologies, but *secular professionals*. This *migration* of demonological themes into a quintessentially modern sphere of familiar authorities—therapists, psychiatrists, police, television talk-show hosts, feminist writers—suggests that larger patterns in the construction of evil were in action in our culture. It is these larger patterns that this essay will address, through their representation in *Rosemary's Baby*.

For an historian of religions, of course, treating a popular movie as both a cultural artifact and a work of literature makes for a bit of a challenge, but we can learn much from the work of anthropologist Birgit Meyer on popular cinema in Ghana. A large portion of movies shown in contemporary Ghana concern the allures and dangers of Satanic power, which seems to offer riches and sexual fulfillment but at the inevitable cost of family and life. The movies delve into Satanic underworlds that their audiences believe to exist, but in the end make clear that flirting with such powers leads to disaster—a theme reflecting current Pentecostal ideology but neatly exploited by the filmmakers. In Meyer's work, which has involved observing audience interaction with the films as well as interviews with actors and film-makers, movies about Satanic powers function as *revelations* of what people imagine really to be "out there." They are "considered to offer a deeper vision than the one provided by one's own eyes, a vision similar to the special eyes of traditional priests and to the so-called 'spirit of discernment' which allows Christian preachers to penetrate into the realm of darkness."[5] *Rosemary's Baby* can serve as a cultural artifact of the same type: not as Levin and Polanski's unique craftwork but as a potential source of revelation and insight for viewers into the way things really must be.[6] It is not just the brilliance of the Levin–Polanski vision of a Satanist conspiracy but, as Meyer teaches us, its reflection of our own assumptions and suspicions that makes *Rosemary's Baby* so effective.

I A conspiracy of Satanists

In both the modern Ghanaian movies and *Rosemary's Baby*—followed by a host of American movies about urban cults, like *The Believers* (1987)—the primary tension that the film progressively resolves is between appearance and reality. Appearances may involve innocent-seeming temptations in Ghana or discon-nected weird events in America. Reality, however, transpires as a vast, timeless, and predatory *conspiracy* of Satanists.

America, we should recognize, has long had an obsession with themes of conspiracy. As organizations flourish and institutions get more powerful, as modernity—urbanism, media, technology—becomes more alluring and more determinative of our everyday experience, as we are forced to trust more and more the appearances of things, we in this culture have kept an eye perpetually cocked for suggestions of suspicion, deceit, and even counter-institutions behind it all. We might recall not only the appeal of movies like *The Manchurian Candidate* (1962) but also the popularity of stories of international white-slavery rings and the perpetual rumors of Catholic, Masonic, Mormon, Jewish, and even extraterrestrial conspiracy over American history.[7]

To a large extent, a myth of conspiracy has always offered a picture of evil, and a revelation of conspiracy through whatever media—the *Protocols of the Elders of Zion, Michelle Remembers,* or Geraldo Rivera—serves as a revelation of evil. For a conspiracy myth lays out current seductions in terms of long-term exploitation; offers a historical, social, and often political framework for the operation of subversive plans; links apparently disconnected, ambiguous, even insignificant events as signs of subversive intent; and inevitably pits a vast, secre-tive, organized, and powerful group against our most precious moral structures and icons, especially our women and children.[8] It is *evil* because the motivations for subversion are divulged to be inhuman and megalomaniacal in their heart-less greed, while the apparently random victims are exploited and brutalized in the most despicable ways.

In the 1960s, when Levin wrote *Rosemary's Baby*, we liked our conspiracies to be broad, political, and insidious, with less moral, intimate danger. It was tradi-tional institutions—communists, Catholics, corporations—that posed the threats. New groups were simply ambiguous, and a discourse of *evil* seemed so primitive that Anton LaVey could start a "Satanic Church" that was little more than a poke at Catholic hypocrisy.[9] But by the late 1970s, in the face of a great variety of discomfiting events, behaviors, and groups, from serial murderers to new religious movements to a surging, chaotic, and libertine youth culture, Americans began to feel an increasing strain between, on the one hand, the moral challenges these phenomena seemed to pose, and, on the other hand, a countervailing moral inclination to humanize, empathize, and contextualize them. Despite our austere Puritan legacy, social scientific enlightenment would not allow us to cast Charles Manson, Jim Jones, and David Berkowitz *out* of the realm of moral comprehensibility. They were mentally ill or products of terrible childhoods, or their worldviews had some weird integrity. And yet, as Andrew Delbanco has pointed out, we very much craved a discourse of Satan and evil to which we could relegate these most extreme figures—and anything morally challenging, for that matter: wayward youth, deviant groups, new sexual perversions, etc.[10]

And so, by the 1980s and 1990s, fuelled by the rise of evangelical Christianity and by cultural confrontation with child sexual abuse, America found new meaning in Satanism and a discourse of stark evil as frameworks for cultural and moral threats. This discourse might enter in a religious vein: that Satan himself was at work in society in advance of the final Tribulation. Or it might take a secular form: as the Colorado religion professor Carl Raschke wrote, the culture had gone so nihilist that only Satan made sense to some people to motivate their behavior. In multiple forms, Satanism—the worship of evil—became the perfect conspiracy. It was a myth that could embrace every publicity-seeking murderer, every allegation of multiple sexual abuse, and every form of deviant religion or religious expression. It could be rooted in ancient heresies and modern immigrations; it could be linked to early modern witches' Sabbat allegations, to Afro-Caribbean cults, to staged deviance among teenagers, and to hoary caricatures of Catholic and Jewish ritual. Indeed, it was the sheer recognizability of a Satanic conspiracy for a culture saturated with Christian apocalyptic demonology that gave it an integrity and authority despite the utter absence of forensic evidence—motivating, for example, innumerable therapists to seek it or foment it among their patients.[11]

Rosemary's Baby was obviously ahead of its time in offering such a revelation of Satanic conspiracy; many of the ideas it raises were not even picked up 20 years later. And yet the revelatory experience it offers the audience—that psychological shift from innocent acceptance of everybody in a tolerant, multicultural society to the terrified awareness of organized "cultic" predation—is one that arose time and time again for television viewers, therapists and their patients, and law enforcement specialists over the 1980s and early 1990s. Out of the mass of communications, interactions, materials, and sights of a busy culture, the presence of a truly horrific and (significantly) ancient religious cult comes into view, yet (we realize) it had always been there, prospering, in the interstices, the ordinary give and take, of society. In the growing awareness of conspiracy we experience an inversion of all things, as familiar people are unmasked as evil predators and unfamiliar, disjointed events are linked as obvious signs. In the final state of "awareness," the world becomes a pulsating series of messages and a network of predatory confederates, as in this instructional page for people attending a Ritual Abuse conference in Hartford, Connecticut, in 2002:

Following are some known [accessing] methods [for secretive organizations and/or cults]. Look for odd hand gestures, such as opening a book, making the shape of a gun with the pointer finger and thumb and "shooting" it, using the cut sign (hand drawn horizontally across the throat), tapping something (a book, the wrist (as in asking for the time), . . . drawing something in the air (like a letter of the alphabet or an unknown sign)). Winks or facial expressions: . . . Though some of these may or may not always signify triggers, it is important to be aware of them.[12]

Or as the Chicago psychiatrist Bennett Braun advised in-patient therapists working with alleged victims of Satanic abuse in 1992, be very careful of the flowers that friends and family might send to patients, for "pink flowers mean suicide, red means cutting. . . . Red roses or white baby's breath means bloody suicide. Pink roses mean hanging. Blue is death by suffocation. Yellow is silence or fire. Green means go ahead and do something. If the card is signed 'Love you,' then that is a danger signal."[13] This was the worldview that Satanic Abuse experts were promoting.

Let us defer condemnation of the many mental health and law-enforcement professionals who got so carried away that they influenced patients, families, and sometimes entire communities.[14] It hardly needs repeating that, while evidence abounded for intrafamilial child sexual abuse, no evidence whatsoever emerged for abusive, infanticidal Satanic cults apart from coerced "memories."[15] But *Rosemary's Baby* may be credited with capturing the experience of a familiar, even familial evil emerging in the consciousness of an educated urban woman, and of that evil coming not so much from a demonic Otherworld as from an association of devotees. New York is represented as a place of innocent excitement, culture, and prospects—hardly the veneer for insidious underworlds that we would see in *Taxi Driver* (1976), *Marathon Man* (1976), and *The Believers* (1987). Rosemary's neighbors are caring, cultured, and elderly—very much the antithesis of those alien traits by which we normally recognize potential danger. Most "cult conspiracy" movies and books make inevitable reference to Arabic, Indian, African, Afro-Caribbean, or subtle Catholic influences. This racial element allows the idea that monstrous predilections that remain safe and even alluring off in their proper domains, out on the periphery, are subversive and predatory as they move in among us.[16] Open-armed elderly white neighbors like Rosemary's, without accents, are quite the opposite. They are completely familiar—although one should note that Ruth Gordon's exaggeratedly Yiddish mannerisms and the distinctively Jewish "cult" obstetrician, Dr. Sapirstein, both recall fairly long traditions of the dangerous Jew.[17]

What makes the process of Rosemary's awareness of Satanic conspiracy so frightening, in fact, is that the neighbors do *not* change personalities or characteristics or clothes. Unlike the Ghanaian Satanist movies, in which seductive women eventually turn into snakes or sink into the ocean or drink blood, Rosemary's neighbors remain very much the same. I am reminded how, during various investigations of ritualized daycare abuse over the 1980s, the solid

reputations and sociable personalities of the accused women and men altogether did nothing to exonerate them or mitigate popular condemnation: they
remained *monsters*. In the popular mind, a 25-year-old mom of a toddler who
worked as a nursery-school aid could *also* be a vicious Satanic child-molester.
The one couldn't erase the possibility of the other. The apparent cannot negate
the veiled, for the veiled is somehow the true, the *real*, by its very nature. This
cognitive factor in the Satanic conspiracy panic, exemplified in *Rosemary's Baby*,
is what allows the conspirators that comfortable latitude *not* to don robes, take
drugs, conduct bloody sacrifices, and build elaborate altars—those perfect
"motifs" of covert evil. The overall terror of the movie lies in the revelation of
conspiracy within a familiar reality, as the mind alternates anxiously between
innocent appearance and covert evil. Overall, "reality" becomes—for Rosemary
and for us—that familiar landscape within which the Satanic is emerging.

II A Satanic cult

But here too *Rosemary's Baby* imagines an especially subtle form of horror.
True, the Devil does appear briefly to impregnate Rosemary and then in the
form of the demonic infant. Yet the evil emerges primarily in the form of
a Satan-worshipping cult. Indeed, it is Rosemary's paradoxical fear near the
time of delivery that this cult will take and sacrifice her baby, the way witches
and Jews in history have been imagined to do. Underneath the conspiracy,
then, is not an insidious group of business or political leaders but a religious
group devoted to some archaic rites and traditions that are altogether deviant.
Let us consider, then, why this image of the cult has for so long served as the
crucible of cultural fears.[18]

From at least the early Roman period, the epitome of conspiracy and moral
subversion lay in illegitimate, subversive rituals especially when they seemed to
function cohesively for some alien group. The "cult," in this perspective, used
cannibalism and incest to bind its members and child-sacrifice for subversive
power, for sorcery. It was a pastiche of Roman notions of impurity and the
night-witch, applied variously to Jews, Christians, and then by Christians to
other Christians; and it contributed to some perfectly lurid scenes in ancient
Roman novels.[19] There was never compelling evidence for real cannibalistic,
incestuous, baby-killing cults then, either; rather, it was a cultural fantasy from
the beginning, a tableau of perversion and evil that served Roman needs to
juxtapose proper civic morality to some dangerous foreign realm of subversion.
And yet, as Norman Cohn showed us in his 1975 study *Europe's Inner Demons*,
this fantasy directly influenced early Christian notions of what "heretics" do.
Beneath all their apparent theology, they eat babies, have orgies, and sacralize
menstrual blood.

All these ideas about heretics were duly inscribed over the fourth and fifth
centuries and then maintained over the centuries to determine how heretics

and their ilk should be understood in later times and places. In the fifteenth century, this same typology for the evil cult arose for suspect Christian practices in Switzerland. Inquisitors believed they had found a broad and subversive Satanic cult that ate babies, used baby parts for magic, engaged in sexual perversions, and swore oaths to do all things evil. This was the beginning of the idea of the witches' Sabbat, which motivated witch-finding movements in large areas of Europe through the seventeenth century. For people in the districts where witch-finders were seeking it out, the Sabbat offered a terrifying specter of coordinated anti-religion and evil. People were really frightened by it. But for many, like the witch-finders and inquisitors, the Sabbat could also provide a fascination, an allure, even theological interest.[20]

So Western culture has in many ways lived with the notion of a Satanic—or simply perverse and infanticidal—cult for countless centuries. Both the conspiracy *structure* and the tableau of perversions have lurked in the western cultural imagination since Roman times as plausible images of Otherness and of evil. But in *Rosemary's Baby*, the ceremonial chanting, anti-Papal jibes, and black-garbed cradle for the demon-baby all signal that another paradigm underlies the image of the cult in the modern American imagination.[21] Listen, for example, to the way psychiatrist Lawrence Pazder reconstructs the Satanic cult that he believes has abused his patient Michelle in the watershed "revelatory" text of the SRA discovery movement, *Michelle Remembers*:

> They seem more complex than ordinary cults or secret societies. Their rituals are very formal and established. . . . Nothing really spontaneous is allowed to happen, you know? All that makes me think this group has a long history. . . . The only group I know that fits your description is the Church of Satan. . . . Most people think they're strictly Dark Ages, but the fact is, the Church of Satan is a worldwide organization. It's actually older than the Christian Church.[22]

Formalism, lack of spontaneity, a long history, and, as Michelle goes on to recall, robes, altars, chalices, and ritual chambers—it all amounts to an extended parody of Roman Catholic rites. This should not make for a surprising background to modern notions of Satanic cults. The Protestant Reformation produced an elaborate series of depictions of Catholic priests and ceremony as cold, formalist, manipulative, hypnotic, cruel, and dependent on symbols and accoutrements to exploit the innocent and unwary.[23] And American culture in particular has a long history of harboring these caricatures as the very images of evil. They have certainly had a great influence on modern notions of "cult" dangers; and it has been important in the recent priest-abuse scandal to separate the criminal behavior of certain priests and the denials of their supervisors from this broader post-Reformation model of the evil cult.[24] The anti-Catholic legacy in Satanic cult depictions really revolve around the ceremonial accoutrements and the cold formalism of the priests. It is no coincidence that Anton LaVey concocted his *Satanic Rituals* (1972) along the lines of Catholic parody.[25]

III Evil and the prurient gaze

It is also important to recognize in the modern depictions of a quasi-Catholic Satanic cult a *voyeuristic* allure similar to that which arose around depictions of the witches' Sabbat. In the predatory and perverse sexuality, the sadistic cruelty, the nudity, and oral/anal concerns, there is as much a prurient fascination with the details as repulsion and an impulse to destroy it. In the late twentieth century as in the sixteenth century, a realm of evil served as a frame for imagining transgression. Because it is configured and understood as evil—because they are Satanists—it is safe to contemplate what they do, and even to enjoy the spectacle as fascinating, even erotic. This may be a surprising idea for some readers, but in the literature of the witches' Sabbat and of Satanic Ritual Abuse both, there is a clear eroticization of monstrosity and the Satanic. Evil became an excuse for imagining all sorts of transgressive scenes.[26]

This erotic, or perversely sado-erotic, feature is quite evident in the Gothic annals of Satanic Ritual Abuse testimonies, where one can read such alleged memories as a Satanic wedding ceremony where "what they were trying to do . . . was to simultaneously blow air up each other's buttocks"[27] or, more graphically:

> I was carried to the toolbench where gibberish was spoken by the four robed adults around me. Rather than water sprinkled, a small, black, wriggling cocker spaniel was held over me and disemboweled with a dagger-like instrument.. . . The long white taper was lit and ceremoniously held over me, wax dripping carefully onto each of my nipples. It was then inserted, still lit, into my vagina. In this way I was welcomed into the faith.[28]

But let us return to *Rosemary's Baby*. For indeed much of the "evil" in this movie revolves around Rosemary's own sexuality and sexual vulnerability. She is alternately childlike and womanly in her behavior and her dress. Cutting her hair short at the beginning of the pregnancy makes her even more childlike—a disturbing sexual contrast to the maturity of the elder neighbors and even her husband. She is thus more of a victim—and yet, as a woman who wants to get pregnant, she is a willing victim.[29]

To refer again to Meyer's work on the Ghanaian films about devil-worshippers, *Rosemary's Baby* shows the viewer "what's really going on," as it were, especially around women's sexuality. If women's sexuality is revealed in the Ghanaian films to be a conduit for Satan's power, it is the focus of Satanic predation in *Rosemary's Baby*—and subsequently in the Satanic cult panic of the 1980s/90s.

The dénouement of this eroticization of evil comes, of course, in the scene of Rosemary's impregnation by the Devil. We see her nude body laid down, then tied down on a mattress, then strange symbols drawn on her body with red paint. In her drugged but aware condition, Rosemary is clearly not responsible for whatever sexual feelings may follow. Her sight of a great number of older, naked adults watching her compounds the voyeurism with which we too, the audience, are complicit: Is this exciting? Is it horrifying? Is it horrifyingly exciting or excitingly horrifying? And then, as the monstrous body and claws of the Devil cover her, we see her face register pleasure before she realizes, "This is no dream, this is real!" In this brief scene, Levin and Polanski captured what would become a central motif of the Satanic Ritual Abuse narratives recited on television talk-shows and dramas, in therapists' publications, and shared in survivor groups: that is, the alternately horrified and eroticized description of the alleged Satanic rites. The idea and the depiction of evil became an opportunity for engaging in transgressive fantasy.[30]

IV From prurience to repulsion, from repulsion to extermination

Conspiracy too, we might say, offers not only terror but also the likelihood that there exists something else beneath the experiences and encounters we have, that randomness is not the way things work, but that another, more powerful realm is at work, controlling things. Maybe it's a positive realm—God and his angels, as in popular evangelical lore; or aliens, as many believe—or maybe an inverse, evil realm, but the excitement comes in peering into it.[31] Evil itself provides a mental and cultural frame both to relegate horrific realities beyond comprehensibility, beyond the spectrum of behaviors with which we think we must empathize, and to imagine things we wouldn't feel comfortable confronting as acceptably human: sexual things, sadistic things, masochistic things, blasphemous things.[32] When we frame them as evil and Satanic, they can be safe to think about.

Unfortunately, in the history of such voyeurism into evil things, there has been an even greater tendency for cultures and their leaders to try to purge that evil from their midst: to expose the witch-cult or Satanic cult, the Jewish or Christian conspiracy—and then to prosecute, torture, execute, and exterminate. The spectacles of perversion associated with the evil cult may be in one sense alluring, but they also fill people with disgust, fear, and a desire not to imagine, not to contemplate—rather, to obliterate all thought and form of transgression. Here is the other side of the "cult next door," for it *is* next door, rather than on some distant island or continent. The sheer intimate presence of such monstrous people with their monstrous ceremonies turns our caricatures and transgressive fantasies into anxiety and terror. They will *steal* my baby, fears Rosemary, and *sacrifice* it to their god. Motivated by a spectacle of transgression from which we cannot turn away, that is totally spellbinding in its obscenity and cruelty, we move systematically and brutally to destroy the cultists utterly, to purify the landscape of them. Lynching, burning, dismemberment, gassing, torture, drowning, exposure, cremation—these are the methods that follow when we conjure evil cults. These are the acts, I would argue, that have historically followed when a community "awakened" to some evil conspiracy.

Notes

1 James B. Twitchell, *Dreadful Pleasures: An Anatomy of Modern Horror* (New York: Oxford University Press, 1985), 300.
2 Cf. Rhona Berenstein, "Mommie Dearest: Alien, Rosemary's Baby and Mothering," *Journal of Popular Culture* 24, no. 2 (Fall 1990): 55–73 and Lucy Fischer, "Birth Traumas: Parturition and Horror in Rosemary's Baby," *Cinema Journal* 31, no. 3 (Spring 1992): 3–18.
3 Levin in Mary McNamara, "The Art of Darkness," *Los Angeles Times*, September 22, 2002, E1, 3.
4 Debbie Nathan and Michael Snedeker, *Satan's Silence: Ritual Abuse and the Making of a Modern American Witch Hunt* (New York: Basic Books, 1995), 34. Also see Berenstein, "Mommie Dearest."
5 Birgit Meyer, "Visions of Blood, Sex and Money: Fantasy Spaces in Popular Ghanaian Cinema," *Visual Anthropology* 16 (2003): 27–28. Cf. "Occult Forces on Screen: Representation and the Danger of Mimesis in Popular Ghanaian Films," *Etnofoor* 15 (2002): 212–21, and "Ghanaian Popular Cinema and the Magic in and of Film," in *Magic and Modernity: Interfaces of Revelation and Concealment*, ed. Birgit and Peter Pels, (Stanford: Stanford University Press, 2003), 218–20.
6 Cf. Carl Raschke, *Painted Black: From Drug Killings to Heavy Metal—The Alarming True Story of How Satanism is Terrorizing Our Communities* (San Francisco: Harper & Row, 1990), 115–16, and Gareth Medway, *Lure of the Sinister: The Unnatural History of Satanism* (New York and London: NYU Press, 2001), 349.
7 Susan Harding and Kathleen Stewart, "Anxieties of Influence: Conspiracy Theory and Therapeutic Culture in Millennial America," in *Transparency and Conspiracy: Ethnographies of Suspicion in the New World Order*, ed. Todd Sanders and Harry G. West (Durham and London: Duke University Press, 2003), 258–86.
8 Serge Moscovici, "The Conspiracy Mentality," in Carl F. Graumann and Serge Moscovici (eds), *Changing Conceptions of Conspiracy* (New York: Springer-Verlag, 1987), 151–69, and David G. Bromley, "The Satanism Scare in the United States," in *Le Défi magique 2: Satanisme, sorcellerie*, ed. Jean-Baptiste Martin (Lyon: Presses universitaires de Lyon, 1994), 49–64.
9 Massimo Introvigne, *Enquête sur le satanisme: Satanistes et antisatanistes du XVIIè siècle à nos jours*, trans. Philippe Baillet (Paris: Dervy, 1997), 257–81.
10 Andrew Delbanco, *The Death of Satan: How Americans Have Lost the Sense of Evil* (New York: FSG, 1995).
11 See David K. Sakheim and Susan E. Devine, eds. *Out of Darkness: Exploring Satanism and Ritual Abuse* (New York: Lexington Books, 1992), and James Randall

Noblitt and Pamela Sue Perskin, *Cult and Ritual Abuse*, Revised edn (Westport, CT: Praeger, 2000). Cf. David Frankfurter, *Evil Incarnate: Rumors of Demonic Conspiracy and Satanic Abuse in History* (Princeton: Princeton University Press, 2006), 189–95.

[12] "Safety Management for Conference Attendees" (2002), http://members.aol.com/smartnews/conference_safety.htm (accessed April 1, 2005). Cf. Patrick Rucker, "Speak of the Devil: Victimized by satanic cults and the CIA or just plain crazy? A look at the recent SMART conference at Windsor Locks," *Hartford Advocate*, September 4, 2003, http://hartfordadvocate.com/gbase/News/content.html?oid= oid:31545 (accessed January 13, 2006).

[13] Bennett Braun, taped presentation given at the Midwestern Conference on Child Sexual Abuse and Incest, University of Wisconsin, Madison, October 12, 1992, quoted in Richard Ofshe and Ethan Watters, *Making Monsters: False Memories, Psychotherapy, and Sexual Hysteria* (Berkeley: University of California Press, 1994), 248.

[14] James T. Richardson, Joel Best, and David G. Bromley, eds., *The Satanism Scare* (New York: De Gruyter, 1991); Sherill Mulhern, "Satanism, Ritual Abuse, and Multiple Personality Disorder: A Sociological Perspective," *International Journal of Clinical and Experimental Hypnosis* 42 (1994): 265–88; Mary DeYoung, "One Face of the Devil: The Satanic Ritual Abuse Moral Crusade and the Law," *Behavioral Sciences and the Law* 12 (1994): 389–407; Lawrence Wright, *Remembering Satan: A Case of Recovered Memory and the Shattering of an American Family* (New York: Knopf, 1994); Nathan and Snedeker, *Satan's Silence*; and Jean S. La Fontaine, *Speak of the Devil: Tales of Satanic Abuse in Contemporary England* (Cambridge: University Press, 1998).

[15] See Gail S. Goodman, Jianjian Qin, Bette L. Bottoms, and Phillip R. Shaver, *Characteristics and Sources of Allegations of Ritualistic Child Abuse* (Washington, DC.: Center for Child Abuse and Neglect, 1994); Nathan and Snedeker, *Satan's Silence*; and La Fontaine, *Speak of the Devil*.

[16] See, for example, Laënnec Hurbon, "American Fantasy and Haitian Vodou," in *Sacred Arts of Haitian Vodou*, ed. Donald J. Cosentino (Los Angeles: UCLA/Fowler Museum, 1995), 181–197.

[17] See Omer Bartov, *The "Jew" in Cinema: From The Golem to Don't Touch My Holocaust* (Bloomington: Indiana University Press, 2005), esp. 3, 13, on principal motifs.

[18] See David Frankfurter, "Ritual as Accusation and Atrocity: Satanic Ritual Abuse, Gnostic Libertinism, and Primal Murders," *History of Religions* 40, no. 4 (May 2001): 352–80, and Frankfurter, *Evil Incarnate*, ch. 4.

[19] Andrew McGowan, "Eating People: Accusations of Cannibalism Against Christians in the Second Century," *Journal of Early Christian Studies* 2 (1994): 413–42; James Rives, "Human Sacrifice Among Pagans and Christians," *Journal of Roman Studies* 85 (1995): 65–85; and Frankfurter, *Evil Incarnate*, ch. 4.

[20] See Frankfurter, *Evil Incarnate*, ch. 5.

[21] Cf. Ira Levin, *Rosemary's Baby* (New York: Random House, 1967), 88: "Roman in a black miter and a black silk robe. With a thin black wand he was drawing designs on her body . . . ."

[22] Michelle Smith and Lawrence Pazder, *Michelle Remembers: The True Story of a Year-Long Contest Between Innocence and Evil* (New York: Congdon & Lattès, 1980), 117.

[23] Frankfurter, "Ritual as Accusation and Atrocity," 357–65.

[24] Cf. Philip Jenkins, *The New Anti-Catholicism: The Last Acceptable Prejudice* (New York: Oxford University Press, 2003).

[25] Cf. Introvigne, *Enquête sur le satanisme*, 276–77.

[26] See Frankfurter, *Evil Incarnate*, ch. 5, drawing on Georges Bataille, *Erotism; Death and Sensuality*, trans. Mary Dalwood (New York: Walker & Co., 1962); Janice Haaken, *Pillar of Salt: Gender, Memory, and the Perils of Looking Back* (New Brunswick, NJ and London: Rutgers University Press, 1998); and Dyan Elliott, *Fallen Bodies: Pollution, Sexuality, and Demonology in the Middle Ages* (Philadelphia: University of Pennsylvania Press, 1999).

[27] Stephen A. Kent, "Deviant Scripturalism and Ritual Satanic Abuse," *Religion* 23 (1993): 237.

[28] Hart in Patricia L. Pike and Richard J. Mohline, "Ritual Abuse and Recovery: Survivors' Personal Accounts," *Journal of Psychology and Theology* 23, no. 1 (Spring 1995): 47.

[29] Cf. Berenstein, "Mommie Dearest," 61–63.

[30] See Haaken, *Pillar of Salt*, pp. 188–90, 232–44; Meyer, "Visions of Blood, Sex and Money," pp. 15–42; and Frankfurter, *Evil Incarnate*, 137–47.

[31] Todd Sanders and Harry G. West, "Power Revealed and Concealed in the New World Order," in *Transparency and Conspiracy*, 1–37.

[32] Harding and Stewart, "Anxieties of Influence: Conspiracy Theory and Therapeutic Culture in Millennial America," in *Transparency and Conspiracy*, 258–86.

Part Two

Philosophical Responses to Evil

Evil and Fault in the Philosophy
of Paul Ricoeur

Alan M. Olson
Boston University

One of my teachers, Erazim Kohak, was fond of quoting Baudelaire's observation that "the cleverest wile of the Devil is to convince us that he does not exist." But Kohak did so in order to refute it by arguing, to the contrary, that "the cleverest wile of the Devil is to convince us that he does exist." Kohak's rejoinder was informed by the notion that wild-eyed assertions regarding the substantial reality of evil coupled with demonic personifications of moral agency are precisely what trivialize the problem of evil. Reduced to fantasy, evil and the demonic become instrumental devices for entertainment, B-movies, political propaganda, and demagoguery. Far from being merely innocent fantasy, however, it is precisely within the domain of political propaganda and demagoguery where an instrumentalist use of the rhetoric of evil is the most dangerous and demonic.

The "is–is not" dialectic that undergirds ontological assertions regarding the existence of absolutes, such as good and evil, is itself very important because it tells us something about "how" we experience and reflect upon evil. And this "is–is not" dialectic is conveyed in a particularly unique and significant way, for Paul Ricoeur, in mytho-symbolic and metaphoric language. Indeed, Ricoeur's choice of the metaphor of *fault* is exemplary, for *fault* elucidates the nature of evil in human experience in a powerful way. On the one hand *fault* has to do with the sphere of finitude and moral culpability, but, on the other hand, *fault* also has to do with geological fissures or physical "rifts" running through reality in its totality. The heart of mankind, of course, is the nexus of the moral and the material, the spiritual and the physical; and in both instances *fault* tells us something about the nature of evil as both suffered and willed. To investigate the problem of evil, therefore, is to take cognizance of a reality both internal and external, at once subjective and objective, in what Ricoeur calls the drama of the "divided self."

It is precisely the drama of the divided self given voice so forcefully by Saint Paul in chapter 7 of his Epistle to the Romans: "Why is it the good that I would do, I do not do; and the evil I would not do, I do? . . . Who will deliver me from this body of death?" This question, or some version of it, is echoed again and again, down through the centuries—most famously, perhaps, in Kant's treatment of radical evil. These thinkers, and many others, inform Ricoeur's bold assertion that "[w]hatever evil is, it is not nothing . . . it is the power of darkness."[1]

In what follows, I begin by saying something about the historical context within which Ricoeur's project, *The Philosophy of the Will*, unfolds and the place of *The Symbolism of Evil* within it. Suffice it to say that Ricoeur's project has fundamentally to do with philosophical anthropology, and this is also true of *The Symbolism of Evil*, which is not a theodicy but a phenomenological hermeneutic of the "experience of evil." It is Ricoeur's view that if we are to obtain a deeper "understanding" of the problem of evil (as distinct from facile "explanations"), we must especially look at the expressions and formulations of evil "prior to the development of theology and philosophy." I will say a few words about Ricoeur's method, his philosophical assumptions, and how he moves from an "eidetics" of the will (in Volume I, *The Voluntary and the Involuntary*) to an "empirics" and "mytho-symbolics" of the will (in Volume II), in order to demonstrate how evil is a phenomenon both "suffered and willed," for what we call evil has both an involuntary and a voluntary dimension. I will also say something about Ricoeur's three phenomenological schemas of evil (defilement, sin, and guilt) and their primary narrative expressions. It is after the production of *Fallible Man* and *The Symbolism of Evil* (Volume II of *Philosophie de la Volunté*) that Ricoeur has his "linguistic turn," as it were, and becomes known as a hermeneutic phenomenologist as distinct from being an existential phenomenologist. Finally, I will focus on Ricoeur's schema of defilement since it is, in many ways, the most powerful symbol of evil, precisely because it is pre-reflective and pre-theoretical. As such, Ricoeur's first and primary schema of evil, the schema of defilement, is particularly helpful in helping us to understand certain aspects of the so-called "Post-9/11 World" we inhabit today.

I The symbolism of evil

Ricoeur commenced *Philosophie de la Volonte* in 1950, a project designed to address what many regard as the essence of philosophical anthropology in the West, namely, the problems of freedom and the will. One thinks, for example, of the sixteenth-century diatribe between the Renaissance Humanist, Erasmus, and the Reformer, Luther, *de libero arbitrio* and *de servo arbitrio,* and the centuries of debate that followed regarding freedom and determinism, whether in Kant, Kierkegaard, Nietzsche, Gabriel Marcel or Karl Jaspers. In each instance, it is fair to say that the notion of *mögliche Existenz* or possible self-Being is fundamentally a matter of the will, and the "more will, the more self" as Kierkegaard put it famously."

Ricoeur designed his project in the immediate aftermath of the European crisis of World Wars I and II, and the more than 50 million casualties of war that had accumulated by mid-century. Hence, the fundamental question "What does it mean to be human?" was posed in the face of the catastrophic omnicide of the twentieth century. It is important to remember, therefore, that basic issues in philosophical anthropology during the mid-twentieth century were not questions of mere academic interest. Rather they were fundamental questions of existential and moral urgency that simply could not be avoided by any serious thinker.

Thus the reality of omnicide informed what, in the mid-twentieth century, came to be known as philosophical anthropology or the philosophy of man. And it is the crisis of self-being and existential estrangement that informs Ricoeur's *Philosophy of the Will,* whether the eidetic structure of the voluntary and the involuntary as disclosed in what it means to-be-in-the-world-through-our-bodies, in Volume I, or, in Volume II, the manner in which we experience culpability, finitude, and evil as realities both "suffered and willed," and how these dichotomies might be transcended by way of a "poetics of the will" and "hope"—in what was to be a never completed Volume III.

Unlike the spate of works on evil that have appeared following 9/11, Ricoeur's work does not provide explanations regarding the reality of evil. Ricoeur's *Symbolism of Evil* is no theodicy and no occasional work. It has nothing in common with hyper-nationalistic attempts to simply explain evil, exploit the fear factor, or justify the creation of political epitaphs and jingos such as "the evil empire" or the "axis of evil." For now let it be said, quite simply, that Ricoeur's philosophy of the will is a phenomenology of the experience of evil, and a hermeneutical discussion of the meaning of its primary narrative expressions.

II Ricoeur's method and his philosophical assumptions

Let us begin by looking at some of Ricoeur's basic propositions and assumptions regarding a proper philosophical analysis of evil:

1. *Evil is not to be equated with contingency and/or finitude.* To do so, as with Descartes, places evil into the ontological sphere too quickly, removing it from the moral and ethical sphere. Nor is evil to be confused with error. By the same token, however, Ricoeur also insists that the element of finitude is not to be discarded by overemphasizing the difference between natural and moral evil, the physical and the spiritual. As a metaphor with split reference, evil is something both "suffered and willed"; that is, evil is something that partakes simultaneously of the involuntary and voluntary dimensions of existence and being. As such, evil has both a material and a moral reference—*material* in the sense that geological faults indicate movements or fissures in the earth's crust that may have a catastrophic impact on the social environment of those living in the proximity of these weaknesses; and *moral*

with respect to the determination of responsibility by those moral agents whose activities have brought about conflict, disaster and suffering, whether intentionally or unintentionally.

2. Determination of intent, of course, can be a tedious process, which is why the courts came up with "no fault" divorce and "no fault" auto insurance. While these policies speed up litigation, the notion of "no fault" has a potentially catastrophic moral implication, namely, a deadening of the existential dimension of fault, in which case, the paradoxical force of Ricoeur's assertion that "evil" is both "suffered" and "willed" is greatly diminished or lost altogether.

3. This is why, as a human action, evil is best understood, for Ricoeur, by way of *action theory*. And as an action, evil is best elucidated through *philosophical anthropology*. In Ricoeur's case, this means through *existential phenomenology*, the goal of which is to deploy all available resources in determining the nature and meaning of evil "as experienced" and not merely "explained."

4. Ricoeur begins his analysis through an *eidetics of the will*—more precisely, an eidetics of a "servile will" both "free" and "bound." By this Kantian strategy Ricoeur repudiates the notion that human beings are either free or determined, and all formulas contending that humans are either "basically good" (as in liberalism) or "basically evil" and "depraved" (as in conservatism), that "man is good and society is evil" (Rousseau), or that "society is good and man is evil" (Hobbes)—positions which assert and/or presuppose that the will is either "free" or "bound" but not both. Choosing between such alternatives is to choose between what Ricoeur calls the "gnostic inventions" that have arisen through over-determinations of human nature. As such, Ricoeur's choice of the paradoxical status of being both free and bound is very close to Luther's enigmatic formulation regarding *Rechtfertigung*: *simul justis et peccator*, and that human beings are simultaneously saints and sinners.

5. Not surprisingly, Ricoeur is very fond of Kierkegaard's *dialectical* notion of "either/or" as a "both-and" reality as evidenced in Kierkegaard's quasi-Hegelian opening to *The Sickness Unto Death*: "A human being is spirit. But what is spirit? Spirit is the self. But what is the self? The self is a relation that relates itself to itself or is the relation's relating itself in the relation; the self is not the relation but is the relation's relating itself to itself. A human being is a synthesis of the infinite and the finite, of the temporal and the eternal, of freedom and necessity, in short, a synthesis. A synthesis is a relation between two. Considered this way, a human being is still not a self" but a self in the making.[2] Ricoeur's proximity to Kierkegaard's paradoxical formulation, and to Jaspers' notion of *mögliche Existenz*, will emerge again in one of his mature works, viz., *Oneself as Another*.

III Ricoeur's three phenomenological schemas of evil

Given his dialectical orientation regarding the nature of the self, Ricoeur's task is to thematize the human experience of evil in ways that will make it more comprehensible. He accomplishes this in two stages or operations, the first phenomenological, and the second hermeneutical. In combination, these two stages or operations represent Ricoeur's version of the hermeneutical circle and the movement between part and whole, namely, the analytical descent to the obscurity limits of the phenomenon-as-experienced, and a dialectical or teleological ascent to the ideality limits of the phenomenon as interpreted.

At the phenomenological stage Ricoeur identifies three basic clusters of symbols of evil as manifest in the following ways: (1) The external or objective manifestation of evil as a physical or material "stain" through the imagery of "defilement"; (2) the internal and subjective manifestation of evil as "sin" understood as the conscious and willful transgression of the moral law defined within the specific social and cultural context of the covenant community; and finally, (3) evil as manifest in the dense and complex symbol of "guilt." Within the phenomenon of guilt there has not only taken place a sublimation or *Aufhebung* of the objective and subjective dimensions of evil; there is also the appearance of something new, namely, the revolutionary development of a confession of moral culpability—or what Ricoeur calls the "it is I" responsible for the condition of evil. And it is precisely the "it is I" that signals the teleo-eschatological element of fulfillment and authenticity "out of the future" so central to Judaism and Christianity. David's Penitential Psalm (51) is a paradigm expression of the phenomenology of confession or *attestation* for Ricoeur: "Have mercy on me, O God . . . blot out my transgressions, wash me from my iniquity, and cleanse me from my sin. . . . Behold Thou desirest truth in the inward parts; therefore teach me wisdom in my secret heart."

These three schemas of evil, however, stain, sin, and guilt, are not merely linear or historical developments for Ricoeur. Rather they are aspects of the symbolism of evil present, in various ways, but with various emphases, throughout the history of human experience and the history of the symbolism of evil. On the other hand, Ricoeur insists, in a quasi-Hegelian way, that "it is from the perspective of *logos* and not *mana*" that we make determinations of historical development—"the perspective of *mana*" being a "first naïveté" forever closed to us.[3] Ricoeur therefore straddles in a quite remarkable way a restorative hermeneutic of "sympathetic reenactment" that Gadamer identifies, on the one hand, with Schleiermacher and Dilthey, and, on the other, with the "integrative" hermeneutic of Hegel and Jaspers.

The second or *hermeneutical stage of analysis* is necessary, Ricoeur insists, to further elucidate the nature of evil as "experienced," since the phenomenologi-

cal stage, left to itself, can be reductionistic. Once again, the phenomenological
stage of analysis, for Ricoeur, represents the downward or analytical movement
of the hermeneutical circle that plummets to the deep structures and obscurity
limits of the phenomenon, obscurity limits he identifies with the bio-energetics
and archetypes of Freudian and Jungian psychoanalysis. The upward motion of
interpretation is dialectical and teleological pressing towards the ideality limits
of the phenomenon as understood and expressed in a narrative of avowal.
These ideality limits Ricoeur identifies, in various ways, with Plato, Hegel, and
idealism generally. That is why Ricoeur insists on the necessity of understanding
the nature of confession or "*attestation*" as the integral narrative process of discovering what evil is "as experienced" rather than "explaining" evil through
theodicy. This *attestation* requires that the analyst and interpreter be released
from the brackets of the phenomenological reduction in order, as Gadamer
puts it, "to speak the text." In other words, and here rather like Dilthey, Ricoeur
believes that an "explanation" of evil is too easy, too premature in the face of
the absence of "understanding," for without understanding there can be no
authentic judgment and appropriation.

It is necessary, therefore, to move from a phenomenological analysis of
symbol to the hermeneutics of myth; it being understood that myth is first and
foremost a narration, and a uniquely symbolic narration through and within
which language becomes transparent to what he calls the "hidden life of
the emotions." Ricoeur's intention to uncover and grasp "the hidden life of the
emotions," cannot be underestimated, for it is precisely in the unconscious
where the imprint of evil "as experienced" is most powerful. This is why Ricoeur
makes a clear distinction between symbols and metaphors: metaphors exist
entirely within the world of logos as "the inventions of language." Symbols, on
the other hand, are like icebergs floating on the surface of the ocean and reveal
only a surface semantic, the vast bulk of meaning remaining buried in the
unconscious or in what cannot be seen in the depths below.

Furthermore, Ricoeur asserts, "Every authentic Symbol has three aspects,"
the *cosmic*, as in Eliade's *axis mundi*; the *oneiric*, or the psychic world of
dreams; and the *poetic*, where the cosmic and the oneiric merge or fuse in *poesis*.
Symbols, then, for Ricoeur, are not merely signs of *univocal* reference as in
symbolic logic. Symbols rather are "layered" precisely because of the aforementioned three aspects of the cosmic, the oneiric, and the poetic. As such, symbols,
for Ricoeur, are *plurivocal* as distinct from being simply equivocal and/or contradictory in the simple sense of being bound by the principle of identity
and contradiction and being either true or false. He also asserts that the tensive
referentiality of symbols is not to be overcome by allegory, for mytho-symbolic
discourse necessarily remains in a state of "hovering" (as Jaspers says of *Cipher-
schrift*) can never be reduced to a single meaning, and, in fact, demands a logic
of double meaning. Ricoeur defines the difference between symbol and myth
as follows: "symbols are more radical than myths. I . . . regard myths as a species

of symbols, as symbols developed in the form of narrations and articulated in a time and a space that cannot be coordinated with the time and space of history and geography according to the critical methods [of empirical historiography and geography]."[4]

Ricoeur's position in *La Symbolique du Mal* can therefore be viewed as a species of realism inasmuch as he argues that the eidetic realm of logos is ultimately parasitic upon the life of particulars (not vice versa), and, moreover, that logos is already present in the mundane life of particulars, incarnate, so to speak, but in a nascent state. That is why he says that the realm of myth and symbol is not "pure." In other words, the primordiality of the mytho-symbolic does not make it "more true" than abstract rational explanations. Ricoeur's position is not "a romanticism of the always anterior" (with which he charges the later Heidegger). It is rather the case that in the realm of myth and symbol we already have an explanation since language, a priori, is the means of its expression, whether that language is verbal or visual. When "the symbol gives rise to thought," as Ricoeur asserts, it gives rise to thought through language—through word (*logos*) and image (*ikon*). The reason that Ricoeur investigates the world of the archaic, then, is not a romantic quest to find an uncontaminated or foundational "truth" (as might be said of Jung and Campbell). His purpose rather is to begin a philosophical investigation from the "fullness of language," that is, with the plurivocal, multivalent language of the mytho-symbolic and with the "surplus of meaning" such language necessarily contains.

Ricoeur provides the primordial symbols of evil, defilement, sin, and guilt, with narrative expression through the prototypical historical myths of the beginning and the end: (1) The schema of defilement is coupled with the ritual vision of the world as evidenced in the oldest theogony/cosmogony, the Mesopotamian *Enuma Elish,* where "Evil is the Past of Being." (2) The tragic vision of injustice, sin, hubris and fate and where "Being Falls on Man," so to speak, as exemplified in the Greek Poets and the Book of Job. (3) The Adamic vision of sin and myth of the fall, which Ricoeur considers the paradigmatic myth of freedom in the Occident, as given voice in Genesis. Finally, (4) the rationalistic and dualistic Orphic vision of guilt and the myth of the exiled soul as expressed in Neo-Platonic, Late-Classical and Medieval Christianity.

Obviously this is not the place to expand on each of these prototypes, except to say that each instance represents a higher and more reified level of mediation regarding the nature of evil. Indeed, by the time one gets to Orphic Neo-Platonism and the reified conception of Being one finds in the privative conception of Augustine, evil is akin to nothingness. But for Ricoeur, "Whatever evil is, it is not nothing," and privative conceptions of evil simply will not do. In his final chapter on "The Cycle of Myths," Ricoeur therefore insists upon the necessity of a "dimming of reflection and a return to the tragic" and the continuation of a rich admixture of the symbolism of sin, guilt, and especially defilement and stain. And with these lengthy preliminary statements, I turn to a discussion of the most powerful schema of evil, the schema of defilement and stain, for this is the primordial symbol to which one necessarily returns "with the dimming of reflection" and metaphysical speculation. It is a schema especially cogent for understanding the nature of evil in our so-called "Post-9/11" world.

IV Ricoeur's schema of defilement

The most primordial and immediate schema of evil, for Ricoeur, is that of "defilement and physical stain." It is a schema consisting of the dialectic of the pure and the impure, of contagion and contamination (at the objective level) and of ethical terror and dread (at the subjective level). Arthur McGill calls this the experience of "infectious contact with trans-human-powerfulness," for example, with disease when one is struck down by unseen powers from a seemingly invisible world. Hence there is the need to ritually build up one's defenses in order to resist and be "delivered from evil"—or at least to co-exist with the "principalities and powers of evil and darkness" in ways that will not lead to one's destruction.

Indeed the paradigm narrative expression of the schema of defilement Ricoeur rightfully locates in the Sumero-Accadian-Babylonian cosmogony of the *Enuma Elish.* It is the prototype cosmogony built upon patricide, regicide and, indeed, matricide, with the ritual rape as exemplified by the dismemberment of Tiamat by Marduk who then recreates the cosmos out of her carcass. It is difficult to imagine a more profound and horrifying conveyance of what Ricoeur calls "Violence as the past of Being"—or, for that matter, a place more suitable for the unfolding of the "ritual vision of the world" than what is presently and ironically the case in Iraq—the origin of the Mesopotamian vision of the world.

The dialectic in this vision is profound in the sense that it definitely is "something" and not "nothing" that infects and contaminates. One's experience of this contamination or defilement is precisely what results in what Ricoeur identifies as "dread," or what we would more mildly call "anxiety," but which, in the case of dread, includes what is material and objective. Most important, perhaps, is the fact that the experience of defilement is precisely what connects us with the higher animals (and perhaps with all higher sentient beings) which have an immediate sense of impending doom and of being endangered, physically defiled, and contaminated by an external power. What makes dread or angst different from fear is that fear (as in *phobos*) has a determinate object, whereas dread has the effect of making one hyperconscious of oneself for no determinate reason.

Ricoeur insists that the cry uttered in the midst of this experience of evil is already an "avowal" with three stages or aspects, dread being the condition anticipating what Ricoeur calls "the vengeful wrath of interdiction." This wrath, as described by Ricoeur in a Hegelian way, has three stages: (1) vengeance of retribution—striking back (objective spirit); (2) expiation—restoration of personal worth (subjective spirit); and (3) expectation of justice—teleo-eschatology (absolute spirit).

If we consider 9/11 in terms of Ricoeur's primal schema of evil as defilement, much of what happened in its aftermath becomes more intelligible and comprehensible. Consider the following points:

1. No event in modern history, other than the incineration of Hiroshima and Nagasaki, has embodied an encounter with trans-human powerfulness more intensely than the destruction of the twin towers in Lower Manhattan on September 11, 2001. The thermo-nuclear annihilation of Hiroshima, and then Nagasaki, was no doubt greater in what the Pentagon calls "shock and awe" and certainly more immediate than the collapse of the twin towers. But there was no CNN in 1945 to convey the immediacy of "shock and awe" to spectators beyond Ground Zero—and to convey it again and again by video, thousands and thousands of times in the months that followed, thereby heightening and intensifying the sense of defilement and contamination felt by all Americans, and, indeed, people all over the world, even those not given to feeling sorry for Americans.

2. Of course there were those in America who felt this defilement more intensely and immediately than others: they were the New Yorkers, especially the New Yorkers of Lower Manhattan and the Washingtonians. For them, especially those working in the Towers, what one commentator described as a "Lo-Tech, High Yield" act of terror was an encounter with evil as the immediate-immediate. By this I mean a pre-reflective, pre-theoretical, emotional event of extraordinary magnitude, an experience followed by what one might call the "stain of shock" and which, for many, did not diminish in intensity for several years.

3. In such a state or condition, critical thinking is impossible. What is possible, indeed natural as a reflexive action, according to Ricoeur, is "the vengeful wrath of retribution," this and this only. One thinks of Hannah Arendt's assertion, out of Hegel, that "evil is the absence of thought," not as banality but pure emotion. Perhaps more clearly, and *apropos* 9/11 and its aftermath, we find ourselves in a situation where critical thinking is difficult, if not impossible, precisely because of emotional intensity.

4. Had the Jihadists targeted another site, for example, the Sears Tower in Chicago, the results might have been different with regard to the collective intensity of "the vengeful wrath of interdiction." But the selected targets in Washington DC and New York City—were ideal to yield the maximum effects of defilement, contamination, and stain on the collective consciousness of the nation. New York is not only the center of finance but, more importantly, the center of the electronic media, the denizens of which, like the Washington establishment, were in a severe state of cognitive dissonance for at least a year or more. Rational dialogue and critique simply disappeared

in an endless bathos of emotion and grief, as if no other country had ever suffered such a catastrophe.

5. Someone in the Bush administration is reported to have said to the President, shortly after 9/11, "Now you can do anything!" Even if this saying is apocryphal, it is true. In the face of this major defilement, citizens rallied around the demigod in charge to plead, "Deliver us from evil!" It was precisely this voluntary submission to absolute authority, for which Bush and also Giuliani became famous, which continues long after the event. And this is why John Mearsheimer observed of the developments leading to the Iraq War, "The Neo-Cons were a necessary but not sufficient condition for invading Iraq. The sufficient condition was 9/11." So it is that the "fear factor" has its own inner logic, and this is why the schema of defilement is so important in understanding the nature of evil prior to considering the nature of sin and guilt.

6. There is an interesting analog to 9/11 in the burning of the Reichstag January 27, 1933. This event caused tremendous distress amongst the German people (even without the benefit of CNN) because the terror was said to be the work of "evil" Communists and Bolsheviks. Even though most historians believe that the Nazis themselves – burned the Reichstag in order to secure absolute power, the parallel is instructive in terms of what followed. The newly elected members of the Reichstag met in the Kroll Opera House in Berlin to consider passing Hitler's emergency *Ermächtigungsgesetz* or the Enabling Act officially known as the "Law for Removing the Distress of the People and the Reich." If passed, it would effectively mean the end of democracy in Germany and establish the legal dictatorship of Adolf Hitler. On February 27, 1933, exactly 1 month after the burning of the Reichstag, the Enabling Act passed by a margin of 441-84. In the United States, six weeks after 9/11, on October 26, 2001, and by an almost identical margin, Congress passed Public Law 107-56, commonly known as "The Patriot Act," by a vote of 98-1 in the Senate and 357-66 in the House.

War fever and what Ricoeur refers to as the "hidden life of the emotions" is not without its inner logic. But a disclosure of the meaning and inner logic of emotionally charged mytho-symbolic language is a demanding enterprise. Ricoeur warns that the emotional life of an individual (or a country), unmediated by reason and understanding, can easily lead to disaster. It is not surprising, in retrospect, that after completing *The Symbolism of Evil* in 1960, Paul Ricoeur spent the next 5 years of his life completing his lengthy *Essay on Hermeneutics* (1965), published in English as *Freud and Philosophy* (1970).

Notes

[1] Paul Ricoeur, *The Symbolism of Evil*, trans. Emerson Buchanan (New York: Harper & Row, 1967), 155. In this essay I rely almost entirely on *The Symbolism of Evil*, which

originally appeared as *La Symbolique du Mal* in 1960. For Ricoeur's treatment of theodicy (25 years later) see "Evil. A Challenge to Philosophy and Theology," *Journal of the American Academy of Religion* 53, no. 3 (1985): 635–48.

[2] Søren Kierkegaard, *The Sickness Unto Death: A Christian Psychological Exposition for Upbuilding and Awakening*, trans. Howard V. Hong and Edna H. Hong (Princeton: Princeton University Press, 1980), 13.

[3] See Ricoeur, *The Symbolism of Evil*, 14.

[4] Ricoeur, *The Symbolism of Evil*, 18.

The Abuse of Evil[1]

Richard J. Bernstein
New School for Social Research

Today our nation saw evil, the very worst of human nature.
George W. Bush, Address to the Nation, September 11, 2001

America has shown its evil intentions and the proud Iraqi people cannot accept it.
Moktada al-Sadr, April 7, 2004

What do we mean when we call an event, an intention, a deed, or a human person evil? What are we referring to when we use evil as a *noun*, when we say, "today our nation saw *evil*"? There is something chilling and powerfully emotional when we speak of evil. We feel that we know precisely what we intend. There is no ambiguity or confusion about what really is evil—even if we are at a loss to define what we mean. And we also feel that there can be no compromise with evil. We must fight to eliminate it. When challenged to clarify what we mean by evil, we may appeal to other expressions such as unjust, immoral, sinful, wicked, malevolent, sadistic, vicious, etc. But none of these are as strong, terse, and compact as evil. To add emphasis—to name the worst—we speak of *absolute, pure,* or *radical* evil. Although we sometimes compare evils and use expressions such as "the lesser of the evils," more often we think of evil in absolute terms. Evil is evil; there are no gradations here.

The concern with evil is as old as civilization itself. It is fundamental to all the major world religions. The greatest philosophers, theologians, poets, and novelists have struggled with the meaning and consequences of evil. Theologians and philosophers speak of "the problem of evil" or theodicy—a word invented by the eighteenth century philosopher Leibniz. If there is a God that is omniscient, omnipotent, and benevolent, then the question arises: how we can reconcile the appearance of evil with the existence of such a God? Some have maintained that evil is only a privation, or that what we claim to be evil is not really evil. Others have claimed that human beings have been given the gift of free will. And it is because they misuse their free will that evil comes about. If we survey the historical literature dealing with the "problem of evil," we will discover that almost every possibility has been explored that would reconcile a benevolent Creator with the existence of evil in this world. Actually, the traditional "problem of evil" is not primarily concerned with describing the meaning of evil. Rather—whatever we take to be evil—the question is how we can reconcile evil with faith in an Almighty God. And sometimes, the problem of evil has also been used to challenge the existence of such a Deity. Dostoyevsky's Ivan Karamazov passionately argues that the gratuitous murder of innocent children cannot be reconciled with a belief in a benevolent God. But it would be a serious mistake to think that the problem of evil is exclusively a religious or theological issue. Non-believers have raised similar questions. They also want to know how to make sense of a world in which evil and suffering seem so intractable. Nietzsche declared that human beings do not repudiate suffering as such: it is *meaningless* suffering that is so intolerable. And Emmanuel Levinas has argued that any attempt (religious or nonreligious) to "justify" or rationalize the horror of evil is a form of theodicy. And we must *resist* the temptation of theodicy—any temptation to justify or rationalize evil.

The twentieth century and the start of the twenty-first century present us with a perplexity concerning evil. Many believe that during this period we have witnessed some of the worst evils that have ever occurred in history. Think of the many of the genocides that have taken place throughout the twentieth century and continue to take place. But at the same time, our moral philosophers tend to avoid talking about evil. They are much more intellectually comfortable speaking about what is immoral or unjust. Even the so-called "problem of evil" has become a very specialized and abstract discussion among philosophers of religion. Andrew Delbanco acutely observes that "a gulf has opened up in our culture between the visibility of evil and the intellectual resources for coping with it. Never before have images of horror been so widely disseminated and appalling—from organized death camps to children starving of famines that might have been averted. . . . The repertoire of evil has never been richer. Yet never have our responses been so weak."[2] The most excruciating and detailed descriptions and testimonies have overwhelmed us; nevertheless our conceptual discourse for dealing with evil has been sparse and inadequate. There have been some notable exceptions to the virtual silence about evil by intellectuals. Hannah Arendt, for example struggled to articulate what she took to be the unprecedented radical evil of totalitarianism. She also coined the phrase "the banality of evil" to describe those desk murderers and "normal persons" who, without *thinking*, commit monstrous evil deeds.

When we look back over the historical attempts to comprehend the meaning and consequences of evil, there is one characteristic that stands out. The confrontation with evil provokes *thinking*. St. Augustine draws on all his imaginative, emotional, and intellectual powers to reconcile evil with his belief in a loving God. Leibniz thought we needed a new discipline—theodicy—to account for the appearance of evil and to explain why everything happens for the best.

Shakespeare, in his poetic thinking, explores the depths of the moral psychology of evil in such characters as Iago, Lady Macbeth, and Richard III. No one poses the dilemmas concerning evil more brilliantly than the characters in Dostoyevsky's novels. Nietzsche provokes our thinking with his genealogy of good and evil.

But something happened on 9/11. Overnight (literally) our politicians and media were broadcasting about evil. We were flooded with headlines about evil and images displaying evil—from the repetitive TV images of the crumbling of the World Trade Center Towers to the smirking faces of Osama bin Laden and Saddam Hussein. Suddenly the world was divided into a simple (and simplistic) duality—the evil ones seeking to destroy us and those committed to the war against evil. What is so disturbing about the post-9/11 evil talk is its immense popular appeal. Few stop to ask: What do we really mean by evil? What are we saying when we label our enemies evil? And who are these enemies? It is presumably self-evident. In a world in which there is both genuine and manipulated fear about the threats of terrorism that can strike at any place and any time, it is psychologically reassuring to label our enemies "evil."

I want to examine this fashionable post-9/11 discourse of good and evil. It is an abuse of evil. It is an abuse because instead of inviting us to *question* and to *think*, this evil talk is used to stifle thinking and obscure complex issues. This is extremely dangerous in a precarious world. This new chatter about good and evil lacks nuance. In the so-called "war on terror" nuance and subtlety are (mis)taken as signs of wavering, weakness, and indecision. If we think that democratic politics requires debate, judgment, and making judicious distinctions, then the talk of absolute evil corrupts politics. It is anti-political. And I also want to argue that despite the religious aura that surrounds so much of the recent talk about evil, there is something about it that corrupts the meaning of religion. As Hannah Arendt notes, "The absolute . . . spells doom to everyone when it is introduced into the political realm."[3] We need to be more self-conscious that this fashionable rhetoric of evil and the "axis of evil" is matched by, and sometimes seems to be the mirror image of, the proclamations of those militant fanatics who are committed to eliminating evil infidels. Consider the statement that I cited at the beginning of this essay by Moktada al-Sadr. If we substitute the phrase "Moktada al-Sadr and his militant followers" for "America," the "proud American people" for the "proud Iraqi people," then we have the type of statement that we hear almost every day from Washington: "Moktada al-Sadr and his militant followers have shown their evil intentions and the proud American people cannot accept it."

Samantha Power succinctly describes the contrast between more thoughtful responses to evil and the new simplistic stark opposition of black (evil) and white (good) in a recent comment about Hannah Arendt.

Arendt used the phrase "radical evil" to describe totalitarianism and this idea has been brought back in circulation. Yet while Arendt did not allow such branding to deter her from exploring the sources of that evil, the less subtle minds who invoke the concept today do so to mute criticisms of their responses. (Who, after all, can be against combating evil?)

But sheltering behind black and white characterizations is not only questionable for moral and epistemological reasons. It poses a practical problem because it blinds us from understanding and thus undermines our long-term ability to prevent and surmount what we don't know and most fear. "Evil" whether radical or banal, is met most often with unimaginativeness. Terrorism is a threat that demands a complex and elaborate effort to distinguish the sympathizers from the militants and to keep its converts to a minimum. Terrorism also requires understanding how our past policies give rise to such venomous grievances.[4]

In order to support my thesis that the post-9/11 popular discourse of evil is an abuse of evil, I want to describe what I call a clash of mentalities. There is a mentality that appeals to absolutes, moral certainties, and stark black and white dichotomies. In opposition to this is a mentality that I will call "pragmatic fallibilism." This mentality criticizes and eschews the appeal to absolutes and fixed certainties. It insists that all claims, epistemological, moral, and political, are fallible—and need to be constantly subjected to ongoing public criticism and debate. Instead of rigid dichotomies, fallibilists insist on the need to make judicious distinctions. When we are faced with difficult moral and political decisions, we frequently are compelled to choose the lesser evil. I also want to challenge the claim that in times of crisis, decisive action can be justified only on the basis firm moral certainties. Finally I want to show how the popular post-9/11 political discourse of good and evil corrupts both politics and religion.

By a mentality, I mean a general orientation—a cast of mind or a way of thinking—that conditions the way in which we approach, understand, and act in the world. It shapes and is shaped by our intellectual, practical, and emotional lives. Mentalities take a variety of concrete historical forms. To understand a mentality we need to examine its historical context, distinctive character, and sources—although we can recognize similarities with other historical examples of similar mentalities. I want to begin with an historical example that has had a great influence on the character of the United States in the late nineteenth and first decades of the twentieth century.

Several years ago, Louis Menand published a fascinating book, *The Metaphysical Club: A Story of Ideas in America*. Menand explores the intellectual history of the American pragmatic movement, and he seeks to situate this movement within the context of American history. (The Metaphysical Club was a discussion group of prominent Cambridge intellectuals who met together in the 1870's.) One of Menand's major contributions is to show how the origins of the pragmatic movement can be understood as a critical response to the excesses of the American Civil War. Menand focuses his attention on four major thinkers: Oliver Wendell Holmes, Jr., William James, Charles S. Peirce, and John Dewey (although he also discusses many of their contemporaries). He makes a bold claim about the influence of these four men. He declares:

> Their ideas changed the way Americans thought—and continue to think—about education, democracy, liberty, justice and tolerance. And as a consequence they changed the way Americans live—the way they learn, the way they express their views, the way in which they understand themselves, and the way in which they treat people who are different from them. We are still living to a great extent, in a country these thinkers helped to make.[5]

What is the bond that unites these four very diverse thinkers? Menand affirms that they shared a common attitude toward ideas.

> What was that attitude? If we strain out the differences, personal and philosophical, they had with one another, we can say that these four thinkers had in common was not a group of ideas, but a single idea—an idea about ideas. They all believed that ideas are not "out there" waiting to be discovered, but are tools . . . that people devise to cope with the world in which they find themselves. They believed that ideas are produced not by individuals, but by groups of individuals—that ideas are social. They believed that ideas do not develop according to some inner logic of their own, but are entirely dependent, like germs on their human careers and environment. And they believed that since ideas are provisional responses to particular situations, their survival depends not on their immutability but on their adaptability.[6]

This "single idea" did not develop in an intellectual vacuum. It emerged in response to the violent extremism of the American Civil War. These thinkers were reacting against the entrenched opposition, the absolute certainty of opposing forces about the righteousness of their cause, the sheer intolerance toward those who held opposing convictions. They were critical of the rigid mentality of stark oppositions that had led to such bloody violence. Holmes fought in the Civil War and was seriously wounded several times. James had a brother who died in the war. Dewey was a young child during the war, but his father fought in it. Menand's thesis is that these thinkers undertook to develop a more flexible, open, experimental, critical, and fallible way of thinking that would avoid all forms of absolutism and appeals to moral certainties. And in their individual and collective ways in doing this, they helped to reshape the ways in which Americans think and act.

Menand captures something that is extremely important about this pragmatic movement. He helps us to understand that when pragmatists criticized all forms of absolutism, when they sought to expose the quest for certainty, when they argued for an open universe where chance and contingency are irreducible, when they stressed the agent's point of view and our ability to respond intelligently to new challenges, they were not exclusively concerned with abstract metaphysical and epistemological issues. They were addressing deep ethical, political, and practical questions that ordinary people face in their everyday lives. They were haunted by the memory of the way in which the conflict of absolutes led to so much violence. They sought to develop a new way of thinking—a new mentality—that would be a genuine alternative to ideological extremism. There is a sustained critique of "the quest for certainty." It is not just ideologists and fanatics, however, who claim to live by absolute certainty. Dewey thought that the quest for certainty had been one of the most basic concerns in the Western philosophical tradition. And he related this quest for metaphysical and epistemological certainty to a quest for *security*, an attempt to flee from the contingency, uncertainty, and ambiguity of everyday life. Many philosophers had tended to valorize what is eternal, fixed, unchanging, and necessary, and to denigrate contingency and becoming. But there is no "escape from peril." According to the pragmatists we are neither playthings of forces that are always beyond our control, nor can we ever completely master our destinies. The pragmatists sought to expose the arrogance and dangers of those who think that they can anticipate, manipulate, and control unexpected contingencies.

Hilary Putnam, who strongly identifies himself with the pragmatic tradition, claims that pragmatism is a "way of thinking" that involves "a certain group of theses, theses that can and indeed were argued very differently by different philosophers with different concerns." He summarizes these key theses as: (1) antiskepticism: pragmatists hold that doubt requires justification just as much as belief;(2) fallibilism: pragmatists hold that there is never a metaphysical guarantee to be had that such and such a belief will never need revision (that one can be fallibilistic and antiskeptical is perhaps the unique insight of American pragmatism); and (3) the thesis that there is no fundamental dichotomy between "facts" and "values"; and the thesis that, in a certain sense, practice is primary in philosophy.[7]

Peirce consistently challenged the idea of epistemological foundationalism— the dream (or the nightmare) of discovering once and for all an incorrigible foundation that could serve as a basis for building the solid edifice of knowledge. Descartes, more than any other philosopher, vividly portrayed what he took to be the grand Either/Or that we confront: *Either* solid indubitable foundations *or* a swamp of unfounded and relativistic opinion. I once called this "the Cartesian Anxiety." It is an anxiety that has haunted us right up to the present. Descartes' search for an Archimedian point is much more than a device to solve metaphysical and epistemological problems. It is the quest for some fixed ground, some stable rock upon which we can secure our lives against the vicissitudes that threaten us. I believe that many of those who claim religious or moral certainty for their convictions and for dividing the world into the stark opposition of good and evil are shaped by a popular form of this Cartesian Anxiety. And they also employ this grand Either/Or in the attacks on their opponents.

For they claim that the only alternative to a foundational moral certainty is to be lost in a quagmire of relativistic and nihilistic opinions.

Now what is distinctive about the pragmatic thinkers is that they rejected this grand Either/Or. The exclusive alternatives—absolute certainty or "absolute" relativism—is specious. We need to exorcise the Cartesian Anxiety, or, to switch metaphors, to engage in a form of philosophical and practical therapy that will release us from its constraining grip. Fallibilism is the belief that any claim is open to ongoing examination, modification, and critique. Peirce originally argued that fallibilism is essential for understanding scientific inquiry because it is a self-corrective enterprise. This is why he placed so much emphasis on cultivating critical communities of inquirers. For it is only in such a community that we can test and validate our hypotheses and theories. But other pragmatists—especially Dewey and Mead—extend fallibilism to the idea of a democratic community, to what Dewey characterized as creative democracy. The pragmatists knew how difficult it is to cultivate and sustain a fallibilistic mentality. It does not come about simply by talking about it or willing it. Fallibilism becomes a concrete reality only when we pay constant attention to developing the proper critical habits in a democratic community. Consequently, fallibilism in its robust sense is not a rarified epistemological doctrine. It consists of a set of *virtues*—set of practices—that need to be carefully nurtured. A fallibilistic orientation requires a genuine willingness to test one's ideas in public and to listen carefully to those who criticize them. It demands that we appreciate the pluralism of different perspectives. It requires the imagination to formulate new ideas to meet new situations. It also requires a high tolerance for uncertainty and contingency, and the courage to revise, modify, and abandon our most cherished beliefs when they are refuted. Consequently, fallibilism involves more than a minimum tolerance of those who differ from us, and who challenge our ideas. We must confront and seek to answer their criticisms—and this requires mutual reciprocal respect.

We can now better understand what Putnam means when he emphasizes the pragmatic claim that one can be a fallibilist and antiskeptical. When Putnam speaks of skepticism he is referring to the philosophical doctrine that calls into question the very possibility of knowledge. Fallibilism is not skepticism in this sense. On the contrary, it clarifies the conditions that are demanded for warranting our validity claims. There is, however, a more common sense idea of skepticism where we can speak of a fallibilistic skepticism. Menand describes the liberating quality of the fallibilistic skepticism that he finds in Holmes, Peirce, James, and Dewey:

> The belief that ideas should never become ideologies—either justifying the status quo, or dictating some transcendent imperative for renouncing it—was the essence of what they taught.

> In many ways this was a liberating attitude.... They taught a kind of skepticism that helped people cope with life in a heterogeneous, industrialized,

mass-market society, a society in which older human bonds of custom and community seemed to gave become attenuated, and to have been replaced by more impersonal networks of obligation and authority . . . Holmes, James, Peirce and Dewey helped to free thought from the thralldom to official ideologies, of the church or the state or even the academy. There is also, though, implicit in what they wrote, a recognition of the limits of what thought can do in the struggle to increase human happiness.[8]

A fallibilistic pragmatic mentality rejects the appeal to ideology, to absolute foundations, to incorrigible truths and certainties, to rigid ahistorical dichotomies including the dichotomy of absolute good and evil. And it seeks to develop an alternative that places the emphasis on critical inquiry, public debate and deliberation, tolerance, and cultivating the flexible habits that enable us to respond intelligently to contingencies.

In the Epilogue to his book, Menand tells us "that a movement of thought that had grown out of the experience of the Civil War appeared to reach an end with the Cold War."[9] With the Cold War a style of thought became dominant that elevated confrontation over compromise. "The notion that the values of a free society for which the Cold War was waged were contingent, relative, fallible constructions, good for some purposes and not good for others, was not a notion compatible with the moral imperatives of the age. [O]nce the Cold War ended," Menand tells us, "the ideas of Holmes, James, Peirce and Dewey emerged as suddenly as they had been eclipsed. . . . For in a post-Cold-War world, where there are many competing belief systems, not just two, skepticism about the finality of any particular set of beliefs has begun to seem to some people an important value again."[10] Menand wrote these words before 9/11— and since that infamous day there has been a radical shift in dominant ways of thinking. One cannot underestimate the consequential differences of the Civil War, the Cold War, and the "war on terror." And yet there are some disturbing similarities in the mentality that gains dominance at these times. There is an appeal to rigid principle, moral certainties, and confrontation. There are no nuances here, but only the black and white opposition of Good and Evil. This is a quasi-Manichean world. It is quasi-Manichean, because the Manicheans believed that God is co-eternal with Satan. Consequently there can be no final victory over evil. But today we are told that ultimately the Good and the Righteous will triumph over Evil. We hear this own political leaders and also from those Islamic fanatics who are absolutely convinced of the righteousness of their cause. Any deviation from this stark opposition is taken to be a sign of weakness. And there is a pernicious sexual subtext here. The alleged "masculine" qualities of toughness, strength, decisiveness are accentuated. Those who oppose them are "feminized." They are weak, too sensitive and indecisive. They are "girlie-men."

I want to emphasize that there is a vital core of the pragmatic ethos—the pragmatic mentality—that transcends the historical context in which it arose.

What we are confronting today is a clash of mentalities. And this is a clash that cuts across ethnic and national differences; it cuts across morality, politics, and religion. It manifests itself in all areas of human experience. It is fashionable today to associate the quest for certainty and absolutes with religion. But the problem is *not* religion. Rather it is a question of which mentality prevails in religion. Pragmatic fallibilism is *not* anti-religious; it is anti-dogmatic. The pragmatists approached religion with the same fallibilistic orientation that they advocated in the range of human inquiry and experience.

Now a critic might object that in drawing this contrast between two opposing mentalities, I am glossing over some tough issues. Pragmatic fallibilism may well be the preferred ethos in those situations where we can expect reasonable deliberation. But this is not our situation today. We have to face the realistic possibility that terrorists may soon have the chemical, biological and nuclear weapons to carry out mass murder. It may well be that there is no single essence or definition of evil, but the deliberate murder of innocent victims has always been an exemplar of evil. The trouble with the pragmatists is that they have always felt uncomfortable to facing up to evil. They speak of contingencies and dangers but they are unrealistic about the real dangers that now exist. Deliberation, diplomacy, and persuasion are, of course, desirable. But—to use a pragmatic turn of phrase—they don't "work" in the extreme circumstances that now exist. We are dealing with ruthless fanatical murderers. We have to be decisive, forceful, and fully committed to fighting this evil. The real weakness with a fallibilistic pragmatic mentality is that it lacks the resources to justify decisive action. Such a commitment depends on a firm conviction—a moral and political certainty of the justice of our cause.

The objection is a serious one and it needs to be confronted. But I want to bring out into the open its underlying fallacious presupposition. It is the assumption that passionate commitment and decisive action presupposes moral certainty. It is a slander to think that robust fallibilism entails indecisiveness and a lack of passionate commitment. There is no incompatibility between being *decisive* and recognizing the *fallibility* of our choices and decisions. On the contrary, this is what is required for *responsible* action. We need to recognize that whatever we do there will always be unintended consequences. Acknowledging and intelligently assessing these consequences may require altering our conduct. Dewey wrote that "only the conventional and the fanatical are always immediately sure of the right and wrong [or the good and evil]."

Many years ago Sidney Hook answered the charge that pragmatists are naively optimistic and unrealistic about the concrete evils that result from human actions. "Realization of the evil that men can do and have done is integral to any intelligent appraisal of history."[11] "The grim fact, however, is that there is sometimes no desire to reason, no wish to negotiate except as a holding action to accumulate strategic power, nothing but the reliance of one party or the other upon brute force even when other alternatives may exist."[12] But branding or reifying something as "evil" results in obfuscation unless we concretely specify what we are talking about and what is the intelligent response and options to the dangers that we confront. Critics of a pragmatic mentality frequently present themselves as "tough-minded realists" and mock their opponents as "tender-minded sentimentalists." Hook's sharp rejoinder to this charge is as relevant today as it was when he wrote it more than fifty years ago:

> This "tough-mindedness" is another expression of the abdication of intelligence. It refuses to discuss specific problems and the specific ways of handling them, smothering all problems under a blanket allegiance to some vaguely defined goal. It wraps itself up in blind faith, essentially religious, that no matter what is done, things will come right in the end. It is impatient with any attempt to judge verbal professions by consequences of fact. It is really not an attitude of toughmindedness at all, for it cannot face or live with the truth. It cannot bear to see its assumptions put into the crucible of doubt. Rather it is a tender-minded sentimentalism that reads its pious wishes into the mysterious "workings" of history.[13]

And Hook's comment about fear might have also been written in a post-9/11 world:

> There is intelligent and unintelligent fear . . . Intelligent fear arms us against real dangers and enables us, by modifying the environment or altering our behavior, to reduce the incidence of terror and pain. Intelligent fear must be proportionate to the dangers. It is the absence of any proportion between the danger and the fear which marks the panicky and hysterical response. Political thinking is often distorted by a failure to distinguish between fears that are ill-grounded or well-grounded.[14]

Let me explain more fully why the post-9/11 popular talk about evil is anti-political and anti-religious. It corrupts democratic politics and distorts the character of religion. I want to draw on some of the insights of Hannah Arendt and John Dewey that have to be incorporated into any adequate conception of democratic politics. Arendt's understanding of politics involves the interweaving of a network of interrelated concepts, including debate, action, speech, plurality, natality, public space, and public tangible freedom. Arendt tells us that "debate constitutes the very essence of political life,"[15] and this claim has a distinctive meaning for her. Debate itself is a form of action, and "action" is the term that Arendt uses to designate the highest form of the *vita activa* (the active life). What Arendt calls "action" is close to what Aristotle called *praxis*, the human activity that is involved in leading an ethical and political life. Action is intimately related to speech. "Action and speech are so closely related because the primordial and specifically human act must at the same time contain an answer to the question asked of every newcomer: 'Who are you?' This disclosure of who somebody is, is implicit in both his words and deeds."[16] This disclosure takes place in a public space where we can debate with each other. The very condition for such action and speech is what Arendt calls *plurality*. "Action, the only activity that goes on directly between men without the intermediary of things or matter, corresponds to the human condition of plurality, to the fact that men, not Man, live on earth and inhabit the world."[17] Plurality has a distinctive political meaning for Arendt. Plurality involves individuality, distinction, and equality. Each and every individual brings a distinctive perspective to a common world. And this plurality of perspectives is rooted in our *natality*, the innate capacity to begin, to initiate action. "To act, in its most general sense, means to take initiative, to begin . . . to set something into motion."[18] Drawing on her interpretation of the Greek *polis*, Arendt tells us that equality—or what the Greeks called *isonomy*—exists only in the political realm where human beings encounter each other as citizens. Returning to the gloss on the claim that "debate is the very essence of politics," we can see that politics involves the mutual and joint action of citizens with their plural perspectives who encounter each other as equals. In this public space, individuals debate with each other form and test public opinions and seek to persuade each other. And persuasion itself is always fallible.

We can deepen our understanding of what Arendt means by politics by seeing how she integrates the concept of "public tangible freedom." The idea of public tangible freedom was central to the *philosophes* of the Enlightenment.

> Their public freedom was not an inner realm into which men might escape at will from the pressures of the world. . . . Freedom for them could exist only in public; it was a tangible, worldly reality, something created by men to be enjoyed by men rather than a gift or a capacity, it was the man made space or marketplace which antiquity had known as the area where freedom appears and becomes visible to all.[19]

Public freedom must be sharply distinguished from liberation. Liberation is always liberation from something, whether it is liberation from poverty, or from oppressive rulers and dictators. The distinction between liberation and freedom is one of Arendt's most important and relevant distinctions. Liberation is a necessary condition for positive freedom, but it is never a sufficient condition for the achievement of public tangible freedom. The latter comes into existence and lasts only as long as citizens deliberate and debate together. Over and over again—especially since the collapse of Communism in 1989—we have to learn the bitter lesson that liberation from oppressive regimes is not sufficient to bring about public freedom. It is a dangerous illusion to think otherwise.

Arendt emphasizes the importance of "elementary republics," "islands of public freedom," "councils"—what Thomas Jefferson called "wards." The flavor of this vision of politics is exemplified when Arendt writes:

> The councils say: We want to participate, we want to debate, we want to make our voices heard in public, and we want to have the possibility to determine the course of our country. Since the country is too big for all to come together and determine our fate, we need a number of public spaces with it. The booth in which we deposit our ballots is unquestionably too small, for this booth has room for only one. The parties are completely unsuitable; there we are, most of us, nothing but a manipulated electorate. But if only ten of us are sitting around a table, each expressing our opinion of others, then a rational formation of opinion can take place through the exchange of opinions.[20]

Whatever criticism we may have of Arendt's conception of politics, I believe that she has captured something that is vital for the core a democratic politics. She is not outlining a blueprint for a democratic politics. She is describing a *permanent human possibility*, one that has manifested itself in the modern age at different times in the most diverse historical circumstances. And her favored example of the politics she describes is the American Revolution itself. The intelligent way to appropriate what she is doing is to read her as reminding us of what is quintessential to *reinvigorate* democratic political life—the fragile achievement of public tangible freedom. It should be clear that there is no place of absolutes, certainties, and rigid dichotomies in this conception of politics. The introduction of absolutes into politics—including absolute evil and goodness—corrupts and destroys politics. I repeat Arendt's warning: "The absolute . . . spells doom to everyone when it is introduced into the political realm."

Although there are many differences between Hannah Arendt and John Dewey, there is a significant overlap in their vision of what lies at the heart of democratic politics. Dewey also warned about the danger of the "eclipse of the public." Like Arendt, he also stressed the importance of the creation of those spaces in which public tangible freedom comes alive—where citizens debate, deliberate and act together. What Dewey wrote on the occasion of his eightieth birthday in 1939 is even more relevant for us today. "We have to recreate by deliberate and determined endeavor the kind of democracy which in its origin one hundred and fifty years ago was largely a product of a fortunate combination of men and circumstances." And in words that echo Arendt, he goes on to declare:

> If I emphasize that the task can be accomplished only by inventive effort and creative activity, it is in part because the depth of the present crisis is due in

considerable part to the fact that for a long time we acted as if democracy were something that perpetuated itself automatically. . . . We acted as if democracy were something that took place in Washington or Albany—or some other state capital under the impetus of what happened when men and women went to the polls once a year or so. . . . We can escape from this external way of thinking only as we realize in thought and action that democracy is a personal way of individual life: that it signifies the possession and continual use of certain attitudes, forming personal character and desire and purpose in all relations of life.[21]

We still need to learn these important lessons from Arendt and Dewey about what is so essential of a genuine democratic politics. Such a politics is contentious and agonistic. In a robust democracy there will be sharp disagreements, and strong opinions among citizens. But when absolutes, certainties, rigid dichotomies are introduced into politics they corrode and corrupt democratic politics.

Finally I want to turn to the question of religion, and to indicate why I believe that the post-9/11 discourse about good and evil has a corrupting influence on religion itself. There is no doubt that the religious right is having a growing influence on American politics. But we must not identify religion with this group. We must not allow any group to "steal" the mantle of religion—especially for dubious political purposes. Alasdair Macintyre gives one of the best succinct characterizations of a living tradition—including a religious tradition. He tells us that "a tradition not only embodies the narrative of an argument, but is only recovered by an argumentative retelling of that narrative which will itself be in conflict with other argumentative retellings."[22] If we examine the history of the great world religions including Christianity, Judaism and Islam, this is what we discover. Living religions are *not* monolithic. There is no such thing as *the* religious understanding of good and evil, nor does it make much sense to speak of *the* Christian, Jewish, or Islamic conception of good and evil. We must always we wary of false misleading essentialism and the reification of a specific conception of good and evil as if it were fixed for all time. Religious conceptions of good and evil are *essentially contested concepts*—and a vital religious tradition is one where there is an ongoing debate about the meaning of these concepts. We must not identity religion with *uncritical* dogmatism or *uncritical* fanaticism. There is the great religious tradition of *faith seeking understanding*. And this seeking involves thinking and questioning. Let me appeal directly to the Bible. Many religious believers (as well as non-religious persons) think of the Book of Job as a primary source for understanding religious faith and evil. But we should not forget that it is Job who *questions* and seeks to understand; it is Job who is not satisfied with the conventional wisdom of the comforters. And it is Job—the questioner—who is finally blessed, not the conventional comforters.

Throughout history we have witnessed the cruelty and extreme violence of those who are absolutely certain that they know what is good and evil. And fanaticism—as we know all too well from the twentieth century—can assume disastrous nonreligious and religious guises. Arthur M. Schlesinger, Jr. has recently declared the greatest threat to civilization today is from religious fanatics:

> Religious fanaticism is the breeding place for the greatest current threat to civilization, which is terrorism. Most of the killing around the world—whether in Ireland, Kosovo, Israel, Palestine, Kashmir, Sri Lanka, Indonesia, the Philippines, and Tibet—is the consequence of religious disagreement. There are no more dangerous people on earth than those who believe they are executing the will of the Almighty. It is this conviction that drives on terrorists to murder the infidel.[23]

I agree with Schlesinger that "there are no more dangerous people on earth than those who believe they are executing the will of the Almighty." That is why it is so disturbing and frightening when we hear something like this from our political leaders and fellow countrymen who think they are defending democracy and freedom. This is just the sort of absolutism that the pragmatic thinkers sought to root out and critique—the absolutism that destroys democratic politics and religion.

I have spoken about a clash of mentalities—the mentality that emphasizes absolutes, certainties, and the stark dichotomies—the mentality that emphasizes fallibility and the need for public debate, criticism, and self-corrective inquiry. This clash does *not* line up the distinction between the religious and the non-religious; both of these mentalities can take a religious or a non-religious form. Let me remind you that in the famous lecture in which William James introduced the idea of pragmatism, the first application of the pragmatic method was intended to clarify and defend his own religious orientation. And throughout his life James sought to show the compatibility of a fallibilistic mentality with the varieties of religious experience. None of the classical pragmatists were anti-religious. They argued that a fallibilistic orientation was just as important and relevant for religion and clarifying one's own faith as it is for dealing with science, ethics, and politics. And in this respect, I think that the pragmatists were attempting to keep alive what is vital to the world religions: the spirit of questioning, seeking understanding, and damning the arrogance and pride of those who claim absolute moral certainty about what constitutes good and evil.

Questioning evil, seeking to comprehend and resist its ever-new forms is a serious and ongoing task—one that I do not think can have any finality. But we must sharply distinguish genuine thinking and reflection from the abuse of evil. The abuse of evil occurs when we appeal to evil to block thinking, to obscure crucial issues, to manipulate fear, to cynically use it for "political advantage." The dominant post-9/11 popular discourse of evil is an abuse of evil—an abuse that corrupts democratic politics and religion.

Notes

[1] For a full elaboration of the argument in this essay, see my book, *The Abuse of Evil: The Corruption of Politics and Religion since 9/11* (Cambridge, UK and Malden, MA: Polity, 2005).

[2] Andrew Delbanco, *The Death of Satan* (New York: Farrar Straus, and Giroux, 1995), 3.

[3] Hannah Arendt, *On Revolution* (New York: Viking Press, 1963), 79.

[4] Samantha Power, "Hannah Arendt's Lesson," *The New York Review of Books*, April 29, 2004, 37.

[5] Louis Menand, *The Metaphysical Club: A Story of Ideas in America* (New York: Farrar, Straus and Giroux, 2001), xi.

[6] *Ibid.*

[7] Hilary Putnam, *Words and Life*, ed. James Conant (Cambridge: Harvard University Press, 1994), 152.

[8] Menand, *The Metaphysical Club*, xii.

[9] *Ibid.*, 438.

[10] *Ibid.*, 441.

[11] Sidney Hook, *Pragmatism and the Tragic Sense of Life* (New York: Basic Books, 1974), 30.

[12] *Ibid.*, 23.

[13] *Ibid.*, 35.

[14] *Ibid.*, 58.

[15] Hannah Arendt, *Between Past and Future* (New York: Penguin Books, 1977), 241.

[16] Hannah Arendt, *The Human Condition* (Chicago: The University of Chicago Press, 1958), 178.

[17] *Ibid.*, 7.

[18] *Ibid.*, 177.

[19] Arendt, *On Revolution*, 120–121.

[20] Hannah Arendt, *Crises of the Republic* (New York: Harcourt Brace Jovanovich, 1972), 233.

[21] John Dewey, "Creative Democracy: The Task Before Us," in *The Later Works, 1925–1953*, vol. 14, ed. Jo Ann Boydston (Carbondale: Southern Illinois University Press, 1988), 225–26.

[22] Alisdair MacIntyre, "Epistemological Crises, Dramatic Narrative and the Philosophy of Science," *Monist* 60 (1977): 461.

[23] Arthur M. Schlesinger, Jr, *War and the American Presidency* (New York: W. W. Norton, 2004), 116.

Evil, Reciprocity, and Rights

Edwin J. Delattre
Boston University

I want to begin by declaring myself on the question of whether diabolical evil is possible, by which I mean the moral condition of a person who chooses to do evil because it is evil, to inflict grievous harm on others for the sake of harming them. I believe the answer is yes. I offer as evidence Eric Harris, a high-school student who committed suicide at the age of 18 after committing mass murder.

You may remember Eric Harris as one of the two students who murdered thirteen people by gunfire at Columbine High School in Colorado on April 20, 1999, one day after the fourth anniversary of the bombing of the Murrah Federal Building in Oklahoma City. The other was Dylan Klebold. Klebold was a depressed and impulsive boy, who evidently did not blame others for his troubles, had probably been suicidal for some time, and might have been helped by perspicacious intervention. Of him, I will have little more to say, although it is clear he was a willing partner to Harris during the year in which they planned the massacre. Physical evidence suggests it is possible—I think it is uncertain what happened at the end—that Harris killed Klebold before killing himself.

I did not know Eric Harris, obviously, but I have known men and women and a small number of boys and girls who resemble him in his most awful aspects. Much of what was published in the popular media in the aftermath of the Columbine shootings about the two shooters was not true. It is not true that Harris and Klebold had been victimized by high-school bullies. They had not been ridiculed and intimidated by athletes or other popular students. They were not friendless loners and outcasts. They were not members of a group at Columbine called "The Trench Coat Mafia." Most of that group had already graduated; neither Harris nor Klebold was included in the Columbine Year-book picture of the group; and high-school classmates did not think of Harris and Klebold as members. Media reporters evidently believed they were members because they wore raincoats on the day of the massacre. Given crimes by gunfire and crime scenes I have seen, I believe Harris and Klebold wore coats simply to conceal firearms and explosives.

Widely circulated, well-intentioned published accounts say that during the massacre, one of the killers asked a born-again Christian girl named Cassie Bernall whether she believed in God, and when she said yes, he shot her to death.

The official investigation, based on eyewitness testimony, concluded that Klebold hit the table where Cassie Bernall was sitting with his hand, shouted, "Peekaboo," and shot her dead.[1] One of the two did shoot a girl named Valeen Schnurr and then asked her if she believed in God, before walking away. She made it to safety and survived.[2]

The media treated the two killers as just another pair of school shooters and made much of the idea that they committed mass murder in reprisal for having been bullied outcasts. The thesis that mass murders in schools can be traced to explosive rage over having been bullied is popular now, far beyond any evidentiary justification, and has led to anti-bullying legislation and anti-bullying research and school practices grants. They seem to me irrelevant to mass murder of the kind that was perpetrated at Columbine. As the FBI summit that was convened shortly after the massacre showed, revenge was not on Dylan Klebold's or Eric Harris' mind. A school shooting was not a very large part of what they, especially, Harris, wanted to do.

On the fifth anniversary of the Columbine massacre, April 20, 2004, Michigan State University psychiatrist Dr. Frank Ochberg and the FBI's lead investigator at Columbine, Supervisory Special Agent and clinical psychologist, Dwayne Fuselier (both of whom served on the FBI summit panel of experts), identified Eric Harris as a remorseless, monomaniacal killer, a psychopath with a superiority complex who felt contempt for the entire human species. Harris, they argued, sought not revenge, but indiscriminate murder on a huge scale. Harris' journal showed that with a grandiosely inordinate sense of proportion, he elevated pet peeves to self-glorifying and monumental contempt for others. He ranted endlessly about his disgust with humanity. He persistently lied for the pleasure and self-aggrandizement of succeeding at it. He feigned regret and remorse and empathy to avoid punishment for wrongdoing. Once, after apprehension for breaking into a vehicle to steal property from it, he sent a written expression of regret and empathy to his victims, while writing in his journal, "Isn't America supposed to be the land of the free? How come, if I'm free, I can't deprive a stupid, f . . . ing dumbshit from his possessions if he leaves them sitting on the front seat of his f . . . ing van out in plain sight and in the middle of f . . . ing nowhere on a Frif . . . ing night? NATURAL SELECTION. F . . . er should be shot." Harris was shrewd and was thought by many who knew him, though certainly not all, to be "nice." They never saw the videotape where Harris and Klebold boasted that at Columbine, they would eclipse the death count of the McVeigh/Nichols bombing of the Murrah Federal Building in Oklahoma City.

Harris did not want Columbine to be remembered as a school shooting at all. He had a history of building homemade bombs, and Columbine was supposed to be a massive massacre by means of such explosives. Law enforcement investigators estimate that if the twenty pound pipe bombs surrounded by propane cylinders Harris and Klebold rigged in the Columbine cafeteria had exploded at eleven o'clock as planned, when 900 students and faculty were scheduled to be there, 600 or more people would have been killed. When Harris and Klebold entered the cafeteria firing their weapons at 11:25, however, and tried unsuccessfully to detonate one of the bombs with gunfire, fewer than 500 people were there. Still, hundreds would surely have died in the structural collapse triggered by the explosions. If the car bombs Harris and Klebold rigged in the parking lot to explode later had gone off as planned, students and school personnel who had fled the high school, injured people, parents, police, firefighters, rescue workers, emergency medical technicians, doctors, nurses, vehicle drivers, media crews, and spectators would have been killed in untold numbers, with all of that carnage recorded on live television, unless or until the camera equipment also was destroyed. If all had gone as planned, Harris and Klebold would also have been positioned to shoot people trying to escape the parking lot carnage.

Harris evidently was not after anybody in particular. He wanted to kill indiscriminately as many people as possible as visibly as possible, with the highest mass murder body count in American history. I believe he sought to achieve massive evil for evil's sake and the eternal fame or infamy that he believed the bombing massacre would bring him. As with others I have met who resemble him, I think he entirely understood that he was deliberately choosing to do evil and took immense pleasure in imagining others, all inferior to him and without any right to exist, dying at his hands. As dreadful as the murder of 13 people and injury of many more were, the Columbine massacre was a dismal failure when measured against Harris' intentions. It demonstrated his overestimation of his competence with explosives and the extent of his self-aggrandizement beyond his capacities. As Ochberg and Fuselier rightly observe, there is no telling how successful Harris might have been in fulfilling his intention of committing the greatest possible evil by massacre, had he waited until he had acquired greater expertise in the use of explosives or found his way into circles with access to other weapons of mass destruction.[3] I conclude from additional conversations with police and law enforcement personnel who know the Columbine case that Eric Harris knew what he was doing, was not psychotic but responsible for his own free choices, and that he was, in his monstrous intentions and actions, all too human.

I also want to argue that the magnitude of evil is not reducible to quantitative terms. I offer as evidence the life and death of a single child, Elisa Izquierdo. As I have recounted in my book, *Character and Cops: Ethics in Policing*, on November 20, 1995, Elisa Izquierdo suffered a brain hemorrhage when her mother, Awilda Lopez, hit her with such force that she crashed headfirst into a cement wall. Elisa died 2 days later, the day before Thanksgiving. Elisa had been born in 1989 addicted to crack, of a mother who was evidently deranged. While in the custody of her father, Elisa was described by adults as a "well-adjusted, lively, intelligent child." Before her father died of cancer in 1994, he requested earnestly that Elisa be placed in custody of his aunt and not of her mother. A court, however, ignored his pleas and placed her in custody of her mother.

There, Elisa suffered terrible beatings, genital torture with a hairbrush, solitary confinement in a small room where she was forced to relieve herself into an overflowing pot and held upside down while her hair was used to mop the floor. Her mother claimed to have stuffed snakes down Elisa's throat to exorcise demons. Before her mother killed her, she broke Elisa's little finger. This painful fracture, with the bone sticking out through Elisa's skin, went as untended as her many other injuries. Scars and wounds covered much of her body. Experienced police who observed her body described her condition, the agony to which she had been subjected, as the worst case of child abuse they had ever seen.

While Elisa was with her mother, members of her late father's family and Elisa's school teachers repeatedly and desperately reported their fears and suspicions about her abuse and suffering and endangerment. Government agencies and courts turned a deaf ear, refusing to separate her from her mother even after being informed that Elisa's mother had withdrawn her from school. Neighbors reported her cries for relief—"Mommy, please stop! I'm sorry"—to no avail. And so, her cries unanswered, terrified, lonely, and violently brutalized, Elisa Izquierdo died.[4]

She was one child. Left to the depravity of her mother, Elisa's life was, in the famous words Thomas Hobbes used to describe human existence in a state of nature, "solitary, poore, nasty, brutish, and short." The enormity of the evil inflicted on her—her agony, fear, and death—could have been prevented by legal intervention and wise judicial action; and that enormity seems to me to refute entirely and by itself the proposition that the gravity of evil must be calculated in terms of numbers.

Elisa's horrible predicament, her utter defenselessness and vulnerability to an adult whom everyone involved knew could not be trusted, should not be thought singular or unique. While I was working with undercover narcotics officers in Philadelphia some years ago, we learned from nearby uniformed officers that the bodies of two young boys had been found in a vacant lot between two tenements. They had been shot to death in the back of their heads at close range within the hour. The story unfolded like this: the two boys were brothers, aged 12 and 10. They and a third brother 9 years old had been given drugs to sell by teenage dealers the night before. The boys went home to rest before hitting the inner city drug markets where suburbanites come at night to buy drugs. While they slept, their mother stole the drugs and, with her friends, used them up. When the teenagers came in the morning to collect, the brothers, hoping to protect their mother, said they had been ripped off on the streets of both the drugs and the money they had collected. The teenagers took them out, assigned them to look out for cops for the morning (a 100-dollar-a-day job for pre-teenagers in a city that then had no budget for truant officers), and then executed them at mid-day. The youngest brother escaped to tell the story when the killers' Mac-10 machine pistol jammed. When the police took the boy home and told his mother that her other two sons had been murdered, she immediately replied, "If them boys are dead, where do I get my rock?" Rock was then the popular name for crack in Philadelphia. She had cast herself into bondage to a single passion—lust for crack—and her sons died for it. She did not intend to kill them, but her theft made their deaths inevitable, as anyone familiar with the conditions of drug trafficking there and at that time would have known.

Third, I want to argue that just as a person can freely choose to do diabolical evil and be diabolically evil, a human being can voluntarily choose a life of radical evil, in the sense that Kant meant it: a life in which a person's principle of choice and action is always to subordinate considerations of moral duty to perceived self-interest and happiness, irrespective of the cost to others. I offer as evidence the conduct of David L. Harding.

Harding was a college graduate with a master's degree in fine arts and drama who became a New York State Trooper. He seemed to be a model trooper: good looking, tall and fit, articulate, a quick learner, courteous, precise in his reports, punctual, conversant with and apparently respectful of the rules and regulations and laws relevant to his work. In time, he went to work in the Bureau of Criminal Investigations in Troop C of the State Police, not far from Syracuse. It was a unit with a high rate of solved crimes, perhaps suspiciously high, that became even higher after Harding's arrival. In 1992, Harding was arrested by the State Police.

The background was this: Harding had learned that the CIA was hiring agents, and he applied for a job. Called for an interview, he went to CIA Headquarters in Langley, Virginia. CIA employment interviews were then conducted as polygraph tests. During the interview, Harding was asked whether he would break the law to complete a mission, if so ordered by a superior. He said yes. Asked how the interviewer could be sure he would do as he said, Harding replied that he had broken the law in many of the cases he had worked as a crime investigator, planting evidence, including fingerprint evidence, coercing witnesses, falsifying reports, giving perjured testimony. The polygraph indicated he was telling the truth.

As required, the CIA notified the Justice Department. The procedure should have had the information in FBI hands in days and in the hands of the head of New York State Police days later. Inexplicably, the actual transfer of information took 9 months.

From 1992 until 1997, the State Police and the New York Attorney General's Office, under the leadership of Special Prosecutor Nelson Roth, spent 119,000 hours investigating Troop C and other Troops, concluding that no one outside the Troop C Bureau of Criminal Investigations was involved in this betrayal of the public trust. Five police investigators were convicted of evidence tampering, official misconduct, and perjury, including Harding. Roth proved that these crimes by police had been committed routinely from 1984 until 1992. Fourteen thousand cases had to be re-examined to see whether the rights of suspects and people convicted of crimes had been violated. The bill for the Special

Prosecutor's Office time and expenses was $625,000. I worked closely with Nelson Roth and the State Police as an advisor during the more than 5-year investigation.

Over the years, I have heard dirty cops try to justify or excuse wrongdoing in their work and investigations by saying they had acted in the public interest, that this suspect or that suspect was an exceptionally dangerous person who had to be put in prison, either by legitimate means or, if necessary, illegitimate ones. The term I coined years ago for this attitude and the conduct that goes with it is "noble cause corruption": "Our mission is so noble that we must not be prevented from accomplishing it by the limiting requirements of the Constitution and the laws."

There was none of that in the Troop C or Harding case. The testimony was that they had to catch or appear to catch the bad guys, and if they could not get legitimate evidence against them, then they had to "put someone, anyone, at the scene of the crime" by planting evidence, and see somebody successfully prosecuted, no matter whom, to maintain the "solve rate." Doing this, Harding and others said, was necessary to satisfy your superiors, get good evaluation and performance reports, have a good chance of promotion, and avoid having superiors make your daily life miserable. Harding was remorseless and unrepentant. He never exhibited the slightest regret. He wanted to be a star, and he was willing to do whatever was required in order to be viewed as one. Interviewed on *60 Minutes* after being sent to prison, Harding clearly relished the exposure. He was as indifferent to the wrongs he had committed in office against the rights of others, in what he believed to be his self-interest at the time, as he had been in the CIA interview.

All of us were perplexed that the background investigation of Harding conducted prior to his being accepted as a police recruit had revealed absolutely nothing in the way of earlier misconduct and had been filled with glowing recommendations. Conducting thorough and reliable background investigations is an essential part of building institutions that the public can trust, and so I recommended that personnel from the State police and the Special Prosecutor's Office retrace the entire background investigation of Harding. Accordingly, they met with the headmaster of a private school where Harding had worked immediately before joining the State Police. He had given Harding top marks in every respect.

The investigators asked whether he had hidden anything from them the first time around. Red-faced, he admitted that he had caught Harding embezzling funds. Harding had repaid the money and begged the headmaster not to tell the background investigators, because doing so would shatter his "life-long dream of becoming a police officer." The headmaster had hidden Harding's criminal acts, he said, "out of compassion for Harding."

Had he not realized, they asked, how much damage a dishonest person can do behind a badge, and how much a person who escapes exposure and punishment for embezzlement might be inclined to think he can commit other wrongs and crimes with impunity? The headmaster replied that he had not thought about that. Imagine: the headmaster of a school, of all people, putting the public at risk by lying to background investigators in telling them Harding's conduct had been exemplary and in hiding his criminal acts. His disrespect for the truth, for the obligations of public servants, and his inattention to our capacity to misdirect our compassion shocked me. His deceit and incompetence had terrible consequences that he did not intend, but for which he surely shares the moral responsibility.

Thoughtlessness so often has dreadful consequences, even with well-intentioned people. In Shakespeare's *Romeo and Juliet*, Friar Laurence marries Romeo and Juliet. Then, to prevent Juliet from having to go through with a different marriage benevolently planned for her by her father, Friar Laurence gives Juliet a potion that will make her appear to be dead for just over 40 hours. Friar Laurence directs a messenger to get word to Romeo that Juliet is not really dead. Circumstances prevent the messenger from reaching Romeo. Believing Juliet is dead, Romeo kills himself. And, learning Romeo is dead, Juliet kills herself. Friar Laurence was a fine maker of potions. He had nothing but good intentions. He seems, though, not to have thought to ask, when he needed to ask, "What will happen if Romeo does not get my message, or gets word instead that Juliet is dead?"

Thoughtlessness is not always well intentioned. In *Eichmann in Jerusalem: A Report on the Banality of Evil*, Hannah Arendt argued that Adolf Eichmann was not a monstrous anti-Semite, intent on genocide, but rather a specimen of the banality of evil. She describes his banality by emphasizing his thoughtlessness. Arendt concluded that Eichmann could speak nothing but "officialese," and explained,

> The point here is that officialese became his language because he was genuinely incapable of uttering a single sentence that was not a cliché. . . . The longer one listened to him, the more obvious it became that his inability to speak was closely connected to an inability to think, namely, to think from the standpoint of anybody else. No communication was possible with him, not because he lied but because he was surrounded by the most reliable of all safeguards against the words and the presence of others, and hence against reality as such.

Arendt went on to say that during Eichmann's trial, "everybody could see that this man was not a 'monster,' but it was difficult indeed not to suspect that he was a clown." He was clownish, she said, in the inconsistencies of his testimony, where he moved from one cliché to another, oblivious to the inconsistencies, depending on his "changing moods." Yet, she insisted that Eichmann was not stupid.[5]

We should note, in contrast, that in a 1990 conversation with Philippe-Michael de Saint-Cheron, Elie Wiesel said, "I remember that when I saw Eichmann in his glass cage, I was frightened, even though he was powerless. But he was still frightening, because he was Evil itself, and Evil is always frightening."[6]

There is no contradiction between being thoughtless in the sense that Arendt took Eichmann to be and being very frightening. Quite the opposite. Whenever I encounter anyone, no matter on which side of the law, who seems to me either unable or unwilling to take the place and point of view of another for the sake of giving moral consideration, I take myself to be in the company of someone who is potentially dangerous, maybe very dangerous. It does not matter to me whether I judge the person to be stupid, or indifferent and uncaring, or caught up in clichés that sustain moral blindness and make others morally invisible, or thoughtless in the sense of incapacity that Arendt meant, or wicked, or radically evil. I never risk thinking of such a person, criminal or bureaucrat, urban gang member or politician of especially raw ambition, as clownish.

I recall meeting shortly after 9/11 with one of the most powerful of United States' Attorneys. We discussed the question of how best to address the problem of the illegal entry during the 1990's of some 300,000 immigrants who might be sympathetic to terrorism against the United States, at least 10,000 of whom were strongly suspected to be so. He told me, with a poker face, that he expected the Immigration and Naturalization Service to oversee the work of state and local police forces in finding these people and determining whether they were dangerous. This was such an obvious lie that I asked him whether any of the major police chiefs in the country had been informed. He knew I could check that, and he said "no". I then asked whether he really believed INS had anything resembling the capacity, let alone the authority, for such a task. Equally dead pan, he said "no" again. So, we stared at each other briefly, and then I said, "You don't have any plan at all." He did not, but he would have been content to send me away believing otherwise.

I trust it is clear that no one who is diabolically evil, no one who is radically evil, no one who is potentially just as dangerous as they because of thoughtlessness, has to wear fangs and horns or be otherwise out of the ordinary. The diabolically evil and the radically evil often do the morally right thing because it is in their interest to do so. So do the thoughtless, even when their thoughtlessness is deliberate or a matter of settled disposition, a sign of radical evil rather than incapacity (as perhaps it was with Eichmann the ambitious bureaucrat).

No one can do evil all the time or at every possible opportunity; a person who tried to do so could not survive for a day. Eric Harris went to school, did his homework at least some of the time, partied with friends and acquaintances, ate in restaurants and paid the checks, stayed out of trouble for the most part, although evidence has been secured of graphic warning signs and of run-ins with others pointing to Harris' intention to commit the massacre. David Harding participated in many legitimate investigations where there was no need to commit wrongs and break the law to get what he wanted. Some crime investigations are easy, especially when the perpetrators behave so incompetently that their identities are unmistakable or they are caught in the act.

Cops who commit acts of corruption for profit also do their jobs in perfectly normal ways at other times. "Grass eaters" are opportunistic cops who wait for such crimes as burglaries to be committed and then steal whatever of value the burglars have left behind.[7] They know the initial burglars will be blamed. They turn around and do right for the rest of their work shifts, no matter how demanding their duties may be. So do "meat eaters"—aggressive cops who initiate burglaries and vehicle thefts, rob drug dealers, traffic in the stolen drugs, and then launder the money.[8] Meat eaters do not wait around to graze for profit. They search for prey. Often, they are much admired for physical courage and relentlessness in the pursuit of dangerous criminals. I have known some who were unflinching in confrontation with grave danger.

Fraudulent and violent people can be intelligent, shrewd, and perceptive. The most effective of them wear no labels. Even if they never enter the place and point of view of another person for the sake of giving the person moral consideration, they enter the minds and hearts of others quite adeptly for the sake of exploitation, manipulation, and deception. Their doing so enables them to use others as means merely to their own goals with great success and to prevent others from obstructing them. It seems that Eichmann was not even very good at this; he never rose to high rank, despite his ambitions.

But effective torturers and interrogators do have this capacity. James Bond Stockdale, the ranking prisoner of war in the Hanoi Hilton who was held in solitary confinement for eight years and tortured repeatedly, wrote ten years later:

> [I]n that brutally controlled environment [of a prison camp] a perceptive enemy can get his hooks into the slightest chink in a man's ethical armor and accelerate his downfall. Given the right opening, the right moral weakness, a certain susceptibility on the part of the prisoner, a clever extortionist can drive his victim into a downhill slide that will ruin his image, self-respect and life in a very short time.[9]

Stockdale identified a need for affection or approval as one of the most dangerous weaknesses a prisoner of war can have.

Police interrogators understand what my friend, Jim Stockdale, knows. The best of them can enter and plumb the mind of a suspect, no matter how shocking and disgusting their discoveries. I have known three women interrogators who could enter in depth the mind of a violent pedophile. They could discern how best to persuade him that they fervently wished he had performed sexual acts with or on them when they were children. Their discernment enabled them to bring the suspect to open up in remorseless confession, describing in detail and bragging about his actions, while sadistically relishing in outspoken and vivid memory the reactions of the children. (Notice the relevance of this work to constructing psychological profiles of serial killers by reconstructing the likely behavior of their murdered victims, from what the victims' intimates knew of their personality and character, to discover what excites and gratifies the killer.)

Such interrogation is an ordeal for the interrogator and for most observers. I once held the shoulders of one of those women as she vomited into a wastebasket immediately after an interrogation I had watched through a one-way mirror. She was unable to make it to a rest room only a few yards away. While interrogating the suspected and in fact guilty pedophile, however, she never once gave the slightest clue that she was anything but thrilled, excited, and even sexually aroused by his description of his repetitive and savage sexual assaults on several children. I have been to Hollywood, and I have been to Broadway, but I believe hers was the most courageous dramatic performance I will ever see.

Involvement in investigations and interrogations of remorseless perpetrators of horrific crimes takes a toll in the lives of law enforcement personnel. One of my friends who spent substantial portions of his career immersed in such work has told me of "the horrors that bark in the night" for years afterward. The sacrifices such public servants make for our safety fill me with admiration.

Philosophers sometimes speak of three kinds of knowledge: knowing that, knowing how, and knowing what. By knowing what, they mean knowing what to feel, what is morally right to feel, in different circumstances and with and toward the people who are involved. Moral discernment of this kind involves the people who figure in our lives and matter to us and also others our actions may affect, and even those whose conduct or circumstances we witness at a distance. Much of the time, knowing what to feel is uncomplicated, as in the appropriateness of sympathy with people who have lost someone they love or who are suffering the consequences of some natural disaster, or the appropriateness of outrage at learning that someone has victimized innocent people by violence or fraud. But knowing what to feel is not always this simple.

When I have witnessed interrogations of remorseless pedophiles and rapists, talked with them myself, and learned their histories and records in detail, I have felt the sense of humility and gratitude that goes with the awareness, "there but for the grace of God go I." So, too, with high-level drug traffickers who remorselessly murdered or arranged the deaths of honest cops, judges, or other public officials who stood in their way; and with street pimps who addicted youngsters to drugs in order to prostitute them, taught them that only homosexual men can get or transmit AIDS, and sent them out to do business knowing that they were HIV positive or afflicted with the full-blown disease. I have felt pity and compassion more strongly for the victims of their crimes, especially children who may forever suffer because of the cruel destruction of their innocence. Above all, I have felt a towering fury and indignation against the most savagely remorseless of these criminals. I have wanted them to be forever unable to victimize anyone again, and I admit that I have wanted some of them dead. The key word is remorseless.

In the child pornography and prostitution industries, where huge illegal and legal profits are reaped world wide, pedophiles are routinely called "chicken hawks." It is a term of derision among those who get rich by sacrificing children to exploit the lusts of their customers. Among most of the police and corrections personnel and almost all of the prison inmates I have known during the past 30 years, pedophiles are called "short eyes." They have eyes for short people. This is a term of contempt. Left among the general population of a prison, no inmate known to have "short eyes" can survive. Many convicts have children of their own, nieces and nephews, younger siblings, and only the strongest among them, those with power in gangs or organized crime, can reach beyond prison walls to protect their children and other young relatives. But they can safeguard all children from future assault by eliminating any pedophile who comes within their reach. Many inmates, especially those serving sentences that leave them with little or nothing to lose, will kill any pedophile they can, and not mercifully.

Corrections and law enforcement personnel can virtually guarantee that a prison sentence for a pedophile is a death sentence. They need only to let the word out quietly that the newcomer to the prison has "short eyes," and then fail to isolate and protect the pedophile by solitary or very selective confinement. Or, when a known pedophile refuses selective or solitary confinement, they can remain silent, instead of telling him he is committing suicide. (In federal prisons, similar conditions obtain for traitors and spies. Many criminal profiteers consider themselves patriots and will kill traitors given the chance.)

What do we owe, what do cops owe, the most remorselessly savage and deadly of criminals? What should cops feel, and what may they, morally speaking, rightly do?

You may recall that Dante's *Inferno* is not populated with the souls of mere sinners, but rather only of remorseless, unrepentant sinners. In *Canto VIII*, Dante the Pilgrim and his guide, Virgil, encounter the weeping and miserable spirit of the remorselessly proud and wrathful sinner, Filippo Argenti. For the first time in his descent into Hell, Dante the Pilgrim expresses intense righteous indignation. He says to Argenti, "in weeping and misery, accursed spirit, may you stay. I know you for all your filth." Virgil embraces Dante in enthusiastic approval, saying, "indignant soul, blessed is she that bore you in her womb." Virgil's words are close to those referring to Christ, in Lk. 11.27: "Blessed is the womb that bore you."[10] In the notes to *Canto VIII* of her commentary on the *Inferno*, Dorothy L. Sayers cautions, "Humanism is always apt to underestimate, and to be baffled by, the deliberate will to evil." *Canto VII*, she explains, is where Dante first "sees (in the image of the damned soul) sin as it is—vile, degraded, and dangerous—and turns against it."[11]

In *Canto XXXII*, Dante commits an act of violence against the spirit of a sinner who committed violent treachery in battle, and in *Canto XXXII*, Dante commits fraud in the form of a false promise to the spirit of a treacherous sinner who had his banquet guests murdered. In these actions, commentators such as Mark Musa stress, Dante the Pilgrim is showing "a spiritual development in the right direction, away from pity for the sinner toward hatred of his sin."[12]

In his 1954 commentary on Dante, H. R. Huse argued that through these episodes, Dante, as author of *The Divine Comedy*, was also delivering a secular, political lesson. Specifically, Huse drew from Dante that "ordinary rules of conduct are inapplicable to the completely depraved: one must keep away from them or act according to the code they have established. This is the realistic Gresham's Law of competitive behavior."[13] Gresham's Law, formulated in the middle of the sixteenth century, is that where money is used as a legal medium of exchange or tender, "bad money drives good money out of circulation." That is, if bad money (say, gold coins with shaved edges which thus contain less gold than unshaved coins with the same face value) and good money are simultaneously in circulation, users will naturally hoard the good money and spend the bad. By analogy, if bad people enjoy all the benefits of their own acts of fraud and violence and also all the benefits of moral treatment by good people, they will dominate, drive good people out of power, and ultimately rule the earth. Huse added, "[G]olden rules and codes of honor presuppose a certain uniformity in the social group. To apply them without discrimination is merely to favor and give superior survival value to the fraudulent and dishonorable."[14]

As tempting as this view may be, and as much as it captures the attitude of some cops who commit noble cause corruption, Huse's account seems to me not faithful to Dante. For Dante, only the dead can be known to be forever unrepentant. Indeed, exposure to moral consideration and treatment may be the occasion of a living person's becoming repentant even late in life. Our fallibility of judgment disqualifies us from deciding who among us will never in the future feel remorse and become repentant. Obviously, we would be fools not to take perfectly justifiable measures, prudent steps, to safeguard ourselves from those who would prey on us by violence or fraud, but self-defense is different from predation and vigilantism.

What, then, of the government that is supposed to protect us, and of those who serve in it? The United States is a constitutional republic. Our Declaration of Independence declares the self-evidence of the proposition that human beings are "endowed by their Creator with certain inalienable rights" and that "to secure these rights, governments are instituted among men." The precision of this language is deliberate: it is not the part of government to grant rights, or to take rights away. It is the purpose of government to *secure* rights granted to the citizenry by their Creator. Government, the Founders of this country knew, is to be composed of public servants, not tyrants. The Preamble says our

Constitution is ordained to "secure the blessings of liberty to ourselves and our posterity." In Federalist 52, James Madison wrote of "the rights secured to [the people] by the Federal Constitution."[15]

When a person enters government, as every criminal justice official, every cop, every law enforcement officer does, with an oath or affirmation to uphold and defend the Constitution, the person commits to *securing* the rights of each individual citizen, no matter how dreadful, savage, dangerous, and remorseless the person, no matter how heinous the person's acts. The Bill of Rights protects all citizens. Police discretion in abridging rights for the sake of the public safety and the safety of the innocent and helpless is not a license to ignore the security of rights. No criminal justice official has the right to violate constitutional limits on search and seizure, impose cruel and unusual punishment, compel self-incriminating testimony, or use force beyond what is reasonably necessary.

Obviously, there are times when the use of deadly force is not only right, but obligatory, and therefore entirely justified. There is no justification for killing someone on the streets for past offenses, or allowing anyone to be killed in prison because of past crimes. I am familiar with cases of both, and they are intolerable. There are also times when the use of deception is both legal and morally legitimate, especially where the public interest cannot otherwise be protected, as I have suggested in examples above. Rightful uses of deception are also limited. Tampering with medical reports mailed from a doctor to a suspect or a prisoner would be illegal and morally intolerable.

Everyone is entitled to the presumption of innocence. The presumption of innocence has nothing to do with epistemology. Saying a person is innocent until proven guilty does not mean we do not know whether the person committed the act in question, because often it is certain that the person did so. The presumption means that the person may not be punished by government, or anyone in government, without having enjoyed due process, without having been found guilty of a crime and been duly sentenced. No one in government has the right to decide that a duly passed sentence is unjust, and add to it by the infliction of pain, suffering, or exposure to danger. Anyone who acts otherwise is acting as a tyrant, not a public servant, in violation of the Constitution and the laws and the principle of government instituted to secure rights.

I have worked on ethics in policing and law enforcement at the federal, state, and local level in the United States and other countries during the past 30 years. The work has brought me face to face, either at crimes in progress, at crime scene investigation, or in the course of subsequent criminal investigation, with most of the forms of motivation for violence and fraud traditionally associated with wickedness and evil. Not all wicked and evil actions are illegal, and not all illegal actions are wicked or evil. Not every serious crime is inevitably motivated by wickedness or evil intent. Desperation, helplessness, extortionate pressure and coercion, susceptibility to adverse peer pressure, exposure to bad examples and destructive attitudes, impulsiveness, incompetence, and ignorance can spawn acts of violence and fraud with severe, even dreadful, consequences.

Furthermore, we need not venture into the domains of illegality to encounter the seven deadly sins: pride; lust; wrath; spiritual, moral, intellectual, and physical sloth; greed; gluttony in all its varieties of intemperate excess; and envy. These are to be found on both sides of the law, in every walk of public and private life, and often, by honest appraisal, in ourselves. The seven deadly sins are not by definition criminal. Rather, the potential for them is sown in human nature and transcends cultural custom and positive law, just as does our fallibility of judgment.

Human nature itself therefore offers the greatest warning against the temptation to forgo morality, to override the security of the rights of citizens, even when we have to deal with the diabolically evil, the radically evil, and the thoughtlessly deadly. Our moral sensibilities, whether we are sworn to uphold the Constitution and the laws or we work in some other walk of life, should bring us to feel outrage over immoral and criminal predation. But if we care about the security of human rights, including our own, we will not want to meet a cop with a badge and a gun, or a bureaucrat with a pen, who believes it is his place, as a member of government, to decide whether or not to grant rights, rather than to respect and act for their security.

When I think of that arrogance in a member of government at any level, I think of the words of a former LAPD cop, Rafael Perez. In 1996, Perez helped to frame an innocent man by falsifying evidence and committing perjury. The man was sentenced to 23 years in prison. Perez also participated in the murder of another person by shooting the victim, planting a gun on him, and cooking up a story while standing over him and watching him die. Interviewed after apprehension for these and other crimes, Perez said, "When I planted a case on someone, did I feel bad? Not once. I felt good. I felt, you know, I'm taking this guy off the streets."[16]

What a cop should feel above all is the imperative of fidelity to the oath of office. The rest of us should feel the weight of our civic obligations.

Notes

[1] Http://en.wikepedia.org/wiki/Cassie_Bernall.

[2] Http://en.wikepedia.org/wiki/Columbine_High_School_Massacre#1997.

[3] Dave Cullen, "The Depressive and the Psychopath: At Last We Know Why the Columbine Killers Did It," *Slate Magazine* (April 20, 2004), http://slate.msn.com/id/2099203. See also David Brooks, "The Columbine Killers," *New York Times*, April 24, 2004, A: 25.

[4] Edwin J. Delattre, *Character and Cops: Ethics in Policing*, Washington, DC, 4th ed. (London: The AEI Press, 2002), 260.

[5] Hannah Arendt, *Eichmann in Jerusalem: A Report on the Banality of Evil* (New York: Penguin Books, 1977), 48, 49, and 55.

⁶ Elie Wiesel and Philippe-Michael de Saint-Cheron, *Evil and Exile*, trans. Jon Rothschild (Notre Dame, IN: University of Notre Dame Press, 1990), 190.

⁷ New York City Commission to Investigate Allegations of Police Corruption and the City's Anti-Corruption Procedures, *The Knapp Commission Report on Police Corruption* (New York: George Braziller, 1972), 4.

⁸ *Ibid.*

⁹ James Bond Stockdale, *A Vietnam Experience: Ten Years of Reflection* (Stanford, CA: Hoover Institution, 1984), 29.

¹⁰ Dante Alighieri, *Inferno*, trans. Robert and Jean Hollander (New York: Anchor Books, 2002), 151.

¹¹ Dante Alighieri, *The Comedy of Dante Alighieri the Florentine, Cantica I: Hell*, trans. Dorothy L. Sayers (Baltimore, MD: Penguin Books, 1949), 120–21.

¹² Dante Alighieri, *The Divine Comedy of Dante Alighieri, Volume I: Inferno*, trans. Mark Musa (New York: Penguin Books, 1984), 144.

¹³ Dante Alighieri, *The Divine Comedy of Dante Alighieri*, trans. H. R. Huse (New York: Rinehart and Company, Inc., 1954), 154.

¹⁴ *Ibid.*, 160.

¹⁵ *The Federalist*, ed. Jacob E. Cooke (Middletown, CT: Wesleyan University Press, 1961), 354.

¹⁶ See Delattre, *Character and Cops*, 320.

How Banal Is Evil?[1]

Manfred Kuehn
Boston University

I Radical evil

In *The Origin of Totalitarianism* of 1951, Hannah Arendt wrote the following about the German Nazis:

> In their effort to provide proof that everything is possible, totalitarian regimes have discovered without knowing it that there are crimes which men can neither punish nor forgive. When the impossible was made possible, it became the unpunishable, unforgivable absolute evil, which could no longer be understood and explained by the evil motives of self-interest, greed, covetousness, resentment, lust for power, and cowardice; and which therefore anger could not avenge, love could not endure, friendship could not forgive. Just as the victims in the death factories or holes of oblivion are no longer "human" in the eyes of their executioners, so this newest species of criminals is beyond the pale even of solidarity in human sinfulness.[2]

She thought that something similar was true for the Russian Bolsheviks. The evil embodied by Hitler or Stalin was radical evil. It represented something that had never before existed, something qualitatively different from any of the crimes so far committed by humankind, something she calls "radical evil."

Arendt took the phrase "radical evil" from Kant, but what she meant by it was very different from Kant's notion. Radical evil for her has four distinct parts. It is (1) unforgivable, (2) unpunishable, (3) rooted in motives so low that no one can understand them, and (4) traceable to a flaw in human nature. She claimed that Kant suspected that this kind of evil existed but then attempted to explain it via motives that anyone could understand.[3]

Just 10 years later, Arendt modified this definition, if it is a definition, to the point that one may say she abandoned it altogether. In her essays on Adolf Eichmann's trial of 1961—appearing first as a serial in the *New Yorker* and then later in revised form as *Eichmann in Jerusalem* with the subtitle, *A Report on the Banality of Evil*—she withdrew the third criterion, namely, the claim that radical evil must be understood as being rooted in motives so base as to be inexplicable. One of the reasons for this retraction seems to have been that she felt she could no longer speak of a truly *radical* evil, an evil that has deep roots in human nature, and understood evil as a surface phenomenon or something that is essentially superficial.[4]

As the Eichmann trial began in Jerusalem and Arendt was able to observe him personally, her conviction that evil was radical in the sense of "deep" was shaken. Arendt became convinced that Eichmann's crimes were based less on maliciousness than on thoughtlessness. As she once described it, Eichmann was "genuinely incapable of uttering a single sentence that was not a cliché."[5] Moreover, "the longer one listened to him, the more obvious it became that his inability to speak was closely connected with an inability to *think*, namely, to think from the standpoint of somebody else."[6] This made communication with him impossible, "not because he lied, but because he was surrounded by the most reliable of all safeguards against the words and the presence of others and hence against reality as such," namely thoughtlessness. This complete lack of imagination on Eichmann's part is the very thing that Arendt takes to be the banality of evil:

> When I speak of the banality of evil, [i.e., in reporting on Eichmann] I do so only on the strictly factual level, pointing to a phenomenon which stared one in the face at the trial. Eichmann was not Iago and not Macbeth, and nothing would have been farther from his mind than to determine with Richard III "to prove a villain." Except for an extraordinary diligence in looking out for his personal advancement, he had no motives at all. And this diligence was in no way criminal; he certainly would never have murdered his superior in order to inherit his post. He *merely*, to put the matter colloquially, *never realized what he was doing*. . . . He was not stupid. It was sheer thoughtlessness—something by no means identical with stupidity—that predisposed him to become one of the greatest criminals of that period. And if this is "banal" and even funny, if with the best will in the world one cannot extract any diabolical or demonic profundity from Eichmann, that is still far from calling it commonplace.[7]

Eichmann's "sheer thoughtlessness," combined with his incapacity for judgment and lack of imagination, allowed him to deceive himself. And this self-deception, for Arendt, was both Eichmann's crime and the necessary condition for his survival in the Reich.

This change in opinion actually brings Arendt closer to Kant, who argued that radical evil is the root of all moral evil and refers to a universal propensity or *Hang* in human beings that is the precondition for adopting moral maxims that are immoral. Henry Allison has therefore argued that Arendt's analysis of evil has not only some of the same structural features as Kant's, but also provides us with a framework for making more sense out of Arendt's account.[8] It is perhaps only an historical irony that Arendt ended up with an account that is closer to Kant's than her original intuitions, for there is no reason to presume the latter account is better than the first. Nor do I think that Arendt and Kant are ultimately very close.

It should perhaps be pointed out that, in making this move, Arendt aligned herself with the majority view of philosophy during the twentieth century. Thus, the Tübingen philosopher Otfried Höffe has observed quite correctly, I think, that there is almost "a complete lack in the twentieth century of discussions of evil." And he traces this shortage of philosophical reflection of evil not to "good arguments," but rather to a state of "thoughtlessness" among philosophers and intellectuals in general.[9] It is certainly true that the problem of evil cannot be included among the more frequently discussed themes in philosophy during the twentieth century.[10] Though one might find essays with titles such as "Is Evil a Philosophical Problem?", "Discourse Ethics and the Problem of Evil," or "Radical Evil, Freedom, and the Accountability of Actions; Reflections on Kant and Habermas," a bibliography of the last century's philosophical contributions toward this theme would be rather shorter than one might have expected.

This is especially striking given how easy it is to find examples in the twentieth century of what would generally be considered evil. The mass extermination of the Jews in Germany is as much an example of it as are the mass murders in Stalinist Russia or any of the other especially gruesome crimes that have either happened or continue to happen. It is in fact fair to say that for many contemporaries the twentieth century represents one epoch in world history for which hardly any other predicate than "evil" can serve, a fact which makes the near absence of sustained philosophical reflection on either the general theme of evil or on any of the specific examples of evil in recent history all the more glaring.

While this has changed during the last 4 years, at least in the United States, I am not sure that it has necessarily changed for the better, as many of the discussions of evil seem to me motivated by other reasons than those having to do with a better understanding of what evil is. Even if Arendt is right in saying that evil is rooted in motives so low that no one can understand them, this does not mean that we should characterize everyone and everything we do not understand as evil. I have had, for instance, to sit through a paper by an "expert on evil" last year, ostensibly on Hannah Arendt on evil, in which George Bush was accused of being "evil" in almost the same way as a German Nazi. I find such performances inexcusable and just another example of thoughtlessness among philosophers.

I do not consider myself an expert on evil. Nor do I consider myself a moral philosopher or public intellectual who would be in a position to tell others what the most important issues that move our present age are. Usually, I am more or less content to investigate the history of philosophy and try to find out why it is that we think what we think. So, you may consider the following discussion of evil as being out of character, an excursion into territory that is for me not as familiar as the eighteenth century and its discussion of evil. I hope you will excuse me, therefore, when I address only a very limited aspect of the problem of evil. Taking some of Arendt's pronouncements in *Eichmann in Jerusalem: A Report on the Banality of Evil* as a starting point, I want to examine more closely how meaningful it is to speak of the "banality of evil" at all. In doing so, I will take for granted not only that there are phenomena that may be described as evil, but also that evil has determinate characteristics, even if they may be hard to describe, including "banality." Since the belief that evil in some sense "exists" is far from universally accepted, I will begin with some remarks on how we can justify accepting the existence of evil before going on to the question of how it is we are to understand evil itself.

II Vocabulary of evil

There is a sense in which the existence of something like "evil" [*das Böse*] cannot be doubted. Apart from its verging on a daily topic of conversation, the discussion of evil pervades our theological, philosophical, literary, and political traditions. We have no problem referring to the "evils of humanity" [*bösen Menschen*] or describing someone as "evil"; we know "evil acts" [*böse Taten*], "villainy" [*Bösewichte*], and "maliciousness" [*Bösartigkeit*], and none of this is particular to the German language. I know of no language—and I think there is no such language—in which one is unable to distinguish between "good" and "evil" or in which this distinction does not play a foundational role. Common sense and ordinary language attest to the phenomenon of evil. Furthermore, the opposition between good and evil is a fundamental part of religion and ordinary morality: some of us pray to God that he may "deliver us from evil," and our moral struggle is to be good and avoid all evil, whatever it may be.

In fairly stark contrast to tendencies prevalent from the Middle Ages until about the middle of the twentieth century, we tend to avoid today the rash distribution of morally negative predicates. Augustine, for example, was convinced that he himself was evil by nature and was therefore prepared to find evil in others. His search for this was unsuccessful, however, and, as he wrote in his confessions, "I looked for the source of evil and my search was itself evil, but in all my investigations I never saw evil itself." Accordingly, when I first read his *Confessions* I was ready to find him owning up to some real misdeeds and was rather disappointed to find nothing but a garden variety of acts that almost no one today would consider particularly bad. Referring to sins like the ones that Augustine reports, Eduard von Hartmann wrote of "normal evil" or an immoral evil which simply represents the other side of morality and was thus something essentially minor on the scale of wickedness.

When we speak of evil today, we generally have grave or unusually brutal assaults or crimes in mind. Evil appears to us as something that is somehow related to incomprehensible or inexplicable behavior and that concerns acts of which we consider ourselves incapable. While we are thus prepared to recognize the unspeakable brutality with which Hitler and his executioners tormented and tortured people as evil, we avoid calling our own acts of everyday villainy "evil." The BTK killer is evil; we are just imperfect. Evil is nothing ordinary but rather something spectacularly and horribly bad that goes far beyond the norm. "Evil" and "perversion" are close cousins these days. Indeed, "evil" has the shades of the strange and even exotic that some people find titillating, as the prevalence of horror movies shows.

This raises the question of how we should relate "normal evil" to its more radical kin. Is it "more of the same," or is it different in kind, perhaps even something *sui generis* or one of a kind, something in every way out of the ordinary? I tend to think that it is.[11] The phenomena that were investigated in the Eichmann trial are indicative of misdeeds that go far beyond the ordinary. And even if many Germans may be described as Hitler's "willing executioners," most would not have been capable to do what (quite a) few did, in fact, perpetrate. And even among those who did, there were some who could not go on. This can be seen from Himmler's description of what an ideal Nazi would be. He would be someone who could butcher people with *Gelassenheit*, i.e., remaining cool, calm, and collected, even as the victims were pleading for their lives. This was not imagined to be easy by those in charge. "An execution must always be the hardest thing for our men," Himmler said. "And despite it they must never become weak but must do it with pursed lips." As a matter of fact, many of the executioners did not find it easy. Some became alcoholic, some committed suicide, others thought of their own wives and children, but some remained hard. For Himmler, it was "the curse of greatness that it must step over dead bodies to create new life . . ." "Most of you know what it means when 100 corpses are lying side by side, or 500, or 1,000. To have stuck it out and at the same time—apart from exceptions caused by human weakness—to have remained decent fellows, that is what has made us hard. This is a page of glory which has never been written and is never to be written." And Himmler also volunteered that it would be "a great burden for [him] to bear."[12]

We do not have to believe that it was a great burden for Himmler to bear what he did bear, but we should observe the fact that he could make appear heroic what was for many Germans morally reprehensible. Hitler himself said:

> My ideal of education is hard. Whatever is weak must be hammered away. In the fortresses of my militant order a generation of young people will grow to strike fear into the heart of the world. Violent, masterful, unafraid, cruel youth is what I want. Young people must be all that. They must withstand pain. There must be nothing weak or tender about them. The free—magnificent predator must flash from their eyes again. I want them strong and beautiful. . . . That way I can fashion things anew.

In preparing their deeds, the Nazis developed a vocabulary that came to be generally accepted and used by Germans at that time. It was in use even as I was growing up. The last and perhaps most serious criticism my father had for me was that I was "soft." If only for this reason, it appears to me true that the vocabulary we use to talk about evil is more important than is generally realized.

III Theories concerning evil

Theories concerning evil have traditionally associated the phenomenon with egotism or self-interest. To give an example, Paul Häberlin, in his book *Das Böse: Ursprung und Bedeutung* (1960), distinguishes between evil understood as whatever set of circumstances may be hindering our interests, and thereby deemed to be "evil" by us, with the kind of evil that is based on egotism and which works to create hindrances or undesirable circumstances for others. "Circumstantial" evil is for him something purely external to the ego and is therefore a predicate attributed to things or to characteristics of things. Evil as an attribute of the subject, however, is based on egotistical interests such as the desire to inflict a nasty state of affairs on someone else. Awareness of this type of evil is thus arrived at only via attention to one's self. Which is to say, as Häberlin puts it, that "the judgment of evil is originally a critique of one's self," a judgment "intentionally undermining the egotistical claim" at the same time that it itself represents an expression of ego.[13] Egotism allows for the possibility that one can be affected by circumstantial evil just as it serves as the ground for the possibility of one's own evil conduct toward others. For Häberlin, "Without egotism there is no evil," and evil as an attribute thus belongs on the side of intentions rather than acts: evil exists precisely in the will-to-evil [*Böswilligkeit*].[14]

Walter Schulz characterizes evil in a similar manner, writing, "What we mean by evil is a very real fact, analogous to an anthropological 'primordial phenomenon,' whose source is egotism and whose most striking expression is the inclination to be cruel to others." Schulz understands cruelty to be a form of radical evil representing a constant threat and a danger the presence of which no one should forget. Viewed from the perspective of history and language, maliciousness or the will-to-evil may mean many things, but it is characteristic of his position that in his discussion of Kant, Schulz speaks of a "falsity of the heart" or a "perversion of myself."[15] The possibility of evil thus seems to be based ultimately on the possibility of placing particularity and arbitrariness above the common good.

This view has its roots in Judeo-Christian anthropology and metaphysics, where evil is located in the turn away from God and towards man and his truths. Gen. 3 reports Adam's fall as the source of evil in mankind, and Adam's sin stems from his will to ignore God's warning. For Christianity, this arrogance is the source of "original sin," and while philosophical thinking since the Enlightenment has almost unanimously rejected this doctrine, thinkers remain tied to the notion so long as they regard egotism as the source of evil.

There are clear guidelines as to what is good and what is evil. Indeed, evil is exactly the opposite of good, and good has no truck with evil. It is either the one or the other. As Plato is taken to have proved against the Sophists for whom the distinction between "good" and "evil" could be reduced to the phenomena of pleasure and pain, the grammar of "good and evil" is different. We may be somewhat in pain and still feel at the same time pleasure. Indeed, there is a large class of pleasures that presupposes deprivation or pain. So the opposites of pleasure and pain are different from the opposite of good and bad. One might therefore argue that the "good" and "bad" contrast functions in the way that other contrast terms function, like "right" and "left," which carve up the world into different regions, and which make no sense in isolation from one another. Just as there cannot be any "right" side without a "left" side, so there cannot be a anything "good" without there being something "bad." This con-clusion should come as no surprise. According to a separate tradition that goes back at least to the Sophists, "good" and "evil" are understood as opposites whose grammar is comparable to that of other contrasts such as "left" and "right." What exists to our left is not independent of what exists to our right or, more specifically, what we regard as to our left or to our right depends on our standpoint. Right has no deeper meaning than left. Both are nothing other than spatial relations and orientations. They are, to use Löwith's words regard-ing the good, "nothing positive in the things themselves, but stand, rather, only in relation to we who are ourselves but one part of the entirety of nature."[16] The conceptual pair "good" and "evil" belong to the set of opposites taken by some of the Presocratics as part of an authoritative explanation of the world. Just as "wet" and "dry," "finite" and "infinite," and "over" and "under" were used by Greek philosophers to explain phenomena, so "good" and "evil" represent prin-ciples for the explanation of the universe and our place within it. Some of the sophists argued that "good" and "bad" were no different from the other oppo-sites in that they were indicative of mere human laws or *nomoi* and not of natural laws or *physis*.

This was not an option for Plato because it would imply radical relativity, since if any object may be to the left of one thing, it may also be to the right of another thing. Something might be good with regard to some frame of refer-ence and bad with regard to another. Someone in Athens might consider something good that someone in Sparta considers bad. Plato wants to avoid this conclusion just as much as the earlier claim because it would make the good less than absolutely good. But if good is absolutely good, there cannot be an absolute evil as well. Evil cannot possess the same dignity of being as good, and this is not just a matter of grammar, but of ontology. Indeed, Plato regarded evil as something having no "independent being" and existing therefore only as a *causa deficiens*, as a mistake or defect.

Aristotle agreed, at least up to a point. He believed that evil destroys itself, that it is incapable of existing if "met with in its pure form." He noted in his *Nichomachean Ethics* that while "Nobility is simple, the gleam of evil is hundred-fold." That is, if achievement of "the real mean" between extremes is the goal of morality and yet moral virtue is only one point within that mean, then those points outside become multiple and evil takes on "the character of a thing without limits . . . whereas the good, by contrast, is naturally bound." It is therefore easy to be evil and correspondingly difficult to be good. In Aristotle's words, "It is easy to miss the goal, difficult to meet it. For this reason excess and deficiency are signs of the immoral, the true mean, by comparison, is the mark of a moral disposition." The concept of evil is thus far more complex than that of the good. What this complexity entails, however, is that only through the simplicity of the good can evil itself be made intelligible.

The saying "*Bonum ex causa integra, malum ex quolibet defectu* [the good arises from a perfect case, the bad from some defect]" seems almost to have been valid as a universal truth for every philosopher from the beginning of Western thought with the Greeks, through Augustine and Leibniz, to the start of the Modern age. Leibniz distinguished between three types of evil or malevolence (*mal* or *malum*): metaphysical, physical, or moral evil. While metaphysical evil exists in imperfection, and physical evil in passion, Leibniz agreed with Augustine that moral evil lies in sin (*péché*) or guilt (*culpa*). Though Leibniz took moral evil to be the most serious manifestation of evil, he also understood it to make sense only in connection with the two other types since the problem of the evil will is connected with theodicy or God's justification. How can an all-knowing, omnipotent, omni-benevolent God create a world in which there is evil? For Leibniz the answer was relatively simple: the world in which we live is the best of all possible worlds. The evil to be found there was permitted by God only because it contributed to the greater good of the world. And the greatest good in the world, for Leibniz, was moral goodness, which itself can be meaningful only so long as there is moral evil as well.

It appears as though this theological or, perhaps better, metaphysical background of philosophy has been almost completely lost—and with it, the concept of evil as well. Friedrich Nietzsche's *Beyond Good and Evil* is only one symptom of this historical process. Karl Löwith, teaching in Marburg at the beginning of the last century, claimed, for example, that given the "decline of a theological setting for sin, judgment, and redemption," the moral question of evil has itself disappeared. For him, the "discussion of more or less complete things, as well as that of the beautiful and the ugly, the good and the bad," must seem to be "essentially irrelevant" when there is either no God or only a pantheistic one such as Spinoza had presented. Under these terms evil remains at the level of naturalistic or anthropological understanding. Evil in this sense, "because merely relative to our all too human goals, desires, and affects, of which the divine nature is free" can appear from the metaphysical perspective to be in fact banal. For here, "Good and evil identify nothing positive in the things themselves, but stand, rather, only in relation to we who are ourselves but one part of the entirety of nature."[17]

IV Banality of evil

This is the context in which we must understand Arendt's theory of evil, if we may call it a "theory." She rejects egotism as an explanation. Egotism, or, in Arendt's words, "self-interest, envy, hunger for power, resentment, cowardice, or whatever else may be given," are simply inadequate for explaining the existence of evil. The kinds of motives that evil acts would seem to require are motives that according to Arendt would have to be so base as to be incomprehensible to normal people.

Here I agree with Arendt, not because I accept the claim that radical evil has nothing to do with egotism, but because I think that egotism *per se* does not have any particular relationship to evil. Not only is it *not* the case that selfishness contradicts the good, but selfishness can also often work for the good. A perfect egotist, if such a person existed, would probably be one of the most moral people who ever lived. This is not to say that self-interest must be viewed, with Thomas Hobbes and Herman de Mandeville, as the only source of morality, but rather to recognize with Bishop Butler that egotism and morality often go hand in hand and thus only rarely find themselves in conflict. All of which means that distinguishing between generous motives and egotistical impulses becomes a somewhat difficult project for reason. If egotism were the source of moral evil, then none of us would be good in the moral sense. Or, as Butler expresses it, "As long as self-love does not exceed the real mean, it is no worse or reprehensible than any other human inclination . . . the most extreme form of moral depravity that we are capable of representing to ourselves [is] disinterested cruelty."[18]

Arendt's generalizes her observations on Eichmann in her later work. Eichmann became the very prototype of evil. Therefore she became convinced that baseness of motives has very little to do with evil at all: it is nothing other than thoughtlessness.

> It is indeed my opinion now that evil is never "radical," that it is only extreme, and that it possesses neither depth nor any demonic dimension. It can overgrow and lay waste the whole world precisely because it spreads like a fungus on the surface. It is "thought-defying" . . . because thought to reach some depth, to go to roots, and the moment it concerns itself with evil, it is frustrated because there is nothing. That is its "banality." Only the good has depth and can be radical.[19]

Evil qua evil has no independent existence; it is *inessential* and thus uninteresting, very much as Plato, Augustine, Leibniz and other metaphysicians had claimed. Take away the robust metaphysical underpinnings of their theory of evil but keep their view of the priority of good over evil, and you end up with something rather banal. The "banality of evil" is a consequence of this very maneuver. I believe this point has remained rather under-appreciated and deserves to be emphasized.

But be that as it may, in her book on *The Life of the Mind* of 1971, Arendt once more made explicit remarks concerning the banality of evil. Here she tries to explain that "no thesis or theory" lies behind the concept of the banality of evil but that she nonetheless "suspects" that "this formulation goes against our literary, theological, and philosophical traditions" according to which evil is something demonic or Satanic.[20] She refers to the "shallowness" of culprits and criminals who must be seen as "ordinary" and "average."[21] But the experience with Eichmann leads her directly to another theory. In particular, Arendt is now forced to ask the following question:

> Could the activity of thinking as such, the habit of examining whatever happens to come to pass or to attract attention, regardless of results and specific content, could this activity be among the conditions that make men abstain from evil-doing or actually even "condition" them against it?. . . To put it differently and use Kantian language: after having been struck by a fact that, willy-nilly, "put me in possession of a concept" (the banality of evil), I could not help raising the *quaestio juris* and asking myself "by what right I possessed and used it."[22]

If evil exists in thoughtlessness then thinking becomes the answer to the problem of evil, and volume one of the *Life of the Mind* is indeed nothing less than the attempt to show this.

But what exactly does Arendt mean by "thinking"? It is not the kind of thinking that we engage in when we consider how to reach a certain goal, and it is also not the kind of thinking that we describe today as "instrumental thought." The kind of thinking that Arendt has in mind is one concerned with the search for meaning, referring us, then, to the Kantian sense of "reason" [*Vernunft*] over "understanding" [*Verstand*]. The use of reason entails not only asking unanswerable "ultimate questions" but is involved in every reflection that does not concern cognition and practical needs and goals.[23] Thinking does not lead—and here one may notice Heidegger's influence on Arendt's philosophy—"to knowledge"; it "does not produce usable practical wisdom," "does not solve the riddles of the universe," and "does not endow us directly with the power to act."[24] It is thinking understood as "non-positivistic" in Theodor Adorno's sense, and Hannah Arendt believes that this kind of thinking would have checked Eichmann and kept him from doing what he did. And this is rather doubtful, I would say, as this kind of thinking did not prevent Heidegger, the *maître penseur*, from arguing that mass murder was no worse than industrialized agriculture.

It may be that Arendt is completely correct in her description of Eichmann's spiritual make-up. It may be that in Eichmann we find a remarkable connection between thoughtlessness and evil. It may even be that similar connections between thoughtlessness and criminal activities can be found in the case of other criminals. And it is also possible that a certain type of thoughtlessness predisposes one to do evil. But none of this means that evil can be reduced to thoughtlessness or that evil is nothing other than thoughtlessness. At best it shows that an evil-doer might also be thoughtless because there was one evil-doer who was thoughtless. But even that is doubtful, for we know just as little as Hannah Arendt that Eichmann was thoughtless in the required sense. As a dedicated Kant scholar I am more scared by his claim that he always used to carry in the breast pocket of his uniform a copy of Kant's *Critique of Practical Reason* and that he shored up his appeals to duty with appeals to Kant's discussion of it. Furthermore, there are many people who, according to Arendt's definition, have spent their entire life in a state of thoughtlessness but have never done anything evil. And there were and are others who have thought in the required sense and who have done evil in the sense required by her later definition. Thoughtlessness should therefore neither be identified with evil—something Arendt at times appears to be doing—nor should the two concepts be brought into such close connection with one another, a connection one always finds in Arendt. Thoughtlessness is certainly not the heart of darkness, and it is simply wrong to assume that thinkers are incapable of evil. Thinking, even thinking in Arendt's sense of the word, is no guarantee against evil activities—as history well shows.

V The jargon of authenticity

Arendt believes that her theory of evil is essentially new and that it contradicts the traditional "literary, theological, and philosophical considerations of evil." As some of my remarks have shown already, this cannot be entirely correct. Although Arendt breaks with tradition by offering clear and important arguments against the reduction of evil to egotism, her doctrine of the banality of evil is in part indebted to the Platonic–Augustinian world view. With its insistence on the role of thinking, it shows a similar influence of Stoic and Kantian rationalism, fatally influenced by the "jargon of authenticity," as Adorno called it. And even within her immediate intellectual milieu in Marburg, there were theories that went much further than hers. We can see, for example, a sense in which Arendt was reacting to claims made by Löwith and quoted above. Her theory, in other words, was not without its debts.

Arendt's approach is non-metaphysical in the sense that it cannot be embedded in a two-world theory where "true being" is contrasted to "mere appearance." In such a view, everything given is appearance and even God judges us only according to appearances. This means, in turn, that good and evil themselves have the status of appearances. This means, that, strictly speaking, Arendt's claim that we only mistakenly assign depth to evil or, to be more precise, and that "only goodness has depths and can be radical," would itself be a problematic claim, as nothing should have depth. Goodness could only be as deep as evil, and Arendt would have to say the same thing about goodness that she did about evil: "It has neither depth nor a [deeper] dimension. It . . . remains on the surface. This is how it resists any consideration that wants to penetrate into the deep and finds nothing there. That is its banality."[25] This would ultimately mean that goodness would only be as banal or non-banal as evil, which, in my opinion, is actually the case. One could therefore say that Arendt's theory presents us with a dearth rather than a surplus of radicalism. Don't we know (or haven't we been led to believe) at least since Diderot's *Rameau's Nephew*, Hegel's *Phenomenology of Spirit*, and Nietzsche's *Beyond Good and Evil*, that the putative contrast between good and evil is simply an assumption that we should attempt to avoid?

The majority of thinkers in the nineteenth and twentieth centuries were unified in thinking that the problem of human existence turns on the relationship between good and bad, not good and evil, and that the latter terms are something we have inherited from a bad sort of metaphysics, something which has continuously led us into error, and something which must be overcome. It has therefore been historically irrelevant whether one was a socialist, Marxist, or liberal when it came to rejecting the pairing of good and evil: once "evil" is considered to be something antiquated and outdated, it becomes useless if one is intent on improving the human condition. This is the real reason that the problem of evil "has gotten lost" in philosophy. Evil has lost its place in the philosophical discussion as a result of deliberation, not thoughtlessness. Indeed, neither Marx nor Rawls could do much with such a concept, and we find "evil" only mentioned, if at all, as a peripheral problem in their works.

Quoting freely from Marx, Berthold Brecht says, "It's the circumstances," and "First comes feeding (*das Fressen*), then morality (*die Moral*)." Rawls suggests that we begin with mankind as possessing a sense of justice and the ability to conceive of the good. Everything else—and that means, above all, evil—will be ignored. Philosophers seem therefore to have consciously excluded evil. But one might also argue that philosophers have long looked in the wrong direction for evil—in a direction where it could not have appeared differently to them—namely toward a transcendental realm. Having disposed of the metaphysics behind the traditional conception of evil, they also believed to have disposed of evil. But, as I would claim, even under the best of circumstances, there are people who do evil. And this evil is far from banal, as ordinary language already serves to show.

Walter Schulz is one German thinker who is vehemently opposed to the view that ethics needs to be made non-metaphysical or, positively expressed, made scientific. Were this to be the case, according to Schulz, "the concepts good and evil [would become] irrelevant." It appears to me that he is entirely correct.[26] If we take the perspective of science or naturalism and regard the behavior of human beings as objectively as "natural things and events, occurrences in the course of nature whether caused or accidental," then all moral categories must become irrelevant as guides for the practitioner. To use them would conflict with the account of the physio-biological processes that one calls human life. "Considered from an exclusively physio-biological standpoint," such things as good and bad acts cannot be given. We may, of course explain how these categories came to be, but from this perspective the world must "appear to be colorless in the literal and moral sense." What we normally identify as moral acts or judgments are from this standpoint nothing other than the natural or artificial reactions of a living being such as man. From the point of view of physio-biology, what we in everyday life call "good" and "evil" are simply mechanisms that enable us to live together. We could perhaps explain why they exist, why they always develop in societies, and what function they fulfill, but we cannot at the same time take up the ethical standpoint since to do this would mean the loss of objectivity. Perhaps the return to a certain kind of metaphysics or the realization that naturalism is just another kind of metaphysics is one way to avoid problems. But perhaps there are other ways as well.

I am aware that what I just proposed needs to be defended and that what I am going to propose needs even more defense, but in my view something similar holds for non-scientific or non-naturalistic reductions of ethics to things non-ethical. In the last section of this essay I would like to show that Arendt's attempt to define evil as thoughtlessness is burdened with the same problems as naturalism since she too attempts to explain a fundamental category of ethics with psychological, phenomenological, perhaps even pseudo-psychological and pseudo-phenomenological, constructions.

VI Understanding evil, judging evil

Let us be clear: the concept of "evil" is a moral concept, not a concept of psychology, biology, or physics. As Kant already noted two hundred years ago, there are two standpoints that we can take. One is theoretical, the other is practical and moral. In his words, "When by means of freedom we conceive ourselves as causes acting a priori," we take a different position than "when we contemplate ourselves with reference to our actions as effects we see before our eyes." Kant was of the opinion that this observation "requires no subtle reflection"; indeed, "the commonest understanding can make it, though in its own way, by an obscure discrimination of judgment which it calls feeling."[27]

When I look for the psychological causes of an action or a particular mode of conduct or practice, I am of course taking the standpoint from which "we contemplate ourselves with reference to our actions as effects we see before our eyes," that is, from the theoretical standpoint of causality or from natural or social science. I am attempting to explain *why* someone has taken this or that particular course of action. And it is completely legitimate and important to understand how and why we or others decide to take a particular action. However, and this seems important to me, when we ask such questions we are moving into the descriptive realm of psychology and not in the normative region of morals. Moral judgments introduce considerations that differ from psychological descriptions or theories. Admittedly, I do not want to go so far as Kant, who thought that all psychological considerations were irrelevant for morality. But I am worried about whether the importance of understanding is not often exaggerated today. Once one reduces fundamental moral categories to things purely psychological, like "thoughtlessness," one has to wonder indeed whether evil has not become an everyday occurrence. Understanding evil and judging evil do not seem to me as closely connected as many thoughtful people think.

So long as "good" and "evil" are regarded as merely descriptive terms, they lose their particular normative character. In an essay by Peter Strasser called "*Das Böse erklären*" one finds the story of a 17 or 18-year-old student who explains that

> he had heard quite a bit about Auschwitz and the Nazi's concentration camps both in school and from his parents, and that he had also read relevant and informative books about the Nazi period, such as Eugen Kogon's *SS Staat*. Despite this, however, he had never really been able to understand the whole thing. The dull-witted boy was chastised by his schoolmates, who were quite comfortable in their roles as upright anti-fascists. What was there not to understand? Did he perhaps want to say that he would only understand, if he could be in the same position; that to comprehend the motives of those engineering the final solution or of their workers in the concentration camps, he would need to conceive of them as if they could be his own?[28]

No, the boy answered, he did not want to say that. He only wanted to say that it was difficult for him to seek reprisal since he simply could not grasp the whole situation. We could draw the conclusion that "evil" is just the kind of concept that keeps us from grasping "the whole situation."

On the basis of this account Strasser concludes not only that *incomprehensibility* is a real feature of evil but also, like Arendt before him, that

> in dealing with evil [we have to] ask whether avoiding its hypostatization could be the only possibility. We know that evil does not approach any objective existence, that it is much more limited to the negative practice of morally assessing facts. These assessments are only made by people as a result of some subjective consternation; and they are, from time to time, made permanent via the practice of institutionalization.[29]

In other words, Strasser's claim is that we will never know whether evil really exists or not, or whether there is even a way "to begin to understand evil"[30] that is better than what the tradition offers. "Evil" is a concept that makes sense in certain vocabularies and not in others.

This kind of relativism is pushed even further by other contemporary thinkers. "Good" and evil" or "good and bad" belong among the basic limiting categories or concepts that Richard Rorty, for example, considers to be part of a "final vocabulary." As such they are in an important sense indisputable. The claim is that arguments against the traditional discourse on evil must be developed within a given "final vocabulary" just as one tries to change this final vocabulary itself. Given the fact that each participant in a discussion concerning final vocabularies is always caught up in his/her own final vocabulary and that we have "no noncircular argumentative recourse" if the value of our words are questioned, we cannot defend the usefulness of the word "evil," nor can someone else prove to us that it is useless.[31] At this point of "fundamental" or "final" discourse, rational discourse ends for Rorty and the work of persuasion or propaganda for a new framework begins. No *philosophical* theory of evil can therefore be given that escapes one's own cultural framework or the literary, theological, and philosophical considerations of evil prevalent in one's culture. No final vocabulary is closer to the truth than any other. We can only playing off old vocabulary against new ones.

Perhaps it is true that no theory of evil can escape the cultural framework in which it was formulated, but this does not mean that we cannot use the word "evil" in such a way that people from other cultures cannot get what we are talking about when we judge certain actions or people as evil. They may not have any idea about what evil "really is" psychologically speaking, and they may, in fact, doubt that an act that is judged to be "evil" can really be understood as evil by looking at the motives of the perpetrator. But this does not matter.

To say it again: trying to understand evil is different from passing moral judgments or deciding whether particular actions or practices are evil. Even without supporting a consequentialist ethical theory that draws a sharp distinction between "motives for action" and "rules of action" and regards only the latter as actually relevant for judging the morality of the act, one can consider an act to be evil though one does not understand it.[32] One can and should, however, distinguish between the principles supporting a moral judgment on conduct and the principles of moral decision. Kant called the former "principles of judgment" and the latter "principles of execution." The principle of evaluating an action and the reason for which someone committed an act need not mirror each other. I can say that an act is evil without knowing anything about why a perpetrator committed it, and I want to suggest that, whenever we judge an act to be really evil, we should not really care to understand it.

Perhaps we can say that whenever it is necessary to judge the actions of normal criminals, we should attempt to understand them. However, from this it does not follow that we should not judge horrific crimes to be bad or evil, if we are incapable of understanding these acts.

Evil is a moral category and it applies to horrific acts that are by that very fact *not* banal. I would like to return to Arendt's first definition of evil and change it in the light of the preceding to discussion. Evil is what an impartial spectator finds to be a) unforgivable, b) unpunishable, and c) of such a type that it becomes unnecessary for us to understand the motivations behind its practice. One might add perhaps add that d) it can be traced back to a flaw in human beings. But this last point is less a matter for the moral philosopher than it is one for the sociologist, psychologist, or biologist.

When I judge the culprit in an especially gruesome murder case to be evil I do not, therefore, have to be interested as such in what motivated him to commit the act. This does not mean that I am somehow barred from attempting to understand *why* he committed the crimes he did. It means only that when I explain his actions psychologically, sociologically, or biologically, I am doing something different than passing moral judgment. Moral *judgments* and *explanations* of actions have less to do with one another than one is currently inclined to believe. Indeed, even the historical attempt to connect evil with the demonic, to see it as an other-worldly or non-worldly influence, rejects any explanation of evil on the basis of specifically human motives. Nor is it, in my view, necessary to change the limiting concepts or "final vocabulary" of our discourse, if we admit that there is evil. Evil is neither banal nor is it as radically questioned in our cultural milieu as is sometimes claimed. Still, it is difficult to talk about.

When Plato, Augustine, Leibniz and Arendt maintain that evil has "no being," and that, as something purely negative, it cannot be clearly defined, they point towards this difficulty, but it seems to me, that they go too far. Karl Jaspers seems to have thought that, writing as he did in 1932, and perhaps with uncanny prescience, "Evil, never really conceivable, incapable of being grasped, proves itself in its *sudden* existence to be *insurmountable*." It is "the phantom that is always present to the good will as though behind its back."[33] We have to watch ourselves, not to succumb to it unawares. One of the things that follows from this is that we should and must reflect on what we are doing, and that this reflective awareness is one of the necessary conditions of avoiding evil. But reflective awareness is clearly not a sufficient condition for avoiding evil. If it were, the disinterested cruelty of which Butler spoke as the "utmost possible depravity" in the early eighteenth century, would not be possible. Nor is the absence of reflection necessarily identical with evil. I think that this is wrong as well. Reflection may be an important part of our own struggle to avoid evil, but it is no guarantee, even if some philosophers think so. "Could the activity of thinking as such, the habit of examining whatever happens to come to pass or to attract attention, regardless of results and specific content, could this activity be among the conditions that make men abstain from evil-doing or actually even 'condition' them against it?"[34] Perhaps it can "condition" us against evil, but I doubt even that, if only because the culture in which the radical evil arose was one in which "the activity of thinking as such, the habit of examining whatever happens to come to pass or to attract attention, regardless of results and specific content" played a most important role. This kind of thinking, originating in Kant, Fichte, Schelling, and Hegel in the eighteenth and early nineteenth century, vigorously pursued by the Neo-Kantians and many other nineteenth and early twentieth-century thinkers (including Friedrich Nietzsche), certainly did not "condition" Germans against radical evil-doing.[35]

Notes

[1] I wrote this paper originally in German, and I would like to thank Professor Jennifer Mensch (Pennsylvania State University) for translating an earlier version of this paper from German into English. All remaining (and newly introduced) errors are my own, of course.

[2] Hannah Arendt, *The Origin of Totalitarianism* (New York: Harcourt, Brace & World, Inc., 1951), 459.

[3] Arendt, *The Origin of Totalitarianism*, 459: "he rationalized it in the concept of a 'perverted ill will.'"

[4] Elizabeth Young-Bruehl, *Hannah Arendt: For the Love of the World* (New Haven and London: Yale University Press, 1982), 369. As Young-Bruehl has shown, the change in Arendt's theory has to do with the third point in the earlier account.

[5] Hannah Arendt, *Eichmann in Jerusalem: A Report on the Banality of Evil* (New York: Penguin Books, 1992), 48.

[6] Arendt, *Eichmann in Jerusalem*, 49.

[7] *Ibid.*, 287. It is interesting that Arendt often contrasts "thoughtlessness" with "stupidity," saying that evil does not arise from stupidity, but rather from thoughtlessness. Hermann Kasack, a novelist quite popular in post-war Germany, had made a great deal of stupidity and its connection with the evils of Western society in his novel *Die Stadt hinter dem Strom* of 1956 (written between 1942 and 1944 and 1946). It seems as if Arendt is trying to put distance between Kasack and herself. But this is difficult, as Kasack also emphasizes the distinction between spirit (*Geist*) and intellect (*Verstand*), and toward the end of the novel one of his characters blames "the inertia of the spirit" as one of the "deepest roots [*Erzwurzeln*] of evil.

From it come not only superstition, false pride [*Dummstolz*] and superciliousness, but . . . also the rawness of disposition, the cruelty of the heart, and the bestiality of power—in short all that is undignified in human life." But he then goes on to say that reason alone does not help our thinking. What counts is the intensity of the "faithful, ironic [*lächelnde*] knowledge of the entirety of being." Kasack castigates the lack of spirit, the *Ungeist*, *Unvernunft*, and *Unnatur*, and finds that it is not the lie that opposes truth but the stupid. But since the stupid is for him essentially a form of thoughtlessness, the difference between the two is not as large as one might think.

8 This appears to be Henry Allison's view. See Henry E. Allison, "Reflections on the Banality of (Radical) Evil: A Kantian Analysis," *Graduate Faculty Philosophy Journal* 18 (1995): 141–58. Reprinted in Henry Allison, *Idealism and Freedom* (Cambridge: Cambridge University Press, 1996), 169–82, 210–12. It should be noted that Kant's account involves egotism or self-love in a way that Arendt's account does not. And the self-deception required by Kant seems to go rather deeper than anything Arendt says.

9 Ottfried Höffe, "Ein Thema wiedergewinnen. Kant über das Böse," in *Über das Wesen der Menschlichen Freiheit* (Berlin: O. Höffe and A. Pieper, 1995), 11, 14, 15 f., respectively.

10 On this point see also Walter Schulz, *Philosophie in einer veränderten Welt* (Stuttgart: Neske, 1993), 718 ff.

11 My suggestion would be that we reserve "evil" for radical evil and that we do not call "normal" human failings "evil," but "bad" or "immoral."

12 Jonathan Bennett, "The Conscience of Huckleberry Finn," *Philosophy* 49, no. 88 (April 1974): 128; quoted from Roger Manvell and Heinrich Fraenkel, *Heinrich Himmler* (London: Heinemann, 1965), 184.

13 Paul Häberlin, *Das Böse: Ursprung und Bedeutung* (Bern and Munich: Francke Verlag, 1960), 8.

14 "[D]as Böse besteht in der Böswilligkeit." The German allows for a linguistic point here since "Böswilligkeit"—translated literally as maliciousness, i.e., intentionally wicked activity—has the word Böse or "evil" at its root; hence the clumsy "will-to-evil" over "maliciousness." See Häberlin, *ibid.*, 9.

15 Schulz, *Philosophie in einer veränderten Welt*, 718 ff.

16 Karl Löwith, "Die beste aller Welten und das radikal Böse im Menschen," in *Sämtliche Schriften*, vol. 3 (Stuttgart: J. B. Metzlersche Verlagsbuchhandlung, 1985), 275-297.

17 See Löwith, "Die beste aller Welten," 275–297.

18 Joseph Butler, *Five Sermons Preached at the Rolls Chapel and A Dissertation upon the Nature of Virtue*, ed. Stephen L. Darwall (Indianapolis, IN: Hackett Publishing Company, 1983), 21.

19 Hannah Arendt, "The Jew as Pariah," in *The Portable Hannah Arendt*, ed. Hannah Arendt and Peter Baehr (New York: The Viking Library, 2000), 369.

20 Hannah Arendt, *The Life of the Mind* (San Diego, New York, and London: Harcourt Brace Jovanovich, 1978), 3.

21 Arendt, *The Life of the Mind*, 4.

22 *Ibid.*, 5.

23 *Ibid.*, 69 ff.

[24] *Ibid.*, 11. This is from the motto, a quote from Heidegger.

[25] Arendt, "The Jew as Pariah," in *The Portable Hannah Arendt*, 369.

[26] Schulz, *Philosophie in einer veränderten Welt*, 718 ff.

[27] Immanuel Kant, *Groundwork of the Metaphysics of Morals*, in *Immanuel Kant: Practical Philosophy*, ed. Mary J. Gregor (Cambridge: Cambridge University Press, 1996), 98.

[28] Peter Strasser, "Das Böse erklären," *Studia Philosophia* 52 (1993): 42.

[29] Strasser, "Das Böse Erklären," 43.

[30] *Ibid.*, 44 (freely rendered).

[31] Richard Rorty, *Contingency, Irony, and Solidarity* (Cambridge: Cambridge University Press, 1989), 73.

[32] See, for instance, John Stuart Mill, *Utilitarianism*, ed. Roger Crisp (Oxford: Oxford University Press, 1998), 64 ff.

[33] Karl Jaspers, *Philosophie II: Existenzerhellung* (Berlin, Göttingen, and Heidelberg: Springer, 1932), 173 and 172, respectively.

[34] Arendt, *The Life of the Mind*, 5.

[35] There are, of course, some who would argue that it was precisely the kind of thinking that Arendt claims to be the solution was actually responsible for the radical evil that was done in Germany during the 1930s and 1940s. But this is too simple an explanation as well.

Evil as Privation: Seeing Darkness, Hearing Silence

Mark Larrimore

Eugene Lang College The New School for Liberal Arts

In *City of God*, Augustine writes, "To try to discover the causes of an evil will . . . is like trying to see darkness or to hear silence."[1] Augustine's point is not just that it is impossible to know the cause of evil, but that it's impossible because there's nothing there to know. The argument that evil is not a substance but privation of substance will become the ground for over a millennium of thinking on evil in the West. For the last three or four centuries, however, the idea has become close to unintelligible. It seems premised on a metaphysical view— whatever is, is good—which is not only implausible but incomprehensible, a perfect example of the disdain of metaphysically or theologically based views for life. In our late modern or postmodern place we are close to believing the opposite. While the good seems to us merely subjective, evil alone seems incontestably real.

In this essay I want to try to make the idea of evil as privation available again. This effort is not just some kind of philosophical necromancy. I believe that the privative understanding of evil is deeper than most of the views which succeeded it. That doesn't mean we can make it meaningful without considerable effort. I will explore the power of this understanding of evil and the insights it offers not only into evils but into our ways of conceiving them and their dangers. The most obvious import of the view that evil is but the privation of good is the suggestion that you can't talk about or understand evils without an understanding of good. This may be why our contemporary discussions of evil float so disconnected from discussions of ethics. Because of the state of our discourse, I will proceed somewhat elliptically toward an account of the good.

My argument will proceed through three stages, each devoted to an important insight afforded by the understanding of evil as privation. First, the idea that evil is privation takes "evil" in general apart. It rejects "the problem of evil" in favor of the challenges of particular evils—evils to which it argues we are made more vulnerable by a focus on evil in general. The privation view forces us to disaggregate, to see that everything we consider evil is in fact a situation involving goods compromised. As I will suggest, understanding evil as privation is in fact a perspicuous description of the language game of ethics, as individuals and communities discern and articulate problems and explore avenues of response. By comparison, a view which sees evil as substantial and incomprehensible turns out to be dangerously inflexible, leaving us no responses but fight or flight.

Second, the idea that evil is the privation of goods confronts us with the fact that no evil is worthy of the goods which it destroys. The point is not to blame victims but to be vigilant of our own vulnerability, both as sufferers and as agents. Many of the supposedly more serious views of evil are, by comparison, comforting fictions of invulnerability which make us more likely to suffer and do wrong. The awareness of the vulnerability of goods heightened by an understanding of evil as privation helps us see the problem which tends to drive reflection on evil into metaphysics and mythology: the gap between evils and the harm they do, which is often so disproportionate as to be cognitively wrenching.

In my concluding section I will offer an account of the good based on what the exploration of evils of the preceding sections has revealed. Having made our way through considerations of particular evils rather than evil-in-general, we will be in a position to understand that common descriptions of "evil" (and of "good"), while distorting, in fact contain insights into the nature of the goods which evils compromise. Good, a Feuerbachian might say, is the secret of evil. The view of good I will offer is modest and open-ended. It is compatible with many fuller religious and metaphysical views, and may need one or other of them to keep hope alive. Its power and claim on our attention come from being anchored in the language of ethical life and its compatibility with a democratic and pluralistic culture, whose efforts to articulate goods have been stymied by prematurely metaphysicalized religious views and by the culture of commodification.

First, however, I'll tarry a bit with Augustine, whose articulation of the idea that evil is privation has been so influential. My purpose is not to comment on it in particular. The analysis of evil as privation seems to me detachable from his hierarchical metaphysics, as I will try to show. But his analyses are insightful—informed by our experiences of evils and goods, not just religious commitments—and even his moves into metaphysical views I reject are instructive. There may be nothing to darkness and silence, but we can learn something valuable about color and sound from the experience of watching ourselves trying to see and hear them in darkness and silence.

I Evil as privation

The idea of evil as privation is traceable back through Christian thought to Plotinus, but its most influential formulations come in Augustine: "Whatever is, is good," he writes in *Confessions*, "and evil, the origin of which I was trying to find, is not a substance, because if it were a substance, it would be good."[2] This seems at first tautologous. Leibniz found that already in 1710 the idea that "evil is a privation of being" was generally "accounted a quibble, and even something chimerical."[3] There is a sense (which later will be exploited by Schopenhauer) in which it seems no more than a word game which could easily be flipped. Doesn't it make as much sense to see good as the privation of evil—if not, indeed, more? But this is the case only for a language in which the meaning of good and evil lies merely in their opposition. Augustine would find such a language absurdly nihilistic, a symptom of a willful blindness to what is actually going on in the situations we call good and evil.

The idea of evil as privation was part of Augustine's response to Manichaean-ism, and as such, a demythologizing move.[4] Every so-called evil, when properly understood, is nothing but a spectacle of privations and perversions of goods. There is no reason to think that evils have anything in common with each other, let alone a common cause or motive. We understand something as evil when a particular good is compromised, not good in general. (This is why it is not evil for human beings to lack wings.) While it may raise questions about good in general (like its corruptibility, or the place of conflict in it), the understanding of evil as privation is resolutely particularizing.

The idea is more compelling when it gets more specific. In the *Enchiridion* Augustine writes:

> Now what is the so-called evil but a privation of the good? In the bodies of animals affliction with diseases and wounds is nothing other than the priva-tion of health. For, when a cure is worked, it does not mean that those evils which were present, that is, the diseases and the wounds, recede thence and are elsewhere; they simply are not. For a wound or a disease is not a sub-stance, but a vice of the fleshly substance; the substance, surely something good, is flesh itself, its accidents being the aforementioned evils, that is, priva-tions of that good which is called health.[5]

Evil is a parasite which lives on good, sapping the energy and using the power of a substance against its nature, but with this difference: there's nothing there except good substances. Evil does real damage—the sick animal is weakened and may be killed by its illness or led to harm other animals—but evil could not subsist on its own. The damage is done by the powers of the good afflicted.

It may seem that this understanding cannot be generalized to include evil wills, the "moral evil" which is taken by many to be the quintessence of evil. Augustine thinks it can: "In like manner evils in the soul are privations of natu-ral good. When they are cured, they are not transferred to another place; since they can have no place in the healthy soul, they can be nowhere."[6] It may seem odd to think of evil wills as analogous to illness, perhaps because we no longer have an understanding of the "healthy soul." Or do we? Certainly it's not the same as Augustine's, but when we try to understand an evil action we seek to understand it in a diagnostic way. What was she thinking? What did he know? What did they believe? What did he mean to do? What was her end? Etc. Not to do so (Aquinas would point out) would be to fail to take the agent seriously as an agent. A diagnostic approach doesn't yield the ultimate cause of the evil will. But it does tell us a lot, not least about how to address it.

Perhaps the illness analogy is no longer persuasive. After all, we know that the causes of illness are often creatures of their own, whose good consists precisely in the corruption of the good of the host animal. Augustine would be unfazed. Being the parasite's good makes it no less an evil to the animal. The evil is defined with reference to the animal's good regardless its cause, and so is its cure. Augustine doesn't deny that we live in a world in which the goods of different species conflict and compete—he reminds us of the hierarchical order of nature and enjoins us to seek out what useful purposes are served by things[7]— but would warn against generalizing from this. The goods of human beings are not defined in the zero-sum way implied by the model of predator-prey or parasite-host. The point is that the term "evil" only applies where something which ought to be is missing. Something else may be in its place, but this does not alter the lack.

The most common modern criticism of privation is that it's not morally serious. It seems to involve a kind of willful moral blindness—and conceptual blindness, too. Say that evil is not a substance and you are quickly mistaken for the kind of person William James damned with faint praise as being by temperament "healthy-minded." "[T]his temperament may become the basis for a peculiar type of religion . . . [which] directs him to settle his scores with the more evil aspects of the universe by systematically declining to lay them to heart or make much of them, by ignoring them in his reflective calculations, or even, on occasion, by denying outright that they exist."[8] "In some individuals," he notes darkly, "optimism may become quasi-pathological. The capacity for even a transient sadness or a momentary humility seems cut off from them by a kind of congenital anaesthesia."[9] Healthy-mindedness seems remote from the reality of cruelty and pain and waste. There may be some evils which turn out to be goods misdescribed, but these are exceptions. Can the understanding of evil as privation even *see* real evils, the ones you can't explain away as illusory? It seems to undermine the possibility even of talking meaningfully about good: if there's no contrasting term, what can good mean?

But Augustine never denies that evils do real harm, and he certainly never denies that they need to be reckoned with. Think of the devil and his demons, whose nature may be defined by privation of understanding but whose danger to us is very real. Augustine claims that God brings a greater good out of evil, but this is not a part (let alone a necessary part) of understanding evil as privation—and affirms rather than denies that evils are evils, not goods. The same goes for claims that Augustine sometimes makes about the pleasing contrast that evils offer to goods, the view John Hick has taught us to condemn as "aesthetic theodicy," a justification of the goodness and wisdom of God in the face of evil which appeals to aesthetic rather than to moral categories.[10] These views seem related because they seem all to be proffered as answers to the same question—the theodicy question of the problem of evil. Indeed, Hick saw privation as the foundation of the "Augustinian tradition in theodicy," which he challenged us to think beyond.

The understanding of evil as privation is not a theodicy, however. If Augustine was engaged in theodicy at all (a claim that has been disputed),[11] it was not in the idea of evil as privation, which at best re-describes the problem of evil. Augustine seems to modern readers to be engaged in theodicy because he acknowledges the problem of evil in many places. The early *On free choice of the will* is even framed by the question "Is God the author of evil?" But read on and Augustine invariably changes the subject. *On free choice of the will* leaves its opening question behind, unresolved.[12] The question of evil can be a helpful point of departure; it's a dead end if we do not allow ourselves to think beyond it. In different ways in different works, Augustine leads the person who is seeking to understand from the idea of evil to the goods it preys on and then to the person seeking understanding. What does asking this question tell us about ourselves? What in us inclines us to be taken in by evil's claim to be real?

In *Confessions*, the idea of evil as privation helps Augustine move away from Manichaeanism toward Christianity. In this context, what it reveals to him about evil is only a stepping stone. He'd been struggling to believe in the immateriality of God but failing. The realization that evil has no substance finally frees him from a monolithic understanding of substance as material, spatial. The claim is certainly not that God, like evil, is not a substance. Rather, as Rowan Williams has argued, the discovery is that evil must be understood as a *process*, the kind we understand as "loss or corruption."[13] Investigating it further we realize that "we identify [evil] more clearly and truthfully the more we grow in understanding of the whole interlocking pattern of the world's activities."[14] This in turn opens Augustine to see that God is to be understood in terms of "temporal processes of clarification, reconciliation, [and] self-discovery in love."[15] Evil falls away as an issue, but not into substance or into mere nonexistence. It remains a challenge and a lesson, a reminder that the merely spatial view of material substance is incomplete and unable to lead us to the true nature of God or his creation. To the extent that we persist in fixating on the question of evil, we need to repent.

Even in *City of God*, sometimes taken to be a vast theodicy of the Sack of Rome, Augustine's discussion of the nature of evil is remarkably quick. It happens in Book XI and moves in a few pages from the necessary distinction among created things to the discovery of the futility of understanding evil, to reflection on the Trinity reflected in creation, the divisions of philosophy, and human nature.[16] The whole movement takes up barely 1 per cent of the text of the

City of God. The passage from which my title is taken comes in Book XII, as Augustine turns to the Fall: "To try to discover the causes of [an evil will] is like trying to see darkness or to hear silence. Yet we are familiar with darkness and silence, and we can only be aware of them by means of eyes and ears, but this is not by perception but by absence of perception."[17]

Augustine is not saying that darkness and silence simply do not exist. And he is certainly not saying that darkness is really light or that silence is really sound. "We are familiar with darkness and silence," he says. We are "aware of them" and indeed aware of them "by means of eyes and ears, but this is not . . . perception but...absence of perception." There is a type of cognition, a kind of under-standing that transcends perception and the perceptible. Augustine goes on:

> [W]hen we know things not by perception but by its absence, we know them, in a sense, but not-knowing, so that they are not-known by being known—if that is a possible or intelligible statement! For when with our bodily eyes, our glance travels over material forms, as they are presented to perception, we never see darkness except when we stop seeing. And we can only perceive silence by means of our ears, and through no other sense, and yet silence can only be perceived by not hearing.[18]

The senses of sight and of hearing are our way of understanding a most radical kind of difference. Silence isn't one kind of sound among others. Darkness isn't one kind of visible object among others.

And then, having understood this to the extent we can, we should move on. In *City of God* Augustine moves into what Paul Ricoeur has called "anti-gnostic gnosis," a rejection of Manichaean or other forms of dualism which reinscribes dualism in a kind of pathologization of the "nothing" of which we're made.[19] It is unthinkable how an evil choice could be made by an angel or human being, by nature good. The evil choice is somehow its own cause, "deficient" rather than "efficient," and possible in some unspecifiable way due to creation's being *ex nihilo*.

I don't want to follow Augustine here. I'll return to this and some of the other claims about good and evil to which the privative analysis of evils leads him at the end of this paper. The understanding of evil as privation seems to me dis-tinct or at least distinguishable from claims from metaphysics and especially theodicy. You don't need to accept a metaphysics like Augustine's for the priva-tion view to make sense. Indeed it may work without any explicit metaphysics at all. The idea that evil is privation has been misunderstood as a theodicy, one thing it decisively is not. The whole point is to call the bluff of *the* problem of *evil*, as if there were just one. Reifying and generalizing evils blinds us to the various and very real dangers which particular evils pose to particular goods.

II The disaggregating imperative: ethics

The notion that evil is best understood as privation doesn't claim that evil simply doesn't exist, or that it's not a problem. Evils are a very great problem, but a problem which is worsened rather than solved when we take evil to be a substance like the goods on which it preys. A full account of evils always reveals goods compromised—and nothing else. This becomes clear as soon as we resist the temptation to think that the essence of particular evil is revealed by understanding its participation in evil in general. In fact, evils have nothing in common, no shared essence. (Below I'll suggest some reasons why we should be tempted to think otherwise.) If evil is nothing but a privation or a hijacking of a particular good, we learn something very important about goods. Good is vulnerable in ways obscured by the illusion that evil exists merely as a foreign substance, an enemy.

Inquiry should never end with a judgment of evil precisely because evil *is* a danger. To the criticism that it fails to appreciate the real danger of evil by eliding evil with good, the idea of evil as privation retorts that it is the substantialist understanding of evil that misdescribes reality and obscures the fact of our vulnerability to evils. Unpacking particular evils, we learn how they arise in goods, how best to respond to them, and how (in other cases) to prevent or mitigate their arising. Generalizing and substantializing evil disempowers us, leaving us no more intelligent or effective responses than fight or flight.

Understanding—exposing—evil as privation is not only demythologizing but disaggregating. Privation is not about somehow making evils vanish by calling their bluff. Evils' appearance of substantiality vanishes once you better understand the particular goods perverted and corrupted by the evils you are trying to understand, and the vulnerable nature of these goods comes into clearer focus. It's not unlike calming a child who thinks she's seen a ghost or a monster: What is it, we ask? What did it look like? Did it look like this? Did it come in over there? It may be that the child *has* seen something truly dangerous, and we're better off knowing what it is. Indeed, the kind of analysis that the privation theory mandates is the very one involved in the effort to understand and address challenges to good in ordinary life. When you disaggregate evils by considering the goods on which they prey and understanding how the corruption happened, how it might be addressed and might have been forestalled, you are doing ethics.

In a way the disaggregating move is like that made by the first generation of virtue ethicists, resisting the tyranny of the language of good and bad. Ethical life doesn't and couldn't subsist on just these terms, on just this contrast, whatever academic moral philosophers may say. The discernment of ethical challenges and values, the articulation and negotiation of appropriate responses depend on the richer and more variegated language of the virtues. This language also better enables us to navigate a world of ambiguity, conflict, and error. And, the virtue ethicists point out triumphantly, ethical life has never let go of the virtues.

The advocate of the understanding of evil as privation delivers a similar challenge to those concerned with "evil." Doesn't all the content of determinations of evil come from more particular discussions? The claim is not that the language of the negative is dispensable. The claim is rather that the language of evil does not illuminate when uncoupled from the particularities to which analyses of privation draw our attention. It's like an exclamation point, wielded as a club. This is the "abuse of evil" about which Richard Bernstein has recently written.[20] To approach evil through privation is not to let down our defenses before it. Rather it helps us respond by moving beyond deceptive abstraction. And that very process of determining what went wrong, what is threatened, what powers are being commandeered by evil and how, returns us to the awareness of *goods*. The idea that evil is privation is not theodicy but ethics; it returns us from the sterile if not self-defeating attempt to relate to evils in the abstract to the discourses and discussions which help decide appropriate ways to respond to them.

It may seem that privation doesn't really correspond to ethics because often an evil is not an absence but a presence. In many cases the presence is what's left of the compromised good, used against itself and others. But thinking through the implications of evil as privation as I have described them means realizing that the language of ethical discernment and response is not a description of static and fixed substances, where things either exist or don't. The objects of our ethical concern grow, change, interact, and move on. Long before metaphysics, the language of ethical life reports and preserves an understanding of a world of complexity and interaction straining to be more than it is, yearning to be fuller and truer, if often failing. If we find this fullness impeded by an absence, it can just as well be impeded by an excess. The distended belly of someone suffering malnutrition is no less an evil for being bigger than the stomach of a healthy person. As the doctrine of the mean suggests, the living language of good and evil isn't about quantities of substance understood in terms of mere tonnage and volume.

There is another school of ethics to which privation is even closer: the ethics of care. When we think about good actions we are apt to think of noble heroic actions like risking our own lives saving the life of an endangered innocent, preferably unknown to us. The analysis mandated by the ethics of evil of privation doesn't deny the goodness of such acts, but suggests that it's usually too late when the evils they focus on appear. The child rescued from a burning building may have been abandoned by someone who should have been there, or was unable to be there, or has died. The fire may have been caused by faulty wiring, a forgotten pot of coffee, a cigarette in bed, or a young arsonist angry at society.

Atom Egoyan's film *The Sweet Hereafter*, based on the novel by Russell Banks, shows the fatuity of our desire to find a single cause of disaster. As we see all that might have gone wrong, we become aware of all that goes right most of the time, and of how dependent we unthinkingly are on its going right. Aristotle already showed the indispensability of a just society to virtuous and happy lives. The ethics of care adds that maintaining a just society and its citizens is a lot of work.

The success of any human life is dependent on all manner of chance, much of it having to do with the human environment or relationships in which it finds itself. Human beings are not substances which just "exist." We participate in worlds of support and encouragement, given and received. Ethicists of care Joan Tronto and Berenice Fischer have defined care broadly as "a species activity that includes everything that we do to maintain, continue, and repair our 'world' so that we can live in it as well as possible."[21] The privative approach to evils makes us aware of the structures and practices of care which make even minimal human flourishing possible, and the success of which would leave us with fewer occasions to fight or flee evils. The focus of most reflection on conspicuous evils seems a distraction from the ongoing work of maintaining a human world, our best hope in understanding and limiting the evils which threaten us.

Understanding evil as privation shows us that evil (such as it is) is never independent but is always parasitic on goods. It finds entrée because of the interdependence and vulnerability of goods. Many, perhaps most goods are like children needing care and encouragement,[22] or a house requiring maintenance and periodic renovation, or an art requiring discipline and innovation. The ethics of evil as privation makes us attendant to the different ways in which the goods of our lives depend on chance but also on structures of care and creativity.[23] It doesn't promise an end to evils, as friction, scarcity, and often tragic choice seem endemic to the human experience. But it helps us maintain a world which lets us forget these often enough to live and love.

With the help of virtue ethics and the ethics of care, we have moved from an understanding of evil as privation to a deeper, more ethically engaged understanding of the substance of good—all without a word about metaphysics. Once recognized as disaggregating, the idea of evil as privation turns out to be alive and well and living in our ethics. Reflection on care as world-making and -maintaining can help us understand why it's so hard to talk about good. It is not just that the language of good has been privatized and even commoditized in contemporary life and society. World-maintaining care work is often invisible—and not accidentally so. It makes you (relatively) free to lead a good life by letting you take it for granted. If we're constantly reminded of our dependence on care, or not allowed to rely on it, it does not free us but enchains us. Good care like other kinds of good invites us to take it for granted, to make ourselves at home.

Consider, again, health. Most people lucky enough to be generally healthy take health for granted, and, indeed, as their due. But to take it for granted does not mean to think about it. It means to use it. Back in the days when ethics took duties to self seriously, one had a duty to make good use of one's health, and to take steps to maintain it. In some traditions, health is understood as something you owe to your ancestors, or to your descendants. But in all these traditions people need to be reminded to count their blessings because it is not normal to be constantly aware of having health. Having health, being healthy, is in part not thinking about health.

This can explain what may seem the paradox of good: that we notice it most when it is threatened or gone. While in the presence of many kinds of good—better, while participating in the world good makes possible—we don't focus on them. We focus on other things—other people, our projects, the world, God. (We focus on other goods.) But when good is destroyed or endangered, not only it but our living and our freedom are thrown into crisis. The destruction of goods can be so soul-searing because with them we can lose a home in the world.

The disaggregating imperative of the understanding of evil as privation brings our concern with evil in general down to our struggles to maintain a world in which we can live. Evil-in-general gives way to evils and so to goods, the discernment and promotion of which is the life of ethics. It may seem that this picture relies on or mandates universal agreement about goods—an agreement unattainable and inimical to the life of a democratic pluralistic society—but it needn't. (Discussions of evil are in fact guiltier here, asserting and assuming consensus on evils.) The understanding of evil as privation simply plugs us into discussions of ethical challenges already taking place. Some of these may be as hierarchical as Augustine's. There is nothing to prevent such discussions from involving people of different value systems, or to prevent them from deciding to privatize the language of good where possible; democratic societies have been sustained by just such discussions for a while now.[24] The chances for a common working language are in any case much greater if people meet in the context of dealing with shared, real rather than abstract problems, and are attending to the ways in which goods are vulnerable and interdependent.

III A modest metaphysics of good

My discussion thus far has kept metaphysics at a distance. Our understanding of evils and responses to them are better based in the discussions of good which constitute and sustain us than in metaphysical abstraction. The account of good offered in Section II is not metaphysical so much as a description of language games. I've wanted to leave open the possibility of disagreement about goods. I'm not saying there is no place for a more philosophical understanding of the nature of good (and evil). There are features of our experiences of good that open a door to metaphysics and may demand some kind of metaphysical or religious elaboration or solace. Many of the major options in the metaphysics of evil can be seen as reactions to features of our lives that only the understanding of evil as privation fully illuminates. While I believe the analysis of Section II can stand on its own (and should), it seems worthwhile to spell these options out because the weakness of our language for good is in part the consequence of the coming together of some of these metaphysical views with modern consumer capitalism.

You may well have thought that the kinds of cases considered and implied in my account so far are too easy (they are certainly, given the nature of the problem, too few), that the power of evil is fatally underestimated. But in fact, looking at good from the vantage point of evil as privation offers a picture of the need for constant work in world-maintenance and -repair, a near guarantee that this work will be ignored and undermined, and no promise that all will be well. It confronts us with an unsettling view of our abiding vulnerability to evil— both as victims and as its more and less unwitting agents.[25] I've emphasized that the privation view is not a theodicy but a re-description of evils. If anything, the problem of evil is given new force by this re-description.

If nobody were ever hurt by evil, we'd soon find evil boring and evildoers self-absorbed and pathetic, the sorts of people to whom one says "get a life!" But beyond the horror of evil's destructiveness is the horrible mystery that it is *so very* destructive. A single virus, a single error, a single bad law, a single traitor, even a single homicidal madman can wreak entirely disproportionate destruction. This disproportion is part of what makes Hannah Arendt's account of the "banality" of the evil of Adolf Eichmann so disturbing. What the privative understanding of evil implies is that even in the worst cases, evils are not worthy of the goods they destroy. Understanding evil as privation makes clear that this is not something that sometimes happens. It is always the case. Indeed, this is just the privative nature of evil seen from another angle.

If the good destroyed is always greater than the evil which compromises it, must there not be something about good which allows this to happen? Just as we have recognized the world-making sweetness of good, we find it betrays itself—and us. I think the disproportion between evil and its victims made clear by the understanding of evil as privation is the secret of the dread fascination of evil. It is what has made more and less glamorous evil a central topic of our popular culture. It is the secret also of a number of ways we run from a world we can no longer bear to trust into world-negating metaphysics. Let me look briefly at two such metaphysical moves. By seeing what's right and what's wrong in them we can fill out our understanding of the nature of good.

One response to the disproportionate destructiveness of evil is to magnify evil, to make it somehow worthy of the harm it has wrought. An interpretive gulf opens up between precious goods destroyed and the accidents, negligence, misunderstandings, pettiness, mean-spiritedness, and boredom which cause their destruction. There must be more to the story, we feel. Judith Shklar put the point well: "Few people can bear the lesson of Cleopatra's nose. They need causes that are as weighty as the result."[26] This well describes part of the reaction to *Eichmann in Jerusalem*. Arendt's finding Eichmann banal seemed to many somehow to be suggesting that the deaths of the millions he enabled were banal deaths. A monstrous crime seems to require a monstrous criminal. But the understanding of evil as privation tells us that the consequences are never banal, though the causes almost always are.[27] Might this be what leads people to magnify and substantialize evils, to demonize those who have failed to maintain goods and—where the immediate cause resists demonization—to posit demonic possessions, dark forces, the ancient enemy? Paradoxically, it consoles us to magnify the cause of our grief. In Clifford Geertz's terms, it makes suffering more sufferable.[28]

Another version of this response may be observed in Ricoeur's suggestion that evil never seems to happen for the first time, but always feels like part of a "history of evil."[29] The privation-informed view of the unworthiness of evils to the goods they destroy offers a different interpretation than Ricoeur's. We live in a world of vulnerable goods, vulnerable also to our mistakes and malice. The destruction of a good shakes the whole world in which we felt at home. But we would be wrong to conclude that this really *is* somehow a continuous history, a history of the assault on our world by some malevolent force bent on its destruction (and against which we shall need a comparably vast force to defend us). The continuity is not in the evils. It is in the goods, in the world they make up. In saying this I do not deny the acuity of Ricoeur's description. But the depth we feel in the evil is really the gap between the paltriness of the cause and the vastness of the destruction. And the sense of a "history of evil" is really a shadow of the connected world, the world of interdependent and interacting goods.

A second response to the unworthiness of evils to the harm they are able to do takes the form of a kind of cognitive dissonance. It doesn't substantialize and magnify evil in a disempowering metaphysical way, but does so instead with the good. *True* good shouldn't be as vulnerable as this, it reasons, so these goods that can be corrupted can't be true goods. Good is invulnerable, perfect, eternal. This world is a fallen one whose goods are pale imitations at best, dangerous temptations at worst. For Platonists (if not perhaps for Plato himself) true good resides outside the world. For Stoics it is to be found only it in those aspects of our world which are in fact invulnerable to corruption—if there are any. Both reject the goods of this world for their vulnerability, and many have followed them (including Augustine). Good, it turns out, is *too* good for this world.

An understanding of evil as privation suggests this isn't just denial of change and mortality. The good *is* something which is experienced as safe and stable. (That is why we speak of *the* good and not just of goods.) Its stability makes the world a place in which we can move. When something sets that world teetering, it's natural to want to restore or preserve a sense of safety and stability by anchoring it beyond the world of change and loss. The good of imperfect vulnerable goods is preserved and honored—but by being taken away from this world.

But is it really of the essence of good to be invulnerable? Opennness is the sign and consequence of its world-making interrelation and connection. The demand that it be invulnerable looks like affront at this fact.[30] One can see why the dream of a general universal unchangeable good would arise, but does it not kill the good to imagine it so self-sufficient? The analysis of evil as privation suggests that its supposed self-sufficiency is really a displaced description of the way it provides a stable and meaningful world for us to live in—a description of interaction, not of self-sufficiency. (It need not be unchanging to offer us a stable world; indeed the ethics of care suggests that it can't be.) In our time we tend to sense connection, involvement, relation—properly characteristics of world-making good—only in evil, which we see as invading, subverting, destroying, while good seems to us inert and closed. Indeed, connection, involvement, and relation are rendered inert (mere exchange) when not destructive by such a view.[31]

A variant of this reaction to the unworthiness of evils to the goods they destroy stares hard at the disturbing fact that all the forces used by evil are good's forces, are themselves goods. What is it about the stuff of which we and our world are made that makes it so vulnerable to destruction? Is matter itself evil? Is it fatally flawed for being made of nothing? We may find Augustine's anti-Gnostic gnosis distasteful, but it needs to be acknowledged as a tough-minded interpretation of a tough reality. There would be no evil did not good offer it a home.

My intention in these speculations has not been to debunk the religious and metaphysical views mentioned. I've tried, rather, to interpret them as responses to an underlying experience disclosed uncompromisingly but undogmatically by the understanding of evil as privation. It is based, I have suggested, in the language of ethics, not in ontology or theology. This understanding implies that evils are never worthy of the goods they destroy. The things we describe and respond to as evils occur and seem so potent because good offers them a home—perhaps by its very nature, since it is of the world-making nature of good to invite us to make ourselves at home.

It may be that an understanding of the vulnerable goods of this world is the best way to God. Or it may be the First Noble Truth. It may be that the vulnerability of the good discloses our indispensable role as stewards responsible for mending the world. Or it may show us that our energies are best spent gathering treasure in heaven. It may be that, understood for what it is in all its interdependence, we can return to the world of transient goods as to a world of precious jewels of pure enlightenment. Or it may be that tenderness for the vulnerable is misplaced, that life requires an embrace of inevitably destructive creativity beyond good and evil. The understanding of evil as privation discloses a world of interdependent goods whose disruption we notice more than its smooth living and growing, which sustains but also depends on us. This understanding is compatible with all of the religious and metaphysical views I've just mentioned—and the continuing heartbreak of this world require one. But the privative view of evil also challenges us not to let our feelings of grief or betrayal prevent us from prizing the goods whose life we have at last acknowledged.

IV Conclusions

I've covered a lot of ground very quickly. I wanted to make clear the many ways in which understanding evil as privation can help us see through the fatal charms of grand theories of evil—and of good. It takes us to the goods, theorized or not, which our ethics seek to preserve and promote and our accounts of evil memorialize. When followed as a mandate to particularize and disaggregate, the idea of evil as privation does more than demythologize. It traces tasks of world-making, -maintaining and -repair, as, indeed, the world of goods which provides the stable ground for our adventures in living. This analysis already takes place as individuals and communities work to define and address problems that confront them. Virtue ethics and the ethics of care affirm the value of the diagnostic approach to evils demanded by a world of complexity and interdependence, and make us aware anew of how vulnerable human flourishing is, of the great quantities of creative care required to sustain a world stable and life-affirming enough for us to dare to acknowledge the true sweetness of the enjoyment of good, as well as the true bitterness of its loss.

Other accounts of evil, mainly focused on those cases where evil happens on a scale big enough to tempt us to mythologize, blind us to the nature and dangers of evils, in part by downplaying our vulnerability both as victims and as agents. (Who's "healthy-minded" now?) Their vision may be obscured by the tears of grief. The disproportion between the causes and consequences of evil disclosed by the privative understanding of evil is hard to accept. It is tempting to commemorate goods undone by causes unworthy of them by magnifying these causes in a perverse tribute to the destruction they have effected. It is tempting to imagine this world's hurts as unreal, its goods as mere shadows of a true, unchanging good this world cannot sustain. Without a ready vocabulary for seeing change, interdependence and even vulnerability as good, it is hard not to substantialize evil as a cause, indeed as a cause powerful enough not only to destroy particular evils but the whole world which the persistence of evil makes us feel in such jeopardy.

Let me end where I began, with Augustine's claim in *City of God* that to try to understand the origin of evil is like trying to hear silence or see darkness. This is both a warning against losing ourselves in a false view of the world and an invitation to watch ourselves as we try to make out the shape of darkness, the melody of silence, to make darkness the shapeliest shape, and silence the profoundest melody of all. What we discern are in fact projections of the melody of change and harmony, the shape of the stable world in which we live.

But we live in a time in which we feel the frisson of reality more in evil—especially spectacular evil—than in good. That's a problem, but not one without a solution. Contrary to modern criticisms that an understanding of evil as privation is unable to take either evil or good seriously, I've tried to show that it is only this understanding that can acknowledge that the frisson is real without slipping into mythological views which disempower us and deny the goods whose appearances they seek to save. The frisson is real because the goods which evils destroy are real. The evils seem possessed of (or by) a sinister power which eludes our grasp because an evil is never worthy of the good it destroys. The danger of evil seems ancient and abiding because the destruction of goods shakes the foundations of the world in which goods invite us to make a home. We would be mistaken to conclude from this that silence is somehow as real as sound, indeed purer or deeper. (We would be misled about the nature, variety and beauty of sounds, too.) But if we watch ourselves listening to silence we might just notice in ourselves the heartbeat of the vulnerable, care-maintained world in which we are privileged to participate.

Acknowledgments

I am grateful for the helpful criticisms and suggestions of Peter Carey, Beth Eddy, Brian FitzGerald, Ray L. Hart, Robert Neville, Joe Tinguely, and Joan Tronto.

Notes

[1] *Concerning the City of God against the Pagans*, trans. Henry Bettenson (Harmondsworth: Penguin, 1972), 481 (XII.7).

[2] *Confessions*, trans. R. S. Pine-Coffin (Harmondsworth: Penguin, 1961), 148 (VII.12).

[3] G. W. Leibniz, *Theodicy: Essays on the Goodness of God, the Freedom of Man, and the Origin of Evil*, §29 and "Causa dei" §70.

[4] Charles T. Mathewes, *Evil and the Augustinian Tradition* (Cambridge: Cambridge University Press, 2001), 63 and ch. 5.

[5] *Faith, Hope and Charity [Enchiridion de fide, spe et caritate]*, trans. Bernard M. Peebles (New York: Fathers of the Church, Inc., 1947), 376–77 (III.11).

[6] Augustine, *Enchiridion, ibid.*

[7] Augustine, *City of God*, 453 (XI.22).

[8] William James, *The Varieties of Religious Experience. A Study in Human Nature* (Harmondsworth: Penguin, 1982), 127.

[9] James, *Varieties of Religious Experience*, 83.

[10] John Hick, *Evil and the God of Love*, rev. ed. (San Francisco: Harper Collins, 1977), 82–89 and 191–93. Marilyn McCord Adams has encouraged a reappraisal of the

aesthetic in *Horrendous Evils and the Goodness of God* (Ithaca: Cornell University Press, 1999).

[11] Kenneth Surin, *Theology and the Problem of Evil* (Oxford: Basil Blackwell, 1986), 11 and Terrence W. Tilley, *The Evils of Theodicy* (Washington: Georgetown University Press, 1991), 113–40.

[12] Evodius, the questioner, disappears too, but not before mocking his earlier question. That the question is not adequately answered by the discussion is suggested by the concession that "[t]hey might, perhaps, have a valid complaint if there were no Victor over error and lust." See *On Free Choice of the Will [De Libero Arbitrio Voluntatis]*, trans. Anna S. Benjamin and L. H. Hackstaff (New York: Macmillan, 1964), 85 (III.i.2) and 129 (III.xix.18).

[13] Rowan Williams, "Insubstantial Evil," in *Augustine and His Critics: Essays in Honour of Gerald Bonner*, ed. Robert Dodaro and George Lawless (London and New York: Routledge, 2000), 105–23, 121.

[14] Williams, "Insubstantial Evil," *ibid.*

[15] *Ibid.*

[16] Augustine moves smoothly, almost briskly, from reproving humanity for judging the world according to its own "utility" rather than appreciating the "logic" of the "order of nature" (XI.16), through the standard arguments for the existence of evil in God's world—free will (XI.17) and the aesthetic argument that God "enrich[es] the course of world history by the kind of antithesis which gives beauty to a poem" (XI.18)—to the privative character of evil (XI.21), and from there to the proper way of approaching creation: "there are three questions to be asked in respect of any created being," Augustine remarks, "'Who made it?', 'How?' and 'Why?' I put forward the answers: 'God', 'Through his word', 'Because it is good.' . . . [T]his formula is to be regarded as a mystical revelation of the Trinity, the Father, the Son, and the Holy Spirit" (XI.23). From here, Augustine moves into an account of the "tripartite division of philosophy" (XI.25) and the "partial image of the Trinity in human nature" (XI.26).

[17] *City of God*, 480 (XII.7).

[18] *Ibid.*

[19] Paul Ricoeur, "Evil: A Challenge to Philosophy and Theology," *Journal of the American Academy of Religion* 53, no. 3 (1985): 635–48.

[20] Richard J. Bernstein, *The Abuse of Evil: The Corruption of Politics and Religion Since 9/11* (Cambridge, UK and Malden, MA: Polity, 2005).

[21] Berenice Fisher and Joan C. Tronto, "Toward a Feminist Theory of Care," in *Circles of Care: Work and Identity in Women's Lives*, ed. Emily Abel and Margaret Nelson (Albany: State University of New York Press, 1991), 40; quoted in Joan C. Tronto, *Moral Boundaries: A Political Argument for an Ethic of Care* (New York and London: Routledge, 1993), 103.

[22] See Sara Ruddick, *Maternal Thinking: Towards a Politics of Peace* (Boston: Beacon, 1995).

[23] I emphasize creativity as an integral part of care because care is sometimes thought to be instrumental and conservative, merely preservation of something whose value is assumed and unexamined, but this is the case only when ethics is divorced from politics. See Tronto, *Moral Boundaries* for the argument that the ethics of care both needs and can generate a democratic politics. Understanding

care as world-making reveals not only our dependence but our interdependence, our need not only to repair and maintain but also to renew worlds. In this broad sense it covers much that we call good—no wonder that the deepest views of good see it as something we participate in, however haltingly.

24 See Jeffrey Stout, *Democracy and Tradition* (Princeton: Princeton University Press, 2004), especially chs. 4, 11, and 12.

25 It is no accident that the book on evil by Nel Noddings, a leading ethicist of care, should have so decisively made the case for excluding "cultural evils" from the categories of natural and moral evil, which dominate philosophical discussion. See *Women and Evil* (Berkeley, Los Angeles, and London: University of California Press, 1989), 104.

26 Judith Shklar, "Misfortune and Injustice," in *The Faces of Injustice* (New Haven: Yale University Press, 1990), 60; a reference to Pascal: "Had Cleopatra's nose been shorter, the whole face of the world would have changed."

27 Seeing Eichmann's kind of banality as specific to modernity, to bureacracy, to "totalitarianism" is a way of refusing to recognize the universality of banality.

28 Clifford Geertz, "Religion as a cultural system," in *The Interpretation of Cultures* (New York: Basic Books, 1973), 87–125.

29 Ricoeur, "Evil: A Challenge to Philosophy and Theology," 636–37.

30 See Ivone Gebara, *Out of the Depths: Women's Experience of Evil and Salvation*, trans. Ann Patrick Ware (Minneapolis: Fortress, 2002).

31 An understanding of goods as invulnerable and non-interactive plays right into the cheap view of goods of a consumer economy, products and objects that we capriciously desire to possess but can never ultimately satisfy us.

Part Three

Deliver Us from Evil

"For Your Own Good": Suffering and Evil in God's Plan according to One Hindu Theologian

Francis X. Clooney, S.J.
Harvard University

Understanding evil

This paper has taken the large topic of evil, narrowed it to India, confined it to Hinduism within its classical and brahminical forms, and then focused on a contained micro-context: (1) Shrivaishnavism, and in the period after Rāmānuja; (2) "Northern School" (Vaṭalakai) Shrivaishnavism; (3) Vedānta Deśika (fourteenth century); (4) Deśika's *Śrīmad Rahasya Traya Sāra*; (5) chapter 18 of the *Śrīmad Rahasya Traya Sāra*. Despite the loss of comprehensiveness, this narrow focus affords us the opportunity to understand evil as firmly located within a fully integrated intellectual and religious framework. We thus gain not only materials that may be of interest to us in our reflection on evil, but more importantly encounter a highly developed and nuanced theology of evil from 600 years ago in medieval India. My expectation is that this small scale, textual, and theological focus aptly illumines a key example of how evil is understood and managed.

Vedānta Deśika and his
Śrīmad Rahasya Traya Sāra

Vedānta Deśika (Veṅkaṭanātha, 1268–1369) is one of the most interesting and versatile of traditional Indian intellectuals. He was a foremost theologian of the Śrīvaiṣṇava Hindu community, a tradition that roots its heritage and theology in the Sanskrit heritage of the Vedānta, and the Tamil devotional heritage of the Āḻvārs. His late-in-life *Śrīmad Rahasya Traya Sāra* (henceforth *RTS*) is a large and comprehensive exposition of the exegesis, philosophy, theology, practice, and religious sociology of south Indian Shrivaishnavism, an ancient tradition devoted to worship of Nārāyaṇa as the sole Lord, along with his consort, Śrī Lakṣmī. At the core of the practice of this tradition, as enunciated by Deśika, is the act variously described as coming near to the feet of Nārāyaṇa and Śrī (*prapatti*), taking refuge there (*śaraṇāgati*), and laying down one's burden before them (*bharaṇyāsa*). This act dramatically transforms the situation of the human person and the community, creating a new way of living and of understanding the world. (Throughout, I will refer to this essential act, against which all kinds of ostensible evils are judged, as "refuge" or "taking refuge.")

The *RTS* is written for those who have either taken refuge or are in a position to do so. It centers on exegeting the three sacred mantras cherished by the tradition, three utterances encoding the act of taking refuge: a confession of the divine–human dynamic (in the *Tiru Mantra*), the enunciation of the words recited while taking refuge (in the *Dvaya Mantra*), and the divine response to those who have taken refuge (in the *Carama Śloka*). The exegesis of the mantras in chapters 27–29 is balanced by an exposition of the worldview that makes taking refuge plausible (in chapters 3–6); chapters 7–19 spell out the manner and motive of a life lived in accord with the mantras; and chapter 18, the focus of this essay, deals with the sufferings that humans endure and the evils that humans perpetrate.

Evil is described in a number of ways throughout the *RTS*, and here I mention only a few of the key insights to be gleaned in sections other than chapter 18; chapter 1 sets the scene for the entire *RTS*. Ignorance is the real problem, a lack of knowledge of one's true identity in the Lord's presence; to be a human, ordinarily, is to live out a loss of identity, like the proverbial prince, lost in the forest and raised by simple hunters, who only later rediscovers his regal identity. Ignorance is thus given its due importance; education and the eradication of ignorance are put forward as the positive goals of life. Chapters 3–5 give the order of all things—all things and persons are oriented to the Lord on whom they depend and in whom they find completion. Accordingly, evil consists in those ideas and acts militating against the right order of things. Chapter 6, which asserts primarily that Nārāyaṇa with Śrī is the one true God, also assesses the worship of those weaker and dependent gods who, eager to please, often seem quicker in responding to human needs; Nārāyaṇa in his sovereign power guarantees the true and enduring good, but he does not hurry to please, and so may seem unresponsive to pleas for immediate protection and benefits. In affirming the goodness of both devotion (*bhakti*) and taking refuge (*śaraṇāgati* or *prapatti*) in chapters 7–12, Deśika also makes clear how lesser goods may be in a way a kind of evil. Ritual performance, meditation, and devotional practices are lesser goods that may tend to evil effect if they also foster feelings of self-sufficiency or, conversely, indicate perfectionist standards that can hardly ever be met. A hierarchy of goods is required, ordered properly in accord with one's innate dependence on Nārāyaṇa.[1]

Chapters 16, 17, and 19 provide the immediate interpretive context for the consideration of evil in chapter 18. In chapter 16 Deśika argues that the true good particularly pleasing to the Lord is the mutual pleasure and mutual service in the community of believers; conversely, discrimination within the community is condemned here, since devotees who have taken refuge are all equal in the Lord's eyes. The overall well-being of the Śrīvaiṣṇava community is the standard by which good and evil are judged; accordingly, as we shall see in chapter 18, even lesser injuries to other devotees turn out to be greatly offensive to the Lord. The community of believers is ideally a community of good intentions, in which evil or disruptive intentions are the most acute evils that may occur.

In chapter 17 Deśika defines the normative values of the Śrīvaiṣṇava community, emphasizing the importance of adherence to religious rules sanctioned by scripture and tradition; the order of dharma, particularly with respect to religious class (*varṇa*) and stages of life (*āśrama*), obliges devotees even after they take refuge with the Lord, thereby surrendering responsibility. This order never lapses, so a predictable and expected measure of evil is whatever that transgresses dharma and offends the Lord. It is all the more striking that the single issue of orthodoxy addressed at length in chapter 18 is the evil of caste arrogance, using the good of orthodoxy as an instrument for rupturing the community. We shall see in chapter 18 that Deśika is in fact interested in how intention, and not obedience to rules, constitutes good and evil, which are never so clear as to be entirely a matter of legislation. As if preparatory to that turn to intentionality, chapter 17 ends with a verse that lists strategies by which to discern the good and evil in ways that go beyond what law books contain:

> By revelation, texts of tradition, good practice, the workings of one's own
>   mind,
> By the intentions of those who are pure,
> By right customs according to family, clan, and locale,
> By restrictions imposed by proper people,
> By omens, dreams, etc.,
> The wise person learns with nuance
> The intent of the First One, controller of all.

$$(318)^2$$

This "original intent," as we shall see in chapter 18, is the foundation for every assessment of good and evil. The Lord's sovereign will for the good is not to be contradicted, but it takes some skill to discover how the Lord is working in any set of particular circumstances.

In chapter 19 we are told that good and evil may have, or seem to have, geographical specificity. It cautions against living in places wherein righteousness is not observed; Deśika specifically laments that "Āryāvarta"—probably the heartland of northern India —is in a current state of decay (346). For the cultivation of a righteous and spiritual life, one must dwell in places where "the dharma of the four religious classes" remains pure and inviolate, places such as Śrīraṅgam, Tiruveṅkaṭam (Tirupati), and Kāñcīpuram (all Śrīvaiṣṇava centers in the south; 346). Strikingly though, he concedes that it is rather more important to live in a place where devotees of the Lord have gathered, since the good of community lies primarily in the right intentions of those who are devoted to the Lord and to one another. (By extension, chapters 20-22 describe the post-mortem ascent to the heavenly Vaikuṇṭha, where one enjoys bliss in irreversible union with the Lord.)

I have surveyed the content of these chapters primarily to make clear from the start that Deśika's reflections on suffering and evil will have little to do with evil as a dynamic counterpart to the good, or as a problem or mystery beyond understanding. The mystery of the divine good is primary, and evil and suffering are intelligible and manageable within the context of that larger reality.[3]

Evil as impurity, accident, and offense

In chapter 18, "The Avoidance of Transgression" (*Aparādha Parihara*), the first image is that of evil as a kind of material pollution; it sticks and restricts, and can be washed away only with difficulty:

> By divine fortune, and for the extinction of impurity,
> even while still in the body the self receives
> the limpid, sweet, ever-purifying good fortune,
> the gentle Gaṅgā stream of Mādhava's mercy —
> even when that self pollutes its own body
> by the mire exuding from things that have no essence,
> even if not associated with the wise.
>
> (322–23)

The Lord purifies those who have taken refuge, and images of sin as pollution must always give way before the power of God's intention to make good triumph and to make devotees pure.

In most of the chapter, though, the imagery of pollution and purification is not prominent. Rather, as in chapter 17, evil is conceptualized as transgression (*aparādha*) of those religious laws that prescribe a right attitude toward self, community, and the Lord. Transgression is taken very seriously; even if exceptions may be justified in emergency situations, they always remain precisely that—exceptional. In general, the rules are to be kept, and it is evil not to do so. But Deśika expects intentional violations to be rare in this ideal community of people who have taken refuge with the Lord: "By his proper nature the person who has taken refuge is exclusively oriented to the Lord, and delights in service to the Lord in accord with the scriptures. Therefore, in non-emergency situations, intentional offenses will not generally occur, because they are contrary to such a person's commitment to service" (323).

Completing the introductory portion of the chapter, Deśika concedes that merely accidental or circumstantial evils occur, but also that these have no larger significance: "By the force of specific karma that is already under way, by defects in the place, time, and situation, or by accidents in deep sleep, etc., traces of offence will occur—but these we can let go of without a trace" (323). Only what is intentional really matters in the calculation of evil and responses to it.

Why good people suffer

Deśika turns, for the bulk of the chapter, to various cases of evil occurring within the matrix of Śrīvaiṣṇava life. He first considers "bad things happening to good people," asking why physical evils such as disease, disability, early death, and unwanted old age occur among people who have taken refuge with the Lord and whom the Lord has promised to protect. For it is obvious that even those who have taken refuge with the Lord and whom the Lord protects experience suffering in the form of obvious evils such as blindness or lameness. But the Lord intentionally modulates such sufferings according to the sins and needs of the person punished: "In accord with the saying, 'One is punished by the prick of a thorn instead of being stabbed with a spear,' [sinners] become one-eyed or lame, etc.; so it is said in scripture. By minor suffering in this life, the Lord of all promotes ways of uprooting [their faults]; his heat is ever subdued by his forgiveness, love, mercy, and tenderness" (326). Even in the ideal community, misfortunes occur, and these are clearly experienced and classed as evil—until properly understood in light of divine intentions, in the context of the Lord's intention to instruct devotees regarding their own good. While this understanding does not obviate the physical ailment or disability that must still be endured, it does give it meaning.

Two analogies clarify what Deśika means. In the first, the Lord is compared to a ruler who knows how to mete out punishment wisely:

An emperor, worthy of respectful service, responds to offences that very much deserve to be punished. In accord with offences by servants in the harem, princes, dwarves and hunchbacks—all of whom carry his insignias—and in accord with their degree of insider status, and because he is related to them and is lacking in cruelty, he forgives the faults they have committed. But to instruct them regarding their future, he averts his face, has them horse-whipped, expelled, put out by the gates or barred from service for a few days. (326–27)

The second analogy refers to a famous scene from the *Rāmāyaṇa*, in which Lord Rāma inflicts partial blindness on a demon crow rather than killing it: "In the same way, in keeping with the maxim of 'Kāka the demon crow,' by the loss of an eye [the Lord] protects those who have taken refuge" (327). Kāka, a crow and demon, pecked at the bosom of Sītā, Rāma's wife, so Rāma chased the crow throughout the universe seeking to kill it. As Sītā watched with approval, Kāka took refuge at the feet of Rāma who, though sparing his life, blinded him in one eye as a milder punishment and cautionary reminder. Instead of dying, Kāka lost an eye; he suffered by way of instruction and for his own good, suffering in this life rather than meriting an eternal punishment. When good people suffer from natural causes, then, it is most often due to the Lord's intervention in their lives, for their betterment.

Deśika also asks why people die young or, just as bad, linger on when they are yearning to die and be with the Lord; dying young is recognized as evil, but an overly long life too may be experienced as merely a venue for ongoing suffering. By Deśika's calculation, the matter is simple: "Trees to which asafetida has been applied wither at different times, depending on differences in location and other factors. Similarly, there are differences with respect to delay or non-delay in the complete cessation of people's worldly existence" (327). Some people have life spans already set (by the Lord, in accordance with their karma), and their purification and the expenditure of remaining karma must occur within that set span, and thus more intensely. Others, having no stipulated life span, linger for a much longer time; they may find suffering pervasive in their old age, and the longer life itself a punishment: "Some people cannot endure delay and desire liberation right now, in this body; but since they do not have a pre-determined length of life, they will suffer delay and longer lives [as a punishment]" (327). By contrast, others have shorter and more intense lives, often full of suffering: "For those whose life spans are predetermined, [taking refuge] bears fruit within that span" (327), and even their suffering is experienced intensely, in that short time.[4]

In chapter 26, one of four chapters dedicated to resolution of lingering doubts, Deśika uses a Job-like image to assert rather more starkly the instructional nature of suffering:

> "He to whom I want to show favor, his wealth I take away; then his relatives forsake him; he is ever full of sorrow. If a man suffers this way but does not abandon me, I show him that grace which even gods cannot obtain."[5] As a teacher, the Lord makes use of deeds that have begun to yield fruit and are the cause of sufferings; he punishes men with hard hearts in order to correct them, as a father [would] correct a son with a whip. It is therefore proper to think of such punishments as special favors. (586–87)

Deśika also recalls a saying of the esteemed teacher Parāśara Bhaṭṭar and expands it into a lesson on how suffering teaches:

> When the king asked Bhaṭṭar whether a disease could be helpful, he replied that sufferings are a teacher. In the mind of one whose life span is so inalterably

fixed that it cannot be extended, sufferings promote learning; if one's life span can be extended, life's sufferings teach that person not to desire a more extended life along with the things desirable during life. For some, suffering is intended only to reveal their offences along with their consequences, and then conceal them again, [gradually] instilling in them complete indifference (587–88)

Experiences are usually mixed, but whatever occurs will be profitable or not, depending on whether one has learned to discern the meaning of past suffering: "Undesirable experiences are the fruit of past karma. That these should become instructive, so that one becomes immersed in acts of atonement, is a fruit of the means [that is, of taking refuge]. That sufferings are experienced as instructive and so forth can also be the result of good deeds already bearing fruit" (588). Also with reference to chapter 26, the modern commentator Rāmadeśikācārya amplifies this story of the teacher Kūrattālvār's steadfastness in resistance to a Śaiva king's declaration of Śiva's supremacy and consequent persecution of resistant Vaiṣṇavas. The king has Kūrattālvār blinded, but he thanks the king for helping him become more detached from the world.[6]

Everything that happens is governed by intention and can be assessed in terms of increasingly more inclusive and overarching intentions. At the most comprehensive level, the key is always the Lord's determination that everything should work out to the good of all persons, who must realize this by learning how to respond to their own sufferings with the right attitude. Understanding divine intention and the meaning of suffering makes it possible that evils can be revalued as goods.

Conversely, resistance to the Lord becomes a way of life that deforms a person more or less severely, hardening their hearts. By their deeds, people become to varying degrees closed to the Lord, "softer" or "harder." Punishment, in the form of disease, disability, and death, aims at deprogramming persons who are trapped by their karma; it will be more or less severe depending on how hardened a person has become: "The Lord arranges that those who are gentle in nature obtain pardon; he gives particular punishment to those who are hard by nature, as a form of instruction" (327).[7]

Even the fear of suffering can serve a good purpose, chastening the mind and heart of persons needing correction. In the *Rāmāyaṇa*, the encounter of Sītā with her demoness captors illustrates how promises of protection may be usefully coupled with threats of punishment and fear:

When those demonesses deliberately offended Sītā again after saying, "Be our refuge," (*Yuddha Kāṇḍa* 58.90) did she not forgive them? For she had said, "I cannot bear [their sufferings]" (*Yuddha Kāṇḍa* 116.44) and "Whether they deserve punishment for their sins or are auspicious, O monkey [mercy must be shown because of your generous nature; there is no one who has not sinned]" (*Yuddha Kāṇḍa* 116.44). We respond that [despite Sītā's words] the demonesses were afraid that Hanumān was going to hurt them severely, and afterwards were saved from that fear. As with the raising of a sword [as a warning], there were a slight punishment and then forgiveness. (327–28)

Gentle and sensitive people require less instruction—less punishment, less suffering—while the hardened require more severe punishment—or fear thereof—if they are to learn anything. Repeatedly, Deśika refers to how a good ruler punishes, in moderations and by calculated warnings, thus educating his servants, family, and consorts. For this model to work, of course, one must have in mind a very ideal king who has learned not to abuse his power, but for Deśika, the Lord is precisely that kind of king.

Even if suffering is instructive and is best accepted as such, still one can take measures to diminish the lingering ill effects of previous evils. The remedy for evils that carry over from a previous life can be material or spiritual: "Statements such as, 'The sins committed in previous births afflict a man as diseases. They can [be] quieted by medicines, charitable gifts, prayers, fire oblations, and worship' (*Vigāheśvara Saṃhitā*), show that by gifts, prayers, etc., even sins already bearing fruit are destroyed" (332). Interestingly, commentators here notice that in his paraphrase of the quotation, Deśika omits "medicines"—as if to deny that physical suffering cured by medicine is of interest to the theologian exploring evil. Or perhaps we are seeing here a complex of responses to evil, modes for its removal or diminishment, alongside Deśika's more pervasive intellectual insight that even disease is a valuable instruction that need not be avoided.

Social evil, real evil

The divine–human community is a web of intentions that is normative with respect to good and evil. The most intense consideration of evil in chapter 18 occurs with reference to the community comprised of those who have already taken refuge or who are at least disposed to value the act. It should be not surprising then that the latter part of chapter 18 shifts from sufferings such as disease, disfigurement, early death, and old age to evils perpetrated within the community when members fail to treat one another with due respect or intentionally demean one another. Here evil is more subtle and particularly noxious, and particularly offensive to the Lord.[8] Deśika laments this more subtle form of evil as all the more difficult—and evil—because it is not necessitated by karma but rather by ill will, and there ought not to be such disorder in the community. If (as in chapter 16) the supreme good lies in serving the community, the greatest evil lies in harm to the community: "Rāmānuja, the author of the *Bhāṣya*, has pointed out at *Uttara Mīmāṃsā Sūtra* 3.4.51 that among the sins to be avoided, misdeeds done to persons close to the Lord stand in the front rank, like transgressions against a king's wives" (334).[9] By his ongoing royal analogy, the entire community is like the king's household; an offense to anyone in that household is an offense against the Lord.

But for Deśika, this does not mean all are of equal status. Echoing a theme recurring throughout in the *RTS*,[10] he asserts that caste differences are not in themselves evil, because they too are intended by the Lord:

> While persons such as Parāśara, Vyāsa, Śuka, Śaunaka, Nāthamuni and others are superior in caste, qualities, and actions, we can be equal to them in certain matters, such as "being the Lord's people" or with regard to attaining the highest goal. But there will still be differences in their proper nature and in characteristics due to the will of the Lord. This [equality-with-difference] is seen with respect to other things belonging to the Lord [where variety prevails], such as cows and cowherds, tulasi leaves and campaka flowers, cow dung and musk. These differences should not be overlooked. (335)

Even caste differences are good, and they ought not be abolished. Yet they can also occasion inexcusable evils, if members of the community revile one another on the basis of caste. Deeper equality and respect are crucially important, even when differences are still respected (335–336). Just as fire is always simply fire even when it takes on the attributes of the various objects that are being burnt, so too the selves of all persons are equal even when they take on the attributes of this or that body. Devotion makes up for all other shortcomings: "As indicated in *Tiruvāymoli* 3.7 and *Tiruvāymoli* 8.10,[11] there must be no lack of reverence [toward devotees]. Even if there were only this reverence, it would complete the service that is doing everything in accord with one's dependence on the perfect Lord. As has been said: 'Just the very thought, "This man belongs to the Lord," is itself capable of effecting good'" (336–337). Readers might instinctively see the solution rather in the simple abolition of caste distinctions, since they will also be occasions for disrespect and dissension. Yet for Deśika it is crucial to locate the undeniable evils within the larger plan God has for the world, a plan that includes differences. To remove caste, in his view, would be to seek to cure an evil by implementing another, great evil.

Repentance and regret

If the primary form of evil about which Deśika is concerned here is intentional disrespect and misunderstanding within the community, the appropriate response to this evil is also a matter of attitude and intention. For the evil that divides the community can be quieted by humble acceptance of rebuke, even unfair criticism. Humility, apology, and forgiveness are exemplified even by divine beings come down on earth. Deśika recalls how the eagle Garuḍa—who

conveys the Lord between heaven and earth—once offended the ascetic Śāṇḍilī
by his thoughts about her:[12] "Even Garuḍa—described [in Āḷavandār's *Stotra*] as
the Lord's servant, friend, vehicle, seat and emblem on the banner—committed
an offense, a transgression against a good person" (333). But Garuḍa repented
and begged forgiveness of Śāṇḍilī. Indeed, the point of the descents of heavenly beings to earth is to exemplify how to repent, to be forgiven and to forgive:
"When eternal beings [such as Garuḍa] descend as does the Lord, they too act
as if subject to the sway of karma, and must ward off transgressions and so forth.
[This good example] promotes the good of the world" (333).

Similarly, later in chapter 18 Deśika recounts how Sugrīva and Lakṣamaṇa
had to express regret and remorse for their argument when tension was building in the midst of the effort to organize the campaign against Rāvaṇa, captor
of Sītā:

(After transgression) one should at once beg pardon of these devoted servants of the Lord. We should reflect on the manner in which Sugrīva, the great
king, and Lakṣamaṇa apologize to one another in these ślokas: "Since you
have offended, I see no atonement for you other than to seek Lakṣamaṇa's
pardon, hands joined in supplication" (*Kiṣkinda Kāṇḍa* 32.17), "If I have
offended you in any way, either on account of overconfidence or love, you
should pardon this fault of your servant; no one is above committing an
offence" (*Kiṣkinda Kāṇḍa* 36.11), "The harsh words that I uttered to you after
hearing the speech of Rāma who is overwhelmed with grief—these words
should be forgiven by you" (*Kiṣkinda Kāṇḍa* 36.28).[13] In the same way, we
should be reconciled with the Lord's devotees, so that any split that has
occurred is patched up without a visible trace. (337–38)

The stories of Lakṣamaṇa, Sugrīva and Garuḍa exemplify how even the most
respected defer to those they have wronged. Spoiled relations in the community, and the failure to make up for them, are the most worrisome of evils, and
the best solution is to repent and achieve reconciliation, thereby overcoming
evil with a greater good.

Turning rebuke into good: accepting criticism

Deśika goes still further, emphasizing the need to respond humbly even to
the undeniable evil of unmerited criticism. To suffer misunderstanding is for
one's own good, even when the unkindness itself is unjustified: "If the Lord's
people are hostile to a person because he has committed some fault, or even
because he did something wrong in a previous birth though doing nothing
wrong now, he should by some means obtain their pardon and so obtain the
Lord's pardon" (338–39). This willingness to accept seemingly unfair criticism

is what distinguishes the devotee: "He is a Vaiṣṇava who, upon hearing harsh words uttered by others among the Lord's people, prostrates before them and begs pardon (*Laiṅga Purāṇa* II.4.9)" (339). Here too, a proper attitude transforms evil into good.

The lesson is reinforced by suggesting that one should be grateful to such brahmins—evidently, to brahmins prone to give out such evil—regardless of how they act:

It has been said, "Those who are brahmins—they are myself, without a doubt, O king. When they are honored, I am honored; when they are pleased, I too am pleased. Their enemy is my enemy" (*Viṣṇu Dharma* 52.20), and "Though a brahmin strikes a person, curses him, and utters cruel words to him, if he does not reverence that brahmin as I did, he is a sinner. He will be consumed by the wild fire of the brahmin's anger. He is to be killed and punished, he is not mine" (*Itihāsa Samhitā* 30.100). If a man does not act this way, he is beyond the bounds of the Lord's approval; he will lose the proper form that is his Vaiṣṇava nature, that is, his being entirely oriented to other among the Lord's people, and so too the qualities of restraint, control, and so forth. To lose these is the same as punishment and death. (339)

Like today's readers, Deśika too seems concerned that his audience will focus only on respect for brahmins, so he adds a significant clarification: "The word 'brahmin' occurring in such verses has a special meaning, as has been said in the verse, 'He who knows Viṣṇu who crosses all, who is Vāsudeva, he is wise (*vipra*), he reaches the state of being wise (*vipra-tva*),[14] he becomes one who sees reality' (*Mahābhārata, Anuśāsana Parva* 16.2). Or it may be used more generally: if an offence against a brahmin is condemned, then it is all the more so that an offence against one of the Lord's people will be even more worthy of condemnation" (340).

Even caste distinctions are subordinate goods, lesser than the goods of being a devotee, and of treating all devotees with reverence. To remove caste distinctions would in his eyes be an evil, but to reserve dignity to brahmins alone would, sadly, turn out to be the greater evil. Again, the modern reader might well think that the abolition of caste would be a safer path to take in ensuring mutual respect in the community, but Deśika disagrees; nor, of course, would he be the only religious leader to insist on the preservation of hierarchies of religious power despite the dangers inherent in them.

The chapter ends with verses that, in lieu of summary, articulate several major sentiments. Three Sanskrit ślokas indicate that sin can be overcome in four ways, stages that reshape one's intentions:

Remorse, refraining from sin, planning on reparation,
then accomplishing it:

due to these four, one after the other, all sins perish.
For those who were despondent in the past or become so in the future,
the act of taking refuge will not differ even if [the evil] to be terminated
    varies in degree.
Thus, a single act of refuge suffices for quieting at once all lesser and
    greater evils.

(340–41)

This change of heart works with both greater and lesser sins, since the fundamental act of refuge is unchanging and capable of rectifying every situation. Then, a Tamil verse tells us that refuge with the Lord—intentional union, the chosen good—defeats evil and its effects; the innate divine sweetness softens and enlivens hearts previously trapped by their deeds:

With inner dread at powerful, persistent deeds,
    seeking refuge at the lotus feet of the Lord who measured the worlds,
people renounce all that karma flourishing like weeds;
to prevent that infantile situation from recurring,
    there wells up the honey of our Lord's grace.

(341)

A final Sanskrit verse introduces contractual language but still culminates in a very tender image, in order to indicate that evil is stopped in its tracks by the Lord's grace:

The Lord casts aside all prior sins—
    excepting effects are already under way—
and sins happening inadvertently after taking-refuge,
plus any portion [of sin] to which we did not assent,
even if its effects are already under way—
for now we have laid down [the burden]; moreover,
there will arise no later intentional sins,
and even if such occur,
they will be done away with, and
even if a person is hard [of heart],
    by instruction our Lord frees [that person] from taint, and
He embraces him.

(341)

No evil is insurmountable, since the Lord's tender love wins over and keeps restoring to full-life all who have taken refuge.

Evil and good in a community formed through intentions

In conclusion, a few comments on Deśika's project and its meaning in a comparative context. Certainly, he succeeds in thinking of evil in a variety of ways in chapter 18:(1) physical defects and diseases; (2) unintentional but particular intentional transgression of religious law; (3) various degrees of the hardening of the heart; (4) a life shorter or longer than desired; (5) separation from the Lord; (6) evils—dissension, contempt, etc.—perpetrated and suffered in the community; and (7) responding to such evil with ill-will. This list is comprehensive, though not entirely so, since some kinds of evil are *not* considered in chapter 18 (nor elsewhere in the *RTS*). For instance, we hear nothing of large natural disasters or broad social upheavals. Even public disasters of which Deśika might have spoken from personal experience—such as the bloody sacking of Śrīraṅgam relatively late in his life—receive no mention. Instead, he aims to speak "inside" the Śrīvaiṣṇava community, for the most part without comment upon or message to the "outside" world.

His faith perspective makes sense, however, since his intended audience is the set of those able to see the world as God does, or at least with some sense of the divine plan in which nothing is accidental or merely meaningless. All evil exists in a web of interconnections among its various kinds: the natural and the social, linking the metaphysical, religious legal, personal, and social, all with respect to the will of the Lord as determinative of what is evil and good. There is continuity among evils and among goods; experiences of evil bear with them inevitable reference to larger and more important goods. Ill will and sin are inseparable natural evil and social evils of all sorts. Karma itself, now rendered intelligible as subservient to divine and human intentions, is enlisted for the sake of this pedagogical and "intentional" reading of evil, and God uses even the inexorable fruition of deeds for a salutary purpose.

Physical evils—disease, deformity, and death—are therefore not in a separate category; the physical, spiritual and mental, private and interactive/social, are all of a piece. All persons are involved in choices regarding evil and good, and there is no brute evil that is not woven into the matrix of intention and instruction. All evil is reconstrued as a matter of human and divine choices. Gratuitous or unintelligible evil is therefore ruled out, and no kind of evil fails to have a place in the divine plan for those who trust in the Lord. Since the Lord's intentions are good and cannot be frustrated, all evil is therefore re-signified within the realm of the intelligible, and read as serving a good purpose. Accordingly, however, intentional evils that violate the right relationship among members of the community are to be ranked as the worst of evils.

Reflection on evil is therefore reflection on how good people still suffer evil and even do evil; once the intentions underlying suffering are understood, it is also a recognition of how such evil counts to a good purpose. For those who have taken refuge, experiences of suffering are always instructive, communication between a Lord who intends salvation and a devotee who has surrendered her or his life to that purposeful Lord. This Lord has no interest in merely punishing devotees; divine anger is a function of divine compassion, intended to help humans (particularly those who have taken refuge) to live up to choices they have already irrevocably made. The human drama is therefore not really a drama at all, if one has in mind a grand contest between good and evil. There is no question of dualism, nor of an independent force of evil opposed to the Lord and in enmity of humans. In the long run, evil cannot possibly be victorious, and no suffering need be meaningless. Evils, lesser goods, and even the commands of religious law, are subordinate to the immeasurable good of refuge with Nārāyaṇa with Śrī. Deśika weaves all this into a comprehensive and persuasive theology, and it might be concluded, without too much exaggeration, that the *RTS* is a testament to the triumph of theology over evil.

Of course, there are limitations to Deśika's project. We cannot say that the eighteenth chapter of the *RTS*, however richly complex it is, presents *the* typical Hindu view of evil; the many Hindu traditions contain still other views of evil worthy of consideration. But Deśika is a thoughtful interpreter of human experience and of the sufferings that are inevitable for human beings for whom evil is framed by God and God's plan for the world, and we have much to learn from his theology—even if his representation of suffering and evil can be honestly contested by those among us who are less confident about the intelligibility of the world. Certain dimensions of his position may predictably (and to an extent legitimately) be criticized as idealizing and perpetuating a status quo that may work theologically, yet in the end still be insufferable to many of those who cannot escape its reach. And while there is room in his worldview for change and the eradication of evil—a life lived according to chapter 18 of the *RTS* would be better than very many alternatives—it may still seem that too much emphasis is placed on accepting God's will in whatever nature or society brings.

Yet in its specificity lie certain advantages as well. Other religious differences aside, Deśika's theistic religious reading of evil turns out to stand in close proximity to classical Christian understandings of why we suffer and what that suffering means. Consider for instance this small passage from Thomas Aquinas' *Summa Theologica*, on the question, "Can anything happen outside the order of the Divine government?" (I.103.7):

> It is possible for an effect to result outside the order of some particular cause; but not outside the order of the universal cause. The reason of this is that no effect results outside the order of a particular cause, except through some other impeding cause; which other cause must itself be reduced to the first universal cause; as indigestion may occur outside the order of the nutritive power by some such impediment as the coarseness of the food, which again

is to be ascribed to some other cause, and so on till we come to the first universal cause.[15]

Against this background he draws a conclusion very close to Deśika's own:

Therefore as God is the first universal cause, not of one genus only, but of all being in general, it is impossible for anything to occur outside the order of the Divine government; but from the very fact that from one point of view something seems to evade the order of Divine providence considered in regard to one particular cause, it must necessarily come back to that order as regards some other cause.

The first objection and response also share Deśika's sense that evil is forever being transformed in accord with the divine plan:

Objection 1. It would seem possible that something may occur outside the order of the Divine government. For Boethius says (*On the Consolation of Philosophy* 3) that "God disposes all for good." Therefore, if nothing happens outside the order of the Divine government, it would follow that no evil exists.

Reply to Objection 1. There is nothing wholly evil in the world, for evil is ever founded on good, as shown above (I.48.3). Therefore something is said to be evil through its escaping from the order of some particular good. If it wholly escaped from the order of the Divine government, it would wholly cease to exist.

Similarly, the following text from Aquinas's *Summa contra Gentiles* on the topic "That God Frees Some Men from Sin and Leaves Others in Sin" (III.162) echoes Deśika's understanding of God's interaction with sinners. God's plan always includes working with sinners to change them:

Now, although the man who sins puts an impediment in the way of grace, and as far as the order of things requires he ought not to receive grace, yet, since God can act apart from the order implanted in things, as He does when He gives signs to the blind or life to the dead—at times, out of the abundance of His goodness, He offers His help in advance, even to those who put an impediment in the way of grace, turning them away from evil and toward the good.

Even evident sufferings and apparent evils are part of God's overall construction of the good:

And just as He does not enlighten all the blind, or heal all who are infirm, in order that the working of His power may be evident in the case of those

whom He heals, and in the case of the others the order of nature may be
observed, so also, He does not assist with His help all who impede grace, so
that they may be turned away from evil and toward the good, but only some,
in whom He desires His mercy to appear, so that the order of justice many be
manifested in the other cases. Hence, the Apostle says, in *Romans* (9.22–23):
"What if God, willing to show His wrath and to make His power known,
endured with much patience vessels of His wrath, fitted for destruction, that
He might show the riches of His glory on the vessels of mercy which He hath
prepared unto glory?"

Like Deśika, Aquinas precludes taking prior births as a satisfactory explanation:
"By this we set aside the error of Origen, who said that certain men are converted to God, and not others, because of some works that their souls had
done before being united to their bodies. In fact, this view has been carefully
disproved in our Book Two."[16]

There is no reason not to see Deśika and Aquinas as allies sharing the same
goal of putting evil back in its subordinate place, giving meaning to suffering
and hope to those who suffer, more forcefully extolling the goodness of God,
and, in the end, bolstering a comparative project that uses discourses on evil for
the sake of a even greater good than the one that either theological tradition
could have envisioned on its own.

Notes

[1] Throughout, "the Lord" will ordinarily be used as shorthand for "Nārāyaṇa with
Śrī."

[2] Here and throughout, I offer my own translations from the *Śrīmad Rahasyatrayasāra*, using Vedānta Deśika, *Śrīmadrahasyatrayasāra*, edited and annotated by
Śrī Rāmadeśikācāryar Swami, and page references are to this edition (Śrīrangam:
Śrīmad Andavan Śrī Pundarikapuram Swami Asramam, 2000). I have also consulted
the standard commentaries, including the edition by Śrīsaila Venkataranganatha
Mahadeshikar and Raghunatha Tatayaryadasar (Kumbakonam, 1903–1931) that
includes the *Sārāsvādinī* of Vedānta Rāmānuja (cc. 1–12) and Gopāla Deśika
(cc. 13–32) and the *Sāraprakāśikā of Śrīnivasa;* the "Cetlur" commentary by Tiruva-
hindrapuram Cetlur Narasimhacary Svami (Chennai: Rahasyatrayasara Pracarana
Sabha, 1920); and the modern commentary by Uttamur T. Viraraghavacharya,
Śrīmad Rahasyatrayasāra with the *Sāravistaram,* 2 vols. (Madras: Ubhayavedanta
Granthamalai, 1980). Although I offer my own translations, I also recommend for
comparison the English translation by M. R. Rajagopala Ayyangar, *Śrīmad
Rahasyatrayasāra* (Kumbakonam: Agnihotram Ramanuja Thathachariar, 1956).

[3] One additional kind of evil, emphasized in the prefatory "Essence of the Lineage
of Teachers" (*Guruparamparāsāra*) and in chapters 30 and 31, which deal respectively with the duties of the teaching and student, deserves particular mention:
whatever undercuts or threatens the proper transmission of tradition is evil in

a very basic and practical way. Tradition itself is the vehicle of the preservation and transmission of all that is good, and dangers to the community and its transmission of knowledge are a kind of immediate and most pressing evil. The *RTS* itself, it follows, including its teachings on good and evil, is itself an act of the immediate good of enunciating and perpetuating the tradition.

4   On the subordination of karma to sovereign divine intentions in Hindu theology, see Francis X. Clooney, S.J., "Evil, Divine Omnipotence and Human Freedom: Vedanta's Theology of Karma," *Journal of Religion* 69 (1989): 530–48.

5   Attribution uncertain.

6   When the same Bhāghavatam (or Varāha) text is cited in chapter 20, Deśika includes also the *Mahābhārata* story of the deity Kuṇḍadhāra who, called upon with great devotion by a poor devotee seeking worldly benefits, instead instructs him on detachment, teaching him gratitude for his poverty.

7   Evil still has karmic overtones; choices made in previous lives work out here, in what one does, in what others do, and how one suffers. Past evils shape kinds of persons who become harder or softer of heart. But karma operates only within boundaries; it is neither undercut nor allowed to gainsay the dominant intention of persons who have taken refuge with the Lord, and in any case, the Lord uses karma for corrective and salvific purposes. Intention governs both good and evil.

8   Deśika does not consider crimes such as murder, rape, and theft, and presumably is assuming a common disapproval of these; he is concerned rather with more subtle evils within the community.

9   The reference is not clear, since this point seems not to be made at UMS 3.4.51.

10 See particularly chapter 25.

11 These are two of the songs of the most important of the Āḻvār poets of the earlier Tamil Vaiṣṇava tradition; both songs stress devotion to the community of those devoted to the Lord.

12 The Śāṇḍilī–Garuḍa encounter, narrated in the *Mahābhārata*'s "Udyoga Kāṇḍa 112", is a complicated episode involving Garuḍa's selfish intentions and Śāṇḍilī's generous forgiveness.

13 Respectively, Hanumān advising Sugrīva, Sugrīva speaking to Lakṣamaṇa, and Lakṣamaṇa replying to Sugrīva.

14 *Vipra* often indicates a brahmin.

15 Here and below I use the *Summa Theologica* as translated by the Fathers of the English Dominican Province (Notre Dame, IN: Ave Maria Press, Inc., 1948).

16 In *Summa contra Gentiles* II.44 and 83. I have used the *Summa Contra Gentiles* as translated by Vernon J. Bourke (Notre Dame, IN: University of Notre Dame Press, 1975).

Can Evil Be Redeemed? Unorthodox Tensions in Eastern Orthodox Theology

Kimberley C. Patton
Harvard Divinity School

There was a roar and a great confusion of noise. Fires leaped up and licked the roof. The throbbing grew to a great tumult, and the Mountain shook. Sam ran to Frodo and picked him up and carried him up and carried him out to the door. And there upon the dark threshold of the Sammath Naur, high above the plains of Mordor, such wonder and terror came upon him that he stood still forgetting all else, and gazed as one turned to stone . . .

"Well, this is the end, Sam Gamgee," said a voice by his side. And there was Frodo, pale and worn, and yet himself again; and in his eyes there was peace now, neither strain of will, nor madness, nor any fear. His burden was taken away. There was the dear master of the sweet days in the Shire.

"Master!" cried Sam, and fell upon his knees. In all that ruin of the world for the moment he felt only joy, great joy. The burden was gone. His master had been saved; he was himself again, he was free. And then Sam caught sight of the maimed and bleeding hand.

"You poor hand!" he said. "And I have nothing to bind it with, or comfort it. I would have spared him a whole hand of mine rather. But he's gone now beyond recall, gone for ever."

"Yes," said Frodo. "But do you remember Gandalf's words: Even Gollum may have something yet to do? *But for him, Sam, I could not have destroyed the Ring. The Quest would have been in vain, even at the bitter end. So let us forgive him! For the Quest is achieved, and now all is over. I am glad you are here with me. Here at the end of all things, Sam."*

J. R. R. Tolkein, *The Return of the King*[1]

Tolkein's majestic vision of the "end of all things," the destruction of evil itself as embodied in the figure of Sauron, would-be Lord of the Rings, is not Christian "allegory"; Tolkein repudiated any allegorical interpretation for his trilogy. However, with its themes of evil warlord defeated, nefarious purpose thwarted, ultimate darkness exploded, proud height brought low, black tower crumbling, and treachery itself betrayed as fire and chaos consume the world, *The Return of the King* draws as richly from Christian apocalyptic as it does from the Old Norse Ragnarök, its other chief source of inspiration. The downfall is a tale that is told in many religious traditions. In the end, the struggle between the powers of good and evil, inaugurated at the beginning of time, will be resolved, and evil, whatever its origins, will be vanquished forever.

In the Eastern Christian tradition, Satan, the personification of evil twinned with death as a primeval curse upon humanity, is first "mocked" in his abode in Hades by Christ's entry into His realm at the crucifixion.[2] Then he is destroyed in the eschaton, when after his brief release from his thousand-year confinement in the pit, he will be thrown into the "lake of fire and sulfur, where the beast and the false prophet were, and they will be tormented day and night forever" (Rev. 20.7–20); the heavenly Jerusalem will be revealed where God's Lamb, Jesus, will be enthroned. Echoing The Revelation to John, *The Return of the King* tells how after the terrible ordeal of Frodo and Sam at Mordor, the Númenorian heir Aragorn at last accedes to his throne in the shining city of Minas Tirith at Gondor, and is crowned king of Middle Earth. His restoration, which the new king himself "sings in" with an ancient hymn of his ancestral home across the sea, ushers in a messianic age of peace, righteousness, and fertility, one that parallels both the final triumph of good in the Christian Revelation and the greening rebirth of the earth from the depths of the sea in the Norse *Völuspá*.[3] *The Return of the King* is self-consciously bardic eschatology—a modern yet archaizing version of the kingdom of heaven made manifest on earth. As such, it is deeply satisfying to the Western religious imagination insofar as it corresponds to the sacred narratives of the West. For Tolkein, evil's destiny is clear: at the end, the unblinking eye of Sauron, he of the fallen angelic race of the Ainur and servant of the eldest and greatest of them, Morgoth, lies fallen and destroyed. Like the prowling Satan of the New Testament, re-cast by Dante as a teratomatic horror eternally lodged upside-down in the seventh, lowest circle in Canto 34 of the *Inferno*, and by Milton as the self-loathing monarch who cannot escape himself in *Paradise Lost* ("Which way I fly is hell; I myself am hell"), Sauron once aspired to rival Ilúvatar, the God of Middle-Earth, as a creator and source of power. As mythographer David Colbert explains, millennia before the action of the trilogy, Sauron deceived a group of human beings into "defying the angelic spirits. As a result, the beautiful island home of the humans [was] destroyed. The few humans who survive[d] [were] driven to Middle-Earth, just as Adam and Eve [were] driven from Eden."[4] Tolkein himself wrote in a letter that the most important message of *The Lord of the Rings* is "about God, and His sole right to divine honor."[5]

Why is evil allowed to roam the earth, afflicting the innocent before the eyes of a loving, omnipotent God? And what will be the fate of evil at the end of the days we know? Christian theodicy has long struggled for rational coherence between three of its central, apparently irreconcilable tenets. These are, as Paul Ricoeur articulates them in *The Symbolism of Evil*: that God is omnipotent; that God is good; and that Evil exists.[6] The final separation of the admixture of evil and good in a future age has strong scriptural support. There will be a reckoning of those who have chosen the wrong side, along with the ultimate binding and destruction of evil itself, the hypostasis of all that has corrupted God's purposes and thwarted His goodness during the age of the world. Revelation's hallucinatory visions of a final fiery struggle, ending the *agon* between dual powers in an inferno that consumes even the sea, is anticipated in the Gospels by Jesus' own prophecies. Both New Testament and patristic eschatologies insist on a "final solution" to the problem of evil. This is one that despite its ethicizing bears all the characteristics of a cosmic warfare comparable to those known to the Norse or the Aztecs. The last conflict will be accompanied by a complete cleansing of the world, which suffers in the Christian religious imagination from an ancient Greek-style *miasma*, that is, a contamination both ritual and moral that can only be supernaturally cured.

It is a mistake to see the Christian apocalypse only as myth, since early Christians understood their apocalyptic as near-future history. These events would fulfill in time, not outside of it, moral trajectories that had been set in motion at the creation of the world. Eastern Orthodox Christian tradition has absolutely affirmed this "history of the future." In the *parousia*, divine justice will prevail over divine mercy; the human and angelic communities will be sorted between the saved and the damned; and evil will be destroyed forever. All of this will entail eternal and irrevocable transformation. As the contemporary Greek Orthodox theologian John Chryssavgis has written, "The Orthodox Church holds the correct position concerning the relation between God's love and justice. In this present life, God's love for man predominates as He patiently waits for man to repent and return to Him, while during the second coming (and from that point forward), God's justice will be activated and fully operational."[7] In other words, there is a point in sacred history beyond which evil cannot and will not be redeemed. In the traditional view, God's mercy will obtain before death, as repentance continually opens wide the door of reconciliation to God, and the erasure of sin. However, at the Second Coming, God's justice will prevail over his mercy (the tension between these two being a key theme of rabbinical theology, as for example in *b. Berakhot* 7b). Woe will be the lot of those who are cast out from the circle of God's regard, for evil itself will be immolated, burning being the most permanent form of ritualized destruction. All those who have chosen evil will endure eternal torment from unquenchable fire and the undying worm.

The patristic writers developed this idea of a sequential moral evaluation, whereby God's mercy will be superseded by his wrath. For example, in his

commentary on Ps. 100.2 ("Of mercy and judgment will I sing unto Thee"),
St. Basil the Great says:

> He combines mercy with justice, so that the precise judgment may be tem-
> pered with mercy. For he says: "If Thou shouldest mark inequities, O Lord,
> who shall stand?" (Ps. 129:3). . . . He is merciful, but also a judge. For "He
> loves mercy and justice," and this is why the Psalmist now says, "Of mercy and
> judgment will I sing unto Thee.". . . . And Hesychios says: "But before judge-
> ment he projects mercy. For our Judge is merciful; however, not when he
> judges, but now when He does not yet exercise judgment. *So then, mercy is for
> the present time, while judgement for the future.* Singing thusly, we are neither able
> to despair nor able to disregard sin. And Theodoret says: "Christ's former
> appearance contained much mercy, while His second will contain justice. For
> 'we must all appear before the judgement seat of Christ, that everyone may
> receive the things done in his body, according to what he hath done, whether
> it be good or bad' (2 Cor. 5:10)." (Italics mine.)[8]

In patristic theology, "the Last Judgement" will be exactly that,[9] with a definitive
separation of good from evil for all time, followed by the utter annihilation of
the latter.

It is startling, then, to discover a powerful minority opinion on this question
within Orthodox theology, one with an ancient heritage and prominent exponents—not all of them excommunicated, and not all of them dead. This
heterodox, or to be more precise, "unorthodox" tension within Orthodox theology, centers around the question of whether evil in fact *can* be redeemed at
the end of time, and potentially restored along with every other human soul or
demon that had chosen evil over goodness. To this question, theologians of the
stature of Origen, St. Gregory of Nyssa, and St. Isaac the Syrian have answered
yes. The condemnation of evil may not in fact be permanent. Rather, in this
alternative narrative, God's dual attributes of omnipotence and superabundant
love compel even the damned, even the demons, perhaps even Satan himself,
to turn back to the Source of life and be re-absorbed. This view holds that evil
can and in fact must be redeemed, else God's omnipotence and love remain
imperfectly expressed for all eternity. Eternal damnation is impossible, or, as
the Athonite abbot St. Silouan murmured when confronted with a hermit who,
with satisfaction, would not pray for those burning in hell, "Love could not bear
that."[10]

More recently, the possibility of the redemption of all, known as "universal
salvation," has been taken up in modern Orthodox theology: among other
sources, in the *vita* of the aforementioned nineteenth- and earlier twentieth-
century saint Silouan by Archimandrite Sophrony Sakharov; in the writings of

Metropolitan Hierotheos of Nafpaktos, particularly in his defense of Gregory of Nyssa;[11] in the teachings of the late twentieth-century mystic and missionary Father Lazarus of India; and most recently, in the final chapter of the first volume of Bishop Kallistos Ware's *Collected Works,* entitled "Dare We Hope for the Salvation of All?"[12] Ware, perhaps the most important contemporary Orthodox systematic theologian alive today, carefully weighs the arguments for and against the ultimate redemption of evil. He concludes that God's very nature, and the inexorability of his soteriological agency in the world, must necessitate a cautious but well-grounded Christian hope that perdition cannot be permanent, and that there is no such thing as "lost forever," even for evil itself. Evil can indeed be redeemed, and probably will be. Echoing Ricoeur, Ware notes that this must require the final rapprochement of the two principles "God is love" and "Free will exists," and that such "ultimate harmonization remains a mystery beyond our present comprehension." "Hell exists as a possibility because free will exists. Yes, trusting in the inexhaustible attractiveness of God's love, we venture to express the hope—it is no more than a hope—that, in the end, like Walter de la Mare's Traveller, we shall find that there is nobody there."[13]

This is not some kind of well-intentioned contemporary project to tone down hell, and to recover a "kinder, gentler" theodicy within traditional Christian eschatology. Unlike some progressive theology that has selectively searched Christianity for "resources" to ameliorate, in the present day, the tradition's unsavory history of misogyny, anti-Semitism, or the abuse of animals, for example, this unorthodox strand of belief in universal salvation has existed since the earliest centuries of the early Christian Church. It is an authentic challenge to traditional eschatology, one that argues for hope for the damned and the demons. It draws authoritative strength from passages within the New Testament itself, both the Gospels and the Epistles, which seem to propose an alternative view to the Matthean vision of an eternal separation of good and evil. It is an integrative theology whereby evil—or better, those who have completely identified themselves with evil—will actually turn and then return to their Source, changing their nature to good, in order to conform to the nature of the first principle of the cosmos.

That this issue remains a live one, bitterly contested, is attested by a glance at any number of contemporary Orthodox theologians and hierarchs who continue vehemently to repudiate the doctrine of universal salvation. Why is this essential question about the ultimate fate of evil and those who choose it still alive at all in Orthodox theological deliberation? Why was the matter not laid to rest centuries ago, as the members of the Fifth Ecumenical Council intended? In Constantinople in 553 they anathematized Origen's teaching of the *apokatastasis,* the final "restoration of everything," along with his belief in the pre-existence of souls and their ability to reincarnate to the resulting betterment or detriment of their moral condition, so closely resembling ancient

Indian ideas of *karma* and *samsara*. How can the ultimate fate of evil, and the question of whether it can finally be redeemed, still be up in the air in a Church whose central dogmas have been emphatically ratified through conciliar debate and so often written in blood?

Esoteric teachings about exoteric topics

Within this tension, a subsurface roiling beneath traditional theological waters, another important polarity emerges: revelation versus hiddenness. Traditionalists who hold that evil will be ultimately destroyed almost invariably speak with the clarity of certain revelation, or even with a kind of satisfaction, like St. Silouan's hermit ("God will punish all atheists. They will burn in everlasting fire.").[14] We might consider the aesthetic as well as the moral aspect of traditional Christian eschatology: it packs the punch of a final purification, a great "tidying-up" that ends confusion and the ambiguity of the *chiaroscuro* of preceding degenerate ages. The deserving will be rewarded, the wicked punished, and it will all last forever. By contrast, however, the "opposition" has always spoken of universal salvation in the coded language of esotericism or even of apophaticism. Those who hold open the possibility of an ultimate restoration of all and a redemption of evil regard the teaching as unfit for public consumption with volatile and even dangerous potential. As we have seen, Kallistos Ware calls it "a mystery beyond our present comprehension." Thus, paradoxically, the idea of universal salvation at the end of time—an exoteric doctrine if ever there was one—is an esoteric treasure revealed to only a few, and guarded by them with care.

We might note three justifications for this reluctance to assert the redemption of evil with the same emphatic righteousness that attends the theology of the traditionalists. The first is certainly the "face-value" philosophical problem raised by Ware: the doctrine of universal salvation seems to offer a counter-intuitive "take" on divine justice and the notion that free will carries with it the consequences of every human (or angelic) decision. The second reason for esotericism concerns the idea that salvation will ultimately be available to *all* sentient beings with moral capacity. The "danger," and the reason that this possibility has been occulted or represented as a mystery, has certainly to do with its implications for right conduct here and now. Without permanent consequences, what meaning does the gift of free will retain; what power does guilt or repentance have in lived religion; what stands as deterrent to lawlessness or the reckless choice of sin? This justification of the doctrine of the redemption of evil is intimately bound up with moral, religious, and of course societal controls, and it is fed by the fear of the widespread disintegration of the social fabric.

All of this seems understandable. But the level of the teaching that seems to have rendered it most oddly and insistently "esoteric" concerns the redemption of Satan. The language of secrecy represents a reluctance to trespass too far into metaphysics, as many believe Origen did, by contemplating the final fate of evil, in particular of its hypostasis, the devil. That is a question that inspires great uneasiness; speculation enters an arena that does not and even should not concern mortals, just as the four rabbis caught up from the earth into the seven levels of PaRDeS suffered so heinously (*b. Hagigah* 14b). The quasi-gnostic atmosphere surrounding the alternate "future history" of the cosmos, a vision that with its radical universalism challenges the tradition from which it comes, is a chronic feature of these unorthodox tensions in orthodox theology.

Variant monotheistic models of the nature of evil

Why is Satan allowed to attack the human heart and to have free reign in the affairs of the world? In his book *The Savage God*, Zoroastrianism scholar R. C. Zaehner seeks to force monotheists to confront the tensions of a *coinciden-tium oppositorum* in the godhead. He sees this manifest in the divine killing sprees of Biblical Judaism and in the powerful dichotomies of Islamic theology—in his Qu'rānic epithets, for example, God is Compassionate (*Ar-Raḥmān*) and Merciful (*Ar-Raḥim*), but he is at the same time "the Subduer (*Al-Qahhār*)," "the Tyrant (*Al-Jabbār*)," and "the Distresser (*Ad-Dārr*)"; more deceptive than Satan if need be, he is "the best of the wiley ones" (S. 3:54). This "evil in God" is expressed, in Zaehner's view, even in the central event of Christianity, "for it is he who tortured his son to death to 'save' first the Jews and then the Gentiles."[15] "[I]t would appear that there is evil in the very heart of God . . . You cannot put the blame on man or even on Satan; you have to blame, if blame you must, him who is alone responsible, God, the creator of Heaven and earth."[16] Islamicist Peter Awn shows that since in the monotheistic theologies evil is not identified as it is in Indian traditions with the body or illusions of the material realm, sin is therefore interpreted as:

> an act of disobedience against a transcendent God whose ways are ultimately beyond human knowing. . . . In Zaehner's view, the *saevus deus* of Judaism, Christianity, and Islam is not exempt . . . from those paradoxical inner tensions that wreak havoc in the world by creating suffering and pain, whose meaning is inaccessible to human comprehension. In the cosmos governed by the God of revelation, men and women must pinpoint the source of their affliction within the godhead, and not relegate it simply to the material realm.[17]

In certain strands of Sufi thought, such a theodicy is embraced as a logical consequence of radical monotheism. In *The Song of Gabriel's Wings*, for example, the

Persian medieval thinker Suhrawardī draws heavily from pre-Islamic Zoroastrian angelology to describe the archangel Gabriel's two wings. The right one, of pure light, is connected to the Absolute Being of God. But the left is turned from God and toward nonexistence. For the Qur'ān, Suhrawardī reminds us, says, "He made the darkness and the light" (S. 6.1): "This World of Deception is the song and shadow of Gabriel's wing, that is, his left wing, while enlightened souls derive from his right wing."[18]

In the Hebrew Bible, "evil" might almost be conceived as an aspect of the divine. In the ancient Israelite religious imagination, God struggles not against evil per se, but against malevolent forces of chaos known from Near Eastern precedents, often with marine associations, that threaten divine order and will be irrevocably constrained at the end. Biblical "evil" or "wickedness," however, is a deceptive entity that taints the choices of individuals and peoples; unlike in gnostic theologies, or, as we will see, to some extent in Christian scripture, it is not a separate, autonomous force with cosmic status. One can instead read "evil" as a dimension of the God of Israel, its actions and consequences always subject to and never independent from his purview and purpose. In Genesis, the serpent, the ancestor of the devil, beguiles, but does not compel; it is human weakness, specifically attached to Eve, the woman, that introduces into human existence affliction of every kind, including painful, permanent human exile from divine proximity and intimacy. It is extrapolating from the Adamic myth in particular that Ricoeur locates ambivalence in the nature of God, echoing Zaehner, but without the latter's bitter desire to compel monotheistic theology to confront its unacknowledged secret:

> We can speak of a tragic aspect in the Adamic myth, expressed in the deep and shadowy psychology of temptation. There is a sort of fatalistic side of the ethical confession of sins. But there is also an irreducible remainder of the theogonic combat, which can be seen in the figure of the serpent and in other biblical figures related to the primordial chaos. What is more, the essentially ethical affirmation of God's saintliness can never entirely rid us of the suspicion that God is somehow beyond good and evil and that for this very reason he sends evil as well as good.[19]

In Job, Satan, the "Adversary," is a member of God's council, a kind of quality-control agent who spends his time "walking to and fro upon the earth" looking for mortals to test. He is not *God's* Adversary but ours. Indeed, the close reader of the Hebrew Bible may be chilled as the Lord unleashes Satan to test Job's piety and lay waste his children, as the Lord creeps in the form of his angel of death, "the Destroyer," through the streets of Egypt in Exodus 12, as Satan tempts David to conduct an unlawful census in 1 Chronicles, and God in anger strikes down 70,000 innocent Israelites, or as the same named angel of death draws his sword to destroy the entire city of Jerusalem. Silently, ominously standing by the threshing-floor of Ornan the Jebusite, the Destroyer does not sheathe his sword until David, in humility and desperation, purchases the threshing-floor and all its equipment and livestock from Ornan in order to construct an altar and perform a sacrifice: the place becomes the site of the Holy of Holies in Solomon's Temple.[20]

A theodicy that constructs evil as an instrument of God's purpose remains in early Jewish Christian thought prior to its encounter with neo-Platonism. One has to look no further than the Johannine version of the betrayal of Jesus by Judas. Even though "Jesus knew that his hour had come to depart from this world and go the Father" (Jn. 13.1), divine providence does not play out directly but through the workings of evil: "The devil had already put it into the heart of Judas son of Simon to betray him" (Jn. 13.2). Similarly, we have Paul's startling prescription for a man in the Corinthian community who is living with his father's wife: "When you are assembled, and my spirit is present with the power of our Lord Jesus, you are to hand this man over to Satan for the destruction of the flesh, so that his spirit may be saved in the day of the Lord" (1 Cor. 5.4–5).

However, in the majority of the New Testament, the nature and personification of evil has clearly been differentiated from its more integral role in the Israelite godhead. Influenced by the explosion of Jewish angelology and demonology in the Hellenistic period, in turn most likely by the result of historical interaction with Indo-Iranian and proto-gnostic cosmogonies, as well as Babylonian magical systems, the Gospels, Epistles, and Revelation present a far more menacing world. Satan and his legions wage active war against God's son, his people, and every orientation toward good. "Like a roaring lion your adversary the devil prowls around, looking for someone to devour" (I Pt. 5.8). If, *contra* oriental dualistic theologies, the devil and his legions were "created" or at least permitted by God to exist, the contingency of their powers is almost completely suppressed in the guerilla warfare set forth in the New Testament and early Christian writings.

By the same token, the free will granted the first couple in Eden has its consequences. Jesus' own teachings on the matter seem utterly clear. In the end, those who have chronically chosen evil, including Evil itself, and have not availed themselves of repentance, will suffer consequences that are eternal and irreversible. In Matthew 13, Jesus compares the kingdom of heaven to a net that catches fish of every kind, but from which the good are sorted from the bad: "So it will be at the end of the ages. The angels will come out and separate the evil from the righteous and throw them into the furnace of fire, where there will be weeping and gnashing of teeth" (Matt. 13.49–50).[21] This vision, however, is only an allusive anticipation of the unrelenting, final division of the righteous from the unrighteous on the Day of the Lord offered by Jesus in Matt. 25.31–32, in which "the Son of Man comes in his glory, all the angels with him, then he will sit on the throne of his glory. All the nations will be gathered before him, and he will separate people one from another as a shepherd separates the sheep from the goats, and he will put the sheep at his right hand and the goats at his left." For their compassion shown to the Lord when he took the form of a stranger, one who thirsts or hungers, or a prisoner, the righteous will inherit "the kingdom prepared for you from the foundation of the world."

> Then he will say to those at his left hand, 'You that are accursed, depart from me into the eternal fire prepared for the devil and his angels; for I was hungry and you gave me no food, I was thirsty and you gave me nothing to drink, I was a stranger and you did not welcome me, naked and you did not give me clothing, sick and in prison and you did not visit me.' . . . And these will go away into eternal punishment, but the righteous into eternal life. (Matt. 13.41–43; 46)

The place for the righteous—the kingdom—has been ready for them since the beginning of time, although they were free during their lives to choose their destinies. But the place for the accursed, the fire where they will dwell forever, interestingly, was not prepared for them specifically, but rather, "for the devil and his angels." This final fate of evil, its irreversible destruction without hope of redemption, is so definitively expounded in the Gospels, and then so dramatically realized in Revelation, that it is hard to imagine any alternative eschatological scenario.

And yet one exists. The subversive doctrine of universal salvation also has its *locus classicus* in the New Testament, in the Book of Acts, in the phrase ἀποκατάστασις πάντων, "the restoration of everything" to grace. In the name of Jesus Christ, Peter heals a man lame from birth, begging as he did daily at the Beautiful Gate of the temple. He then addresses the astonished crowd:

> You Israelites, why do you wonder at this, or why do you stare at us, as though by our own power or piety we had made him walk?. . . Repent therefore, so that your sins may be wiped out, so that times of refreshing may come from the presence of the Lord, and that he may send the Messiah appointed for you, that is, Jesus, who must remain in heaven until the time of universal restoration [ἀποκαταστάσεως πάντων] that God announced long ago through his holy prophets. (Acts 3.12, 19–21)

What is at stake in Peter's exposition? How far did that "restoration of all things" extend? To the righteous, awaiting the reunion of their souls with their bodies, and their joyous entry into heaven? Even for the wicked, trapped in the fires? What about the devil himself? Acts does not say, but the unrestricted construction of God's nature, salvific for all, even if they do not accept Christ, is a linchpin for Paul's apparent "opening of the door" in 1 Timothy 4.9-10: "Timothy, my son, the saying is sure and worthy of full acceptance. For to this end we toil and strive, because we have our hope set on the living God, who is the Savior of all men, especially of those who believe."

Apokatastasis has a long history in the ancient Mediterranean thought-world. Suggestively, it grew from the notion of *physical* restoration to an original condition, and thus from the beginning occupied the semantic field not of morality but of medicine or "therapy." Plato used the root verb in a physical sense: *kathistanai* in *Philebus* 42d refers to the re-establishment of normalcy following physical alteration. Hence in the corpus of Hippocrates (1258) or of Aretaeus (9.22), the addition of the prefix "apo-" creates a word that means a return of someone who is sick back to health; Hellenistic medical references speak of the *apokatastasis* or "re-setting" of joints. Polybius (4.23.1; 3.99.6) uses it to indicate the re-establishment of civil peace or the re-integration of an individual into his or her family.[22] As is characteristic of earlier Hellenistic thought, whereby physical "salvation" or "restoration" was increasingly sublimated, Origen's extreme spiritualization of the term is already anticipated in "the perfect *apokatastasis* of the soul" of Philo Judaeus in his *Who is the Heir* (293). Philo's usage of term indicates, as Robert Turcan notes, "the philosophical healing that follows the two stages of infancy, first unformed and then corrupt. The soul recovers the health of its primitive state after a series of disturbances."[23] *Apokathistanai* is used by the Septuagint to translate Jeremiah's vision of the end of the exile in Babylon and the return of the Jews to the Holy Land. The word always bears a certain cyclicity, and with it, a sense of *therapeutic intervention* for the ultimate good of the sufferer or the exile. This therapeutic thread mattered deeply to the patristic defenders of *apokatastasis*.

Patristic sources and debates

Origen and Apokatastasis

It was, however, to Greek philosophical and astrological ideas of the *apokatastasis*, later amplified in gnostic apocalypses, that the seminal Christian thinker of the Antenicene period Origen (*c.* 185–254) responded. It is in this intellectual and historical context that he must be read. As far back as Heraclitus and perhaps earlier, and extending forward into the works of Aristotle, Plato, the Stoics, and later Ciceronian and neo-Platonic thought, Greek speculative philosophy featured a "Great Year" of varying lengths involving the entire cosmos. The Great Year cyclically ends with conflagration and palingenesis: the end always circles back to the beginning. The dominant idea, also found elsewhere in the thought of Basilides and in Manichaean *apokatastasis*, is the restoration of original order after a specified series of astral revolutions.

The Alexandrian theologian Origen apparently sought to counter the influence of gnostic cosmogonies by positing a Christian *apokatastasis*, whereby there is "a restoration of true piety toward God," as he wrote in *Against Celsus* 7.3. All souls will return to their original (non-corporeal) state: "For the end is always like the beginning" (*First Principles* 6.2). Origen's doctrine of the final restoration is distinct from its Hellenic and Hellenistic analogues in its temporal constraints. As Robert Turcan notes, "it depends on God (and not upon sidereal revolutions) and is completed once and for all at the end of time, without being repeated indefinitely."[24]

But what was most revolutionary about Origen's *apokatastasis* was his insistence on universal salvation. In *First Principles* 6.1, he wrote, "The end of the world and the consummation will come when every soul shall be visited with the penalties due for its sins. This time when everyone shall pay what he owes, is known to God alone. We believe, however, that the goodness of God through Christ will restore His entire creation to one end, even His enemies being conquered and subdued."[25] In Origenist theodicy, evil, lacking substance or essence, is situated purely in the dialectic of rationality; it is the result of the misuse of the divine gift of free will. Hence one is always, even after death, free to choose the good, the quintessence of being.[26] Origin's metaphysics strongly depends on his doctrine of the pre-existence of souls, and the mechanism of their rebirth along a hierarchy of potentialities. Hence human beings are free through rational exercise of free will to be reincarnated either as angels or as demons. Even demons can indeed be saved, and there is no "point of no return." In Origen's *First Principles*, Peter's idea in Acts of *apokatastasis* receives its most radical expression. It is interesting to note that even in the first formal patristic expression of this controversial concept, later anathematized and rejected in the formulation of conciliar doctrine, there is an esoteric atmosphere. Origen strongly iterates his uncertainty about these matters, and an atmosphere of humility and mystery attends his articulation of the ultimate restoration of all to God and the endless possibility of the redemption of evil. "All *may* be saved, and all *may* fall." "Exactly how it will be is known to God alone, and to those who through Christ and the Holy Spirit are the 'friends' of God" (*First Principles* 6.4).

No stronger or more typical Orthodox response to Origen's eschatology can be found than in the liturgical text "Synodikon of Orthodoxy":

To those who accept and transmit the false and Greek sayings that there is pre-existence of souls and that all things do not come from non-being and who have given out that there is an end to hell or a restoration once more of creation and of human affairs, and for such reasons the Kingdom of Heaven is altogether done away with, and produces an insertion which betrays what Christ our God Himself taught and we have received from both the Old and the New Testaments, that both Hell is unending and the Kingdom is everlasting, who for such reasons destroy themselves and cause eternal condemnation to others . . . Anathema."[27]

And writing out of the modern Orthodox tradition, Oxonian M. C. Steenberg asserts that the efforts of Henri Crouzel, Joseph Wilson Trigg, and Jean Daniélou to rehabilitate Origen as a defender of the faith must be resisted:

> In the end, the doctrine of Universal Salvation cannot be faithfully paired with the more patristic notions of free will or final judgement, even though Origen energetically defends both. . . . He exaggerated the love of God to a degree that downplayed his righteousness: two features which the Church has been insistent to bring *together* in its teachings, rather than to separate. Here we must admit a severe flaw in Origen's thought. Ultimately, his view of universal restoration took the concept of free will full-circle, and ended with its absence; for if all are indeed to be restored to God, then the "choices" one makes in life are really not choices at all—for the ultimate fruit of the decision is already determined by God.[28]

Echoed in the attacks of Bishop Alexander and the more moderate considerations of Metropolitan Hierotheos (below), we see that the issue is still not defunct in modern Orthodox discourse. A teaching of predestination claiming that the exigency of divine Love must redeem all, even the exponents of evil, would seem to fall well outside the pale of Christian doctrine. Yet on this issue Ss. Gregory of Nyssa and Isaac the Syrian themselves stand with Origen, beyond that very pale. Somehow these saints retained their sanctified and communicant status. Why?

St. Gregory of Nyssa

Gregory, the student of Origen, rejects his teacher's teaching on the pre-existence of souls, and hence the possibility of reincarnation as an opportunity for all creatures, even the demons, to improve their ontological status in each successive life through the rejection of evil and the choice of the good. Nevertheless, Gregory's catechetical teachings retain Origen's view of evil as not-being and affirms the doctrine of *apokatastasis*, the ultimate restoration of everything, largely basing his support for this controversial idea on the inexorably compassionate nature of God. Unlike Origen, who argued for any number of future stages of existence before the final consummation and restoration of all, Gregory says that there are only two worlds, this world and the next (the temporal sequence to which we referred earlier). In *De anima et resurrectione* 227, it is in the next world that the ἀποκατάστασις πάντων will be effected through fire: "The avenging flame will be the more ardent the more it has to consume . . . But at last evil will be annihilated, *and the bad saved by nearness to the good*" (italics mine). Then all nature will join in thanksgiving. In *The Great Catechism*, this is presented in therapeutic, even medicalized terms:

For it is as now with those who for their cure are subjected to the knife and the cautery; they are angry with the doctors, and wince with the pain of the incision; but if the recovery of health be the result of this treatment, and the pain of the cautery passes away, they will feel grateful to those who have wrought this cure upon them. In like manner, when, after long periods of time, the evil of our nature, which is now mixed up with it and has grown with its growth, has been expelled, and when there has been a restoration of those who are now lying in Sin to their primal state, a harmony of thanksgiving will arise from all creation, as well as from those who in the process of the purgation have suffered chastisement, as from those who needed not any purgation at all.[29]

But this is exactly to what Bishop Alexander refers when he condemns the still extant view of the fires of hell as "a certain pedagogical method used for the rehabilitation of sinners": Gregory, following Origen and anticipating Isaac the Syrian, extends this therapeutic, corrective, and purifying potential of the flames of hell, which Isaac radically calls "the scourgings of love," into the eschaton. *The punishment of evil is not eternal because evil itself is not eternal.* The temporary, contingent nature of evil is exposed by Gregory's flaming *apokatastasis* and resolved by being burned away, but he who is completely identified with evil will be saved. "The great adversary . . ., as well as humanity, will be purged." The result, as Metropolitan Hierotheos of Nafpaktos courageously describes the consequences of Gregory's system, is clear:

> Not only will men's souls be purified and evil done away with, but also the devil will submit to God, which means that he will be saved. Christ's redemption has proven ultimately to be salvation even for the devil. Christ assumed human nature and died on the Cross, and the devil, trapped by Christ's flesh like a fish on a hook, was obliged to yield up the soul which he had seized. Thus this proved salvation also for the devil.[30]

Because Origen was anathematized and his student Gregory was rather canonized and is venerated today in Orthodox history as a member of the great fourth-century Cappadocian triad (of Ss. Basil, Gregory, and John Chrysostom), the question of hell's nature remains alive and well. Gregory's view of hell would seem to derive from his teacher's, condemned by Bishop Alexander as "the relative sense of a certain period, perhaps lengthy but finite."

Isaac of Nineveh (Isaac the Syrian)[31]

The Syrian mystic of the eighth century, St. Isaac of Nineveh, isolated from the Origenist controversy, nevertheless held a view similar to Origen's on both earth (for the living) and hell (for the dead) as a place of pedagogy and loving correction.

I say that even those who are scourged in hell are tormented with the scourg-ings of love . . .. It is wrong to imagine that the sinners in hell are deprived of the love of God . . . But the power of love works in two ways: it torments those who have sinned, just as happens among friends here on earth; but to those who have observed its duties gives delight. So it is in hell: the contrition that comes from love is its harshest torment."[32]

As Hilarion Alfeyev describes Isaac's cosmogony, "Divine love was the main reason why God created the universe and is the main driving force behind the whole of creation."[33] In Isaac's theology, the love of God for his creation over-rides all other mechanisms, allowing him to patiently suffer the workings of evil, "gently enduring its importunity, the various sins and wickednesses, the terrible blasphemies of demons and evil men,"[34] and essentially overpowers any possi-bility of permanent retributive justice in the next world.[35] Indeed, vengeance and retribution do not pertain to the godhead, either in this world or the next. "He has a single ranking of complete and impassible love towards everyone, and he has a single caring concern for those who have fallen, just as much as for those who have not fallen."[36] Thus while Isaac does not deny the existence of hell before the eschaton, he denies the view that it is a place of punishment. Like God's chastising on earth, the purpose of hell, as Kallistos Ware says of Isaac, is "never retributive and retaliatory, but exclusively reformative and therapeutic."[37] As Isaac wrote in his 45th *Homily*, "God chastises with love. Not for the sake of revenge—far be it!—but seeking to make whole His image. . . . Love's chastisement is for correction, but it does not aim at retribution."[38]

And at the eschaton? Eternal damnation of anything God has created is, in fact, impossible. "It is not [the way of] the compassionate Maker to create ratio-nal beings in order to deliver them over mercilessly to unending affliction."[39] Therefore in Isaac's eschatology, there can be only what he calls "a wonderful outcome," a vision that cannot help but comprise the entirety of the creation that God generated out of such love, subsuming all beings in their original source. God's love will have the inexorable force of tidal waves. Isaac's eschatol-ogy is above all symmetrical: the end will mirror the splendid beginning, which was one of superabundant creation in love. But here again, as does Origen, Isaac deploys the language of "mystery" to describe the final salvation of all, including the redemption of evil. There is an apophatic atmosphere to his anticipation:

What a mystery does the coming into being of the creation look towards! To what a state is our common nature invited! What love served to initiate the creation of the world! . . . In love did he bring the world into existence; in love is he going to bring it to that wondrous transformed state, and in love will the world be swallowed up in the great mystery of him who has performed all these things; in love will the whole course of the governance of creation be finally comprised.[40]

In his *Ascetical Homilies*, Isaac becomes more specific about the fate of hell and its occupants: "I am of the opinion that He is going to manifest some wonderful outcome, a matter of immense and ineffable compassion on the part of the glorious Creator, with respect to the ordering of this difficult matter of [Gehenna's] torment: out of the wealth of His love and power and wisdom will become known all the more—and so will the insistent might of the waves of his goodness."

As with Origen and Gregory, Isaac's foundation for so compelling a view of the end of all things, and particularly of the redemption of evil, is based on his view of God: "There exists with Him a single love and compassion which is spread out over all creation, [a love] which is without alteration, timeless and everlasting . . ."[41] But whereas for Origen, evil will be redeemed at the end of time because of its nature as an unfortunate and hence ultimately correctable exercise of free will, for Isaac, evil will be redeemed because God cannot do otherwise. Hence Isaac can say that at the end of all things, "no part belonging to any single one of [all] rational beings will be lost."[42] Ware rightly invokes the notion of *therapeia* in describing Isaac's view of suffering on both sides of the veil, thus linking his theology to the original meaning of *apokatastasis* as a term of medical healing, which both Origen and Gregory metaphorically affirm. For Isaac, that "healing" or restoration is an ongoing theurgic activity that at the end of time will be fully realized, sublimated, and universalized.

"The Restoration of All": an esoteric secret?

"The end of all things," as Frodo describes the fiery apocalypse before his eyes, scarcely seems as though it could be a more public event. And yet the nature of that event, and in particular the ultimate fate of evil at the end of the world, has remained not only a controversial topic in orthodox Christian theology, but interestingly, an often suppressed one. Even among those who espouse, with Origen, St. Gregory of Nyssa, and St. Isaac the Syrian, the redemption of all, an intriguing quality of hiddenness has obtained: this possibility should *not* be made known to all. Huston Smith describes a week-long trek in the Himalayan foothills in 1964 with Father Lazarus, a missionary of the Eastern Church in India for twenty years, in which the priest responded to Smith's attraction to Hinduism "because of its doctrine of universal salvation. Its alternative, eternal damnation, struck me as a monstrous doctrine that I could not accept."[43]

Father Lazarus told Smith that universal salvation was, in his view, the great secret of Christian wisdom—"the exceptional character of the revelations"—to which St. Paul refers in 2 Corinthians 7. These were the visions to which Paul was privy when he says he knows "a person in Christ" who "was caught up to the third heaven—whether in the body or out of the body I do not know; God knows—" and who "was caught up into Paradise and heard things that are not to be told, that no mortal is permitted to repeat" (2 Cor. 2-4). "Paul was speaking of himself, Father Lazarus was convinced, and the secret he was told in the third heaven was that ultimately everyone is saved. That is the fact of the matter, Father Lazarus believed, but it most not be told because the uncomprehending would take it as a license for irresponsibility. If they are going to be saved eventually, why bother?"[44] Smith observes that "that exegesis solved my problem and has stayed in place ever since."[45] But Father Lazarus was not alone in expressing his fears that widespread knowledge of the extent of divine grace might undermine religious devotion and especially moral behavior. With the threat of punishment removed, what would be the incentive for human righteousness? So goes the thinking. Thus it is not surprising to find that Father Lazarus identifies the content of Paul's secret, learned in his *merkavah*-like ascent into the "third heaven" of the seven identified by the mystics of the rabbinic period, with the "secret" of universal salvation. This is apparently a secret that must be kept at all costs, and not disseminated. It is treated as dangerous, even by those who do not find it heretical. As the nineteenth-century Pietist theologian Christian Gottlieb Barth expressed it, "Anyone who does not believe in the universal restoration is an ox, but anyone who teaches it is an ass."[46]

Esotericism is often married to spiritual elitism, whereby hidden knowledge—"trade secrets"—are known only to a select few who have undergone the ascetical and spiritual training to be able to receive them. It is deeply paradoxical, then, in a tradition like Christianity, in which so much struggle ensued early on to rescue Christ's teachings from any kind of gnosticism or exclusive esotericism, to discover the idea of such democratic, universal salvation *after* death re-sequestered like a precious pearl. Now the secret known only to a few is that all will be saved; but all cannot be told.

"Mind Your Own Business": the redemption of the devil

The possibility that all creatures possessing free will and moral capacity may ultimately be saved apparently causes discomfort among those who entertain it. Kallistos Ware tells the delightful story of a prospective four-hour car ride with a Greek archbishop of Athens, whom he had just met. Thinking that they could pass the time in theological discourse, Ware asked the archbishop as they began their journey, why, "if it is possible that the devil, who must surely be a very lonely and unhappy person, may eventually repent and be saved, why do we never pray for him?" "Mind your own business," the archbishop snapped in reply, and the four hours in the car were spent instead in mutual silence. Ware defends the archbishop, reflecting Origen's rightful hesitation in speaking of the fate of evil: "He was right." The question is beyond human capacity to describe or theologize.

So far as we humans are concerned, the devil is always our adversary; we should not enter into any kind of negotiations with him, whether by praying

for him or in other ways. His salvation is quite simply none of our business . . ..
[T]he devil has his own relationship with God, as we learn from the prologue
of the book of Job, when Satan makes his appearance in the heavenly court
among the other 'sons of God' (Job 1.6-2:7). We are, however, altogether
ignorant of the precise nature of this relationship, and it is futile to try to pry
into it. Yet, even though it is not for us to pray for the devil, we have no right
to assume that he is not totally and irrevocably excluded from the scope of
God's mercy. In Wittgenstein's words, *Wovon man nicht reden kann, darüber muß
man schweigen* ["Whereof one cannot speak, thereof one must be silent."].[47]

Even *The Return of the King*, in its self-conscious, lyrically-realized eschatology,
contains elements of this tension. Frodo, his finger bitten off by the accursed
creature Gollum, argues for purpose and redemption even in the latter's twisted
life of monomania. He reminds Sam of Gandalf's words, *"Even Gollum may have
something yet to do."* "But for him, Sam, I could not have destroyed the Ring. The
Quest would have been in vain, even at the bitter end. So let us forgive him! For
the Quest is achieved, and now all is over." Gollum merits forgiveness; Gollum
can thus be rehabilitated, even if only in memory. In other words, Gollum's
choice of evil was, in the end, usable by Goodness to its own ends and thus was
redeemed.

A thoroughgoing redemption of evil in *The Lord of the Rings*, however, would
not stop with the redemption of Gollum, a being who has freely fallen from
a state of grace and chosen evil. It would go much further. Such an eschatology
would also encompass the redemption of Sauron. A radical application of the doctrine
of *apokatastasis* would find Sauron and his armies of Orcs, Nazgûl, Ring-wraiths,
Mumakils, and hideous mercenaries lifted from the dust, brought back into
the light: transformed, changed, set upon the path of light, goodness, and
reason. These too would be incorporated into the messianic kingdom over
which Aragorn reigns.

This is *not* what Tolkein gives us, for his is a thoroughly orthodox view of
the fate of evil at the end of time. Sauron lies defeated in the dust.

These unorthodox tensions in orthodox theology remain, and probably
always will, a subsonic skirmish. What is strange, as I said, is that such tensions
exist at all, and that the ultimate destruction of evil has not been universally
accepted in modern Eastern Christian theological discourse. Much of the
"unorthodox" alternative to eternal hellfire seems to originate in two related
theologies, the one that sees all creatures, no matter how far gone, and even past
their incarnation on earth, as always capable of choosing the good; the other
that argues that they will be unable to resist a return to the Source of all goodness, a Source which, as St. Dionysios the Aereopagite wrote in his *The Divine
Names,* in turn yearns for them. The latter view, however covertly expressed in
monotheistic contexts, sees evil as an aspect of the godhead, and hence subject
to its redemptive energies, participating in a teleology inaugurated at the beginning of time and hence fully realized at its end in the collapse of all dualisms.

Notes

[1] J. R. R. Tolkein, *The Lord of the Rings* (New York: Houghton Mifflin: 1994 [1955]), 925–26.

[2] See "The Catechetical Homily of St. John Chrysostom," read out from The Lenten Triodion every Pascha in every Orthodox church at the midnight Resurrection Service during the Great Vigil: "It [Hades] was embittered because it was mocked [by Christ's death and arrival into Hades]."

[3] The Eddic prophecy of the seeress roused by Odin at the gates of Hell, where she slept in her grave.

[4] David Colbert, *The Magical Worlds of Lord of the Rings* (New York: Berkley Books, 2002), 129. Colbert notes that "[c]ritic Randel Helms declares the stories of Sauron and Satan align 'point by point.'"

[5] *The Letters of J. R. R. Tolkein*, ed. Humphrey Carpenter with Christopher Tolkien (London: George Allen and Unwin, 1981), 243.

[6] Paul Ricoeur, *The Symbolism of Evil* (Boston: Beacon Press, 1967).

[7] John Chryssavgis, *Repentance and Confession in the Orthodox Church* (Brookline, MA: Holy Cross Orthodox Press, 1988), 11 n. 6.

[8] Basil the Great, *An Interpretation of 150 Psalms of David*, vol. 2, trans. John Chryssavgis (Thessalonika: Orthodox Kypseli, 1981), 630, 646.

[9] This finality is later instantiated in the Nicene Creed: "He will come again in glory to judge the living and the dead, and his kingdom will have no end."

[10] Archimandrite Sophrony (Sakharov), *Saint Silouan the Athonite*, trans. Rosemary Edmonds (Maldon, Essex: Stavropegic Monastery of St John the Baptist, 1991), 48.

[11] Bishop Hierotheos of Nafpaktos, *Life After Death* (*I Zoi Meta tou Thanatou*), trans. Esther Williams (Levadia: Birth of the Theotokos Monastery, 1996).

[12] Bishop Kallistos Ware, "Dare We Hope for the Salvation of All?", in *The Inner Kingdom, The Collected Works*, vol. 1 (Crestwood, NY: St. Vladimir's Press, 2000), 193–215.

[13] Ware, *The Inner Kingdom*, 215.

[14] Archimandrite Sophrony, *Saint Silouan the Athonite*, 48.

[15] R. C. Zaehner, *Our Savage God* (New York: Sheed and Ward, 1974), 278.

[16] Zaehner, *Our Savage God*, 237.

[17] Peter Awn, *Satan's Tragedy and Redemption: Iblīs in Sufi Psychology* (Leiden: E. J. Brill, 1983), 191–92 passim.

[18] Suhrawardī, *Oevures Philosophiques et Mystiques*, vol. 3, ed. S. H. Nasr (Tehran: Imperial Iranian Academy of Philosophy, 1977), 217–22. See also the discussion in Sachiko Murata, "The Angels," in S. H. Nasr, ed., *Islamic Spirituality: Foundations* (New York: Crossroad, 1991), 329–30.

[19] Paul Ricoeur, "Evil," in Mircea Eliade, ed., *The Encyclopedia of Religion*, vol. 5 (New York: Macmillan, 1987), 203.

[20] The later midrash *Mekhilta de Rabbi Ishmael* avers that the place was that of the aqedah, and that God "saw" the blood of Isaac there. Just as he was turned aside in his wrath by the blood of the paschal lamb, the *qorban pesach* smeared above the lintels of the enslaved Hebrew people in Egypt, so his lethal rampage is halted

by the apotropaic power of the life-force of Isaac spilled out in later versions of the Genesis story.

[21] New Revised Standard Version, ed. Bruce M. Metzger and Roland E. Murphy, *The New Oxford Annotated Bible* (New York: Oxford University Press, 1991, 1994).

[22] Robert Turcan, "Apokatastasis," in Mircea Eliade, ed., *The Encyclopedia of Religion*, vol. 1 (New York: Macmillan, 1987), 344.

[23] *Ibid.*

[24] *Ibid.*, 346.

[25] English text, with the Greek and Rufinus' Latin version: *Origen on First Principles*, trans. G. W. Butterworth (Gloucester, MA: Peter Smith, 1973).

[26] This idea of choice continuing after death animates C. S. Lewis's novel *The Great Divorce*, whereby the lost in hell are free to take a bus trip to heaven and stay there anytime they like, if only they will surrender their most cherished character defects—although Lewis wrote with sorrow in *The Problem of Pain* that "some will not be redeemed."

[27] Triodion, ed. Phos, 160 (Gk.), cited in Metropolitan Nikotheos, *Life After Death*, 278.

[28] M. C. Steenberg, "Origen and the Final Restoration: A Question of Heresy," at Monachos.net (http://www.monachos.net/patristics/origen_apokatastasis.shtml).

[29] Gregory of Nyssa, *The Great Catechism*, in *Select Writings and Letters of Gregory, Bishop of Nyssa*, trans. William Moore and Henry Austin Wilson, in *Nicene and Post-Nicene Fathers of the Christian Church*, vol. 5 (Grand Rapids, MI: William Eerdmans [1892], 1972).

[30] Metropolitan Hierotheos, *Life after Death*, 281. He is referring to Gregory's radical claim in *The Great Catechism* Chapter XXVI that "The great adversary must himself at last find that what has been done is just and salutary, when he also shall experience the benefit of the incarnation. He, as well as humanity, will be purged."

[31] I am greatly indebted to the investigations of Isaac's eschatology found in Kallistos Ware, *The Inner Kingdom*, 206–10, and in Hilarion Alfeyev (Hieromonk Ilarion), *The Spiritual World of St. Isaac the Syrian*, Cistercian Studies Series 175 (Kalamazoo, MI and Spencer, MA: Cistercian Publications, 2000), 35–39.

[32] St. Isaac the Syrian, Homily 27, 28, trans. Sebastian Brock, in A. M. Allchin, ed., *The Heart of Compassion: Daily Readings with St. Isaac of Syria* (London: Darton, Longman & Todd, 1989), 53.

[33] Alfeyev, *The Spiritual World of St. Isaac the Syrian*, 36.

[34] Isaac of Nineveh (Isaac the Syrian), "*The Second Part*," *Chapters IV–XLI*, trans. Sebastian Brock, Corpus Scriptorum Christianorum Orientalum 555, Scriptores syri 225 (Louvain: 1995), 10, 18–19. This volume is hereafter referred to as *Isaac the Syrian II*.

[35] For Isaac, we might call the compassionate human heart "theomorphic": "An elder was once asked, 'What is a compassionate heart?' He replied: 'It is a heart on fire for the whole of creation, for humanity, for the birds, for the animals, for demons and all that exists. At the recollection and at the sight of them such a person's eyes overflows with tears owing to the vehemence of the compassion which grips his heart; as a result of his deep mercy his heart shrinks and cannot bear to look on any injury or the slightest suffering of anything in creation. This is why he constantly offers up prayer full of tears, even for the irrational animals

and for the enemies of truth, even for those who harm him, so that they may be protected and find mercy. He even prays for the reptiles as a result of the great compassion which is poured out beyond measure—after the likeness of God—in his heart." *Mystic Treatises by Isaac of Nineveh*, trans. A. J. Wensick (1923), 341; re-translated from the Syriac by Sebastian Brock in A. M. Allchin, ed., *Daily Readings with Isaac of Syria* (Springfield, IL: Templegate Publishers, 1989), 29.

[36] The demons thus cannot be excluded. In the words of Alfeyev, "the providential care of God and his love extend to angels, who were the first product of the divine creative act, and includes those who fell away from God and turned into demons." Alfeyev, *The Spiritual World of St. Isaac the Syrian*, 39, referencing *Isaac the Syrian II*, 40, 2.

[37] Ware, *The Inner Kingdom*, 209.

[38] *The Ascetical Homilies of Saint Isaac the Syrian*, trans. D. Miller (Boston, MA: The Monastery of the Holy Transfiguration, 1984), Homily 45, 48, 230.

[39] St. Isaac the Syrian, Homily 39, 6, trans. Sebastian Brock, cited in Ware, *The Inner Kingdom*, 209 n. 33.

[40] *Isaac the Syrian II*, 38, 1–2.

[41] St. Isaac the Syrian, Homily 39, 13, in Allchin, ed., *The Heart of Compassion*, 174.

[42] *Ibid.*, 176.

[43] Huston Smith, *Why Religion Matters: The Fate of the Human Spirit in an Age of Disbelief* (San Francisco: HarperSan Francisco, 2001), 269–70. This was the same Father Lazarus whom Kallistos Ware encountered in India, and who had such an impact on the latter's conversion.

[44] *Ibid.*, 270.

[45] *Ibid.* That Paul was speaking of himself is almost certain, as he slips into the first person a few verses later when describing his refusal to boast of what he had been shown (v. 6), and of the "thorn" given to him "in the flesh, a messenger of Satan to torment me, to keep me from being too elated" (v. 7).

[46] Quoted in Ware, *The Inner Kingdom*, 214, n. 42; he discovered the passage in Jaroslav Pelikan, *The Melody of Theology: A Philosophical Dictionary* (Cambridge, MA: Harvard University Press, 1988), 5.

[47] Ware, *The Inner Kingdom*, 203.

Desire: Between Good and Evil

Richard Kearney
Boston College

In this paper I will explore two different responses to desire in Western thought. The first conceives of desire as basically evil and gives rise to what I call a hermeneutics of prohibition. The latter views desire as either ambivalent or, at its best, as a function of what is most noble and divine in humans. This I call, with Paul Ricoeur, a hermeneutics of affirmation.

Under the first heading I will consider certain biblical accounts of desire as "an evil inclination of the heart," looking at various passages in Talmudic and Christian philosophy (e.g., *concupiscentia oculorum*). I will also draw here from some Greek accounts of *eros* in Hesiod, Aristophanes, and Plato, which construe desire as an agent of unruly passion and chaos.

Under the second heading, I will identify an alternative and more positive reading of desire in biblical and Greek traditions that has often been neglected. Here desire is recognized as an indispensable function of creation and communion, and is at times even attributed to God. A proper understanding of this function will prompt us to distinguish between ontological desire (the less seeking the more) and eschatological desire (the more seeking the less). One of my underlying hypotheses is that when it comes to "good" *eros*, the old binary opposition between ascending and descending desire is ultimately unraveled and surpassed.

Part 1: The prohibitive reading
(Hermeneutics of Suspicion)

(a) Biblical narratives

In Genesis, Yahweh tells us that the "desire in man's heart is evil from his youth" (Gen. 6.5).[1] The Hebrew term used is *yetzer hara* and is usually translated as "evil inclination of the heart," "evil imagination," or "evil drive." The negative verdict on desire is intimately linked with the role played by the *yetzer* in the Fall of Adam and Eve. The evil desire is what prompted the First Parents to become fascinated and enthralled by the forbidden fruit, desiring to become "like gods" (after the prompting of the serpent in the Garden of Eden). The result was an ignominious fall into mortality, guilt, and shame—Adam and Eve cover their genitals and are hitherto condemned to the shames and labors of menstruation, procreation, and childbirth. But the evil desire of the *yetzer* is more than sexual; it is primarily a desire of desire itself, a desire to possess what the other has, be that other divine or human—in short, a deep metaphysical drive to move from lack to absolute fulfillment. This is why Cain's murder of Abel is attributed to his evil *yetzer*. Cain kills his brother because he covets his relationship with Yahweh. And he then proceeds to blame Yahweh for it, declaring that it was God's fault for creating the "evil yetzer" in him in the first place.

It is no accident, as René Girard explains, that most of the Ten Commandments involve injunctions of one kind or another against the covetous, acquisitive, and idolatrous impulses of mimetic desire. That is, against our human desire to have what we do not have and to do everything possible to acquire it. The root of evil is thus identified with the *yetzer* as a carnal impulse buried deep in the human heart to possess and therefore replace the divine (Genesis Rab. 27, Jalkut Shim. Gen. 44). As Solomon Schecter puts it in *The Evil Yetzer: The Source of Rebellion*, "Sin, being generally conceived as rebellion against the majesty of God, we inquire after the source and instigator of this rebellion. In rabbinical literature the source is entitled *yetzer hara* . . . ."[2]

From this basic prohibition of desire in Genesis and Exodus, we find a whole tradition of suspicion and suppression developing. Let me take just a few examples. First, in rabbinical or Talmudic literature, we find self-denial, contemplation of death and other ascetic practices being counseled as remedies for the erotic drives of the *yetzer*. Indeed, even circumcision is recommended, on occasion, as a means of purging our evil desire: "Remove the evil *yetser* from your hearts so that ye may be all in one fear of God . . . circumcise therefore the foreskin. . . ."[3] A number of other cautionary tales bear out this attitude of suspicion. We read of the Nazarite who had all his hair cut off in order to destroy the *yetzer* that had prompted him to idolize his own image (the rabbinical answer to the Greek myth of Narcissus) (Num. 6.18). Or more dramatic still, we have the case of the Rabbi who prayed for the demise of his nearest of kin when he feared she might become an agent for the power of the evil *yetzer* (Tann. 24a). But above all, the evil desire of the *yetzer hara* is associated with the crime of idolatry—that "strange god" within the heart of man, warned of in Ps. 81.10. As Rabbi Jannai starkly observes, "He who obeys his yetser practices idolatry" (Jer. Nedarim 41b).

In Christian theology also, we find a strong, perhaps even canonical reading of desire in terms of evil. One thinks of a long lineage of suspicion running from the various Patristic warnings against the demonic temptations of sexual desire to Augustine's famous analysis of desire as an evil "lust of the eyes" (*concupiscentia oculorum*) in the *Confessions*. But in the Christian, as in the Jewish, tradition, the desire is evil not primarily because it is some base animal instinct but more interestingly because it is a metaphysical drive to possess what is not ours, and in the most offending instance, what is absolutely not ours is divine power. At its most pernicious, this ocular-erotic drive takes the form of an obsessive *curiositas* with regard to absolute knowledge. "Such empty curiosity," writes Augustine, "is masked by the names of learning and science," but it is really just another name for what biblical language called "the lust of the eyes."[4]

That is why the desire of the eyes, or inner fantasy, is considered even more dangerous than the desire of sexual organs. For while acts of genital eroticism are confined to one person (or at least one person at a time), non-genital or metaphysical eroticism knows no limits. It is by its very nature megalomaniac, serial, endless. Hence it is one explanation for the curious link between sinful *eros* and evil imagination in the biblical tradition (the term *yetzer* is used synonymously of both). Christ too has harsh words for the one who desires to commit adultery with the "eyes": "If a man looks at a woman lustfully, he has already committed adultery with her in his heart" (Matt. 5.27). For here again, it seems, the worst form of desire is not that of carnal fornication but of spiritual fornication—what Luther will call *fornicatio spiritus* or the proud drive to dominate and appropriate what is another's as if it were ours. In other words, we are dealing less with physiological appetite than mimetic or metaphysical craving. And those who wish to reduce the absolute Other to a property of conceptual vision (*visio dei*) are, for Luther, the most egregious perpetrators of evil desire.[5]

I take it there is no need here to track this biblical hermeneutic of suspicion any further in the history of Western Christianity. Reformation Puritanism and counter-Reformational Jansenism offer ample evidence of doctrinal links between evil and *eros* right into modernity and, one might add, into many of the secularized versions of puritan morality that continue to inform our present age, not least in the recent moral crusade led by America's home-grown Burning Bush. Suffice it to say that these various theoretical and doctrinal condemnations of evil desire see it as a spiritual deformation that seeks to replace the fullness of the divine with the emptiness of human fantasy and illusion. Evil desire is above all a sin against the spirit.

(b) Greek narratives

Nietzsche was not correct, however, to claim that it was only Christianity, or the biblical tradition, which gave *eros* poison to drink. The Greek tradition also contributed in its own way to our Western attitudes of suspicion and prohibition. This is particularly so with the allegedly "Platonic" view of things, as we shall see, but already in Greek mythology we find evidence of this mistrust. Hesiod tells us, for instance, that *eros* follows chaos into the universe and so is forever a threat to order and structure. As Thomas Moore comments in his book *Dark Eros*, "This sibling origin of eros and chaos pictures the vast crater that eros can blast when he appears unexpectedly in the center of an ordered life. What is more unsettling than an unsought fall into love? Along with it may come powerful fantasies in which cherished relationships fall apart, or a career collapses, or long-held values crumble."[6] The classic Greek linking of *eros* with a dark underworld or hell is to be found in this famous passage in Aristophanes' *The Birds*: "Then in the infinite bosom of Erebos first of all black-winged Night bore a wind-sown egg, from which in the circling of seasons came Eros. . . . Mingling in broad Tartaros with winged and gloomy chaos he hatched out our race . . ."[7] And so we find that in both of these early Greek sources, *eros* is identified with negative powers of night, confusion, and that gaping emptiness at the bottom of the world known as Tartaros: "A gloomy place through which souls pass on their way to Hades, Erebos is where Eros is born. Erotic experience originates in this gloomy place of the soul."[8]

Plato is the first Western philosopher to formulate a more systematic or rational account of *eros*, but here, I would argue, the "official" Platonic verdict is still ultimately in the negative. (The "unofficial" Plato of *The Phaedrus* and other mystical dialogues is another matter.) In classic and canonical texts like *The Republic* this verdict is pretty unambiguous. We might cite here, for example, the denunciation of poets and artists in Book 10 of the *Republic* to the degree that they foment and foster our passions and desires. Poetry only leads us from reason to confusion, argues Plato, because it "gives us representations of sex . . . and the other desires and passions . . . it feeds them when they ought to be starved and makes them control us when we ought to control them" (Republic 606d).[9] The terms Plato uses in this passage are *to aphrodisia* and *epithumia*.

In the *Symposium*, desire—called variously and synonymously *eros* and *epithumia*—would seem to come off better. But in fact the ultimate account of desire offered by Diotima treats *eros* as a ladder which leads us away from the flesh to a supra-sensible realm of Forms beyond this world. *Eros* is stigmatized here with the character of lack or indigence: Diotima tells us that the mother of *eros* was *penia* or penury. And the ultimate service that *eros* is deemed to offer is to lead us beyond all expressions of flesh or carnality to a zone of immutable ideality. Diotima's ladder, like Wittgenstein's, is really only there to be kicked away again once we have reached the top. The aim is to reach the contemplation of pure and unalloyed Form, "untainted by human flesh and color and a mass of perishable rubbish (*phlearia*)" (212c).[10] Platonic *eros* is, in this influential text, ultimately anti-carnational in character.

In sum, in the canonical Plato *eros* is given pretty short shrift as a human desire for embodied persons or things. There are, it must be said, many contemporary readings which, of course, dispute this orthodox view, suggesting for example that Alcibiades' intervention in the final act of the *Symposium* subverts the Socratic direction of transcendental ascent. But whether we go with the traditional metaphysical reading or the more contemporary rhetorical one, it is safe to say that in Plato's world the divine as such cannot desire. In short, while we mortals may desire the beatific form of the Good (*kalagathon*), it does not desire us mortals. Platonic *eros* moves from lack to fulfillment, never from fulfillment to lack. And since the divine is considered by Plato, then later by Aristotle, as that which knows no lack, insufficiency or movement, divine desire is a contradiction in terms.

For the Greeks, it is true that when desire is considered evil it is more as a failure of knowledge (epistemology) than of spirit or will (ethics). But the fact remains that in the Hellenic texts cited above, no less than in the biblical ones quoted in our first section, desire is evil insofar as it seeks to replace the divine with the human, the timeless with the transient, plenitude with lack, reality with unreality.

Part 2: The affirmative reading (Hermeneutics of Celebration)

(a) Biblical narratives

Having traced what I consider to be some of the most formative readings in the genealogy of evil desire, I now turn to a very different if often neglected reading of desire in Western culture. This involves a hermeneutic of celebration which can also be traced back—like its rival narrative just mentioned—to the very beginning.

Let me start with some biblical sources.

If it is true that several passages in the Torah and Talmud describe desire in terms of "an evil inclination of the heart," there are other passages where desire is recognized as a positive and, at times even indispensable, agency of creation. When Yahweh (*Yozer*) first created (*yazar*) humans with the *yetzer*, deploying the letters of the divine Book of Creation (*Sefer Yezirah*), he said that it was "good" (Gen. 1.31). He spoke likewise of all created things. Indeed the *yetzer* was considered by some to be that "image" of the divine in the human, according to which Yahweh created us. Thus if it is true that the evil *yetzer* led to the Fall, it also led to history and therefore to the promise of a messianic kingdom of peace on earth. And if it is true that Cain reprimands Yahweh for creating him with an evil *yetzer*, causing him to covet his brother's blessings and ultimately kill him, a common rabbinical defense of Yahweh on this front is that God created us free and that we therefore have the liberty to choose whether we follow the evil or the good drives of the heart (the *yetzer hara* or the *yetzer hatov*). Likewise, if it is true that Enosh and Aaron used the *yetzer* to create idols and false Gods, the prophets and psalmists used it to create divinely inspired narratives of salvation, mercy, and justice. (This question of divinely inspired desires and prophecies will also be raised by Plato in some of his mystical dialogues, e.g., the *Ion*, *Phaedrus* and *Timaeus*.)

In his book *Good and Evil*, the modern Jewish philosopher, Martin Buber, offers this illuminating gloss on the activation of the *yetzer*: "The curse conceals a blessing. From the *seat* that had been made ready for him, man is sent out upon a *path*, his own, the human path. This is the path to the world's history, only through it does the world have a history—and an historical goal . . ."[11] Or, as Buber explains, once the desire of the heart is activated and one is no longer content with what one is, one strives for what one *might* be and *could* be and *should* be. The future tense of history enters human consciousness the moment the *yetzer* of desiring imagination is ignited. This is why Joel praises the *yetzer* as the "the hidden one in the heart of man" (Joel 2.20). And one particular Talmudic source even claims that God preferred the songs of humans over the songs of the angels, because only the former possessed the "desire of the heart."[12] It is for this reason that Buber argues that Judaism sees evil as an anthropological rather than cosmological condition. Evil is not some cosmic force that pre-exists the human and somehow overpowers and takes possession of us. Evil, like good, must be seen in terms of human beings' free decisions. Our desires, good or evil, are *our* responsibility—not God's. Thus, as Buber explains,

> If the *yester* in a measure displaces Satan in the rabbinical account of sin, it must be regarded as a movement in the direction of a more ethical and rational conception. For the *yester,* however vividly it is personified, always remains the tendency or disposition of a man's heart. Satan cannot be appealed to for the purpose of explaining the origin of the *yester.* . . . God made the good *yester* also and man is responsible for the evil, or at least for its persistence . . . or the evil *yester* itself is good, or at least inevitable in the world, and men are to turn it to good purposes.[13]

This internal drama of good and evil desires is thought to be at the root of Paul's famous account of his own existential struggle between spiritual intentions and corporeal inclinations.

Indeed, some interpreters go so far as to suggest that the reason God did not create on the Seventh Day was not out of some perverse need for sabbatical self-congratulation, but because he wanted to leave that ultimate phase of creation free for humans to complete. In short, the kingdom of messianic justice is something that humans are called to co-create with God. Buber concludes accordingly that the *yetzer* is *potentially* both evil and good.

> In the midst of it, (our) decisions can arouse the heart's willing direction toward Him (God), master the vortex of the possible, and realize the human figure proposed in creation, as it could not have done prior to the knowledge of good and evil. This is the greatest danger and greatest opportunity at once: to unite the two urges implies to equip the absolute potency of passion with the one direction that renders it capable of great love and great service. Thus and not otherwise can man become whole.[14]

Hence the command to love God with one's "whole heart," meaning with the entirety of one's desiring being.

(b) Eschatological eros in the Song of Songs

It is no doubt within this tradition of affirmative interpretation that we can best locate the erotics of the Song of Songs. For here it is not only human desire that is unashamedly celebrated, but divine desire as well. Or given the dialectical exchangeability of bride and bridegroom in several of the speeches, we might be wiser to talk of a desire that is at once human and divine. The Song of Songs testifies, it seems, to an eros that is at once meontological (moving from lack or non-being/*meon* to fulfillment) and eschatological (moving from surplus towards the least and most lacking of beings). And the "at once" is all important. It is not a matter of either/or but of desire both ascending (*anabasis*) and descending (*katabasis*).

Let's look a little more closely at this revolutionary text, which has caused so much controversy and debate over the centuries in both the Jewish and Christian traditions, but has never actually been banned, despite several attempts. Here *eros* is characterized not as a source of evil but as a source of good.

One of the most revealing verses here is surely the Song of Songs 3.1–4 where the anxious, expectant seeking of the love-struck bride is reversed into a *being-found*, that is, a *being desired*. Here the desire of God is a "hound of heaven" that hunts and finds, a disguised sentinel who finds you out by asking "where are you?"—"Who goes there?"—and you reply, "Here I am! It is me." The lover of God, this verse tells us, exists in the accusative as well as the nominative. It is only *after* the bride has passed the sentinels who "found" *her* that she finds *Him* whom her soul loves!

God, it seems, is the other who seeks me out *before* I seek him, a desire beyond my desire, bordering at times, in the excess of its fervor, on political incorrectness! Solomon's Song is here in keeping with a whole theoerotic tradition which surfaces in a number of texts from Hosea to the Psalms. Ps. 63 is pretty explicit on this score: "My soul is thirsting for you my God . . . My flesh faints for you . . . Feast where all your desires may be satisfied." Here desire takes on the character of suplerfluity and abundance, as in Ps. 34, where we are told that "those who seek the Lord lack no good thing"; or again in Ps. 139, where it is clearly God who now seeks out the human with amorous passion:

> You have searched me and you know me Lord…You search out my path and are acquainted with all my ways . . . You hem me in, behind and before, and lay your hand upon me . . . Where can I flee from you? If I ascend to heaven, you are there; if I make my bed in Sheol, you are there . . . If I take the wings of the morning and settle at the farthest limits of the sea . . . your right hand shall hold me fast. (Ps. 139)

This is a hot God if ever there was one! *Eros* is no longer considered as some fantasy or deficiency but its own reward—excess, gift, grace. Why? Because such desire is not some gaping emptiness or negation (as Sartre and certain existentialists held) but an affirmative "yes" to the summons of a superabundant, impassioned God—"Here I am. Come. Yes, I will Yes, I will Yes."

The lovers' discourse in the Song of Songs is very much inscribed in this theoerotic tradition. It powerfully testifies to the traversing of sensuality by transcendence and of transcendence by sensuality. On the one hand, Solomon compares his beloved's breasts to "two fawns, /twins of a gazelle" (7.4) while she compares his eyes to "doves at a pool of water" (5.1). On the other hand, the amorous passion serves as a *trace* testifying to the unnameable alterity of God: there is even a telling allusion to the burning bush episode of Exod. 3.14 in the beloved's claim that "love is as strong as Death. . . . The flash of it is a flash of fire,/A flame of Yahweh himself" (Song of Songs 8.6). The transfiguring fire of the burning bush here becomes the fire of a devouring desire—the Shulamite woman tells us she is "sick with love"—where the ecstasy of the beloved traverses the incarnational love of God (5.8). And in this crisscrossing of divine lover and human beloved, both are transfigured. Divine desire is embodied. Human desire is hallowed. It is made good.

If Exod. 3 allowed for a God speaking through an angel and a burning thorn bush, the Song of Songs amplifies the range of divine speech to include lovers' bodies and, by analogy, entire landscapes. The landscapes in turn are brimming with fruits (nuts, figs, pomegranates), harvests (wine, honey, wheat), plants (lilies, cedars, roses, apple-trees), and animals (gazelles, stags, and turtledoves). The divine desire of Yahweh's flame here appears to embrace all that is alive. As though the seed of the thorn bush has spread from the dusty heights of Mt. Horeb and disseminated its fecundity throughout the valleys and planes below. But above all, the seed has found its way into the embrace of lover and beloved. The free nuptial love celebrated in this song challenges the cheerless moralism of tribal legalities (the Shulamite's proprietal brothers oppose the relationship). And, in so doing, it miraculously echoes the innocence of *eros* prior to the Fall, when God made the first lovers of "one flesh" and declared it "good" (Gen. 2). And perhaps even more radically, the beloved's desire looks *ahead* to an eschatological kingdom where such innocence may flourish again once and for all. The reference (backward and forward) to paradise is reinforced by the suggestive verse "Under the apple-tree I awakened you?"—an allusion reiterated in the fact that the lover-king-shepherd is himself referred to as an apple tree (8.5). These ostensibly retrospective echoes of a lost Eden are thus transformed here into a celebration of a passionate desire *in the here and now* for a fuller consummation *still to come*. This latter eschatological horizon is powerfully indicated by v. 5.1, among others, which sings of the lover entering a garden full of milk and honey.

It is this underlying eschatological intent which has prompted several contemporary commentators to identify a "subversive" intent behind the Song's lyrical and pastoral tones.[15] We would be mistaken, however, to see this subversiveness as somehow turning the lovers into cardboard characters of abstract allegory. The lovers are not mouthpieces for some spiritual message. They are much more than "personifications" of spiritual wisdom or "representations" of Yahweh's continuing love for Israel in spite of infidelity.[16] These things too perhaps, but much more. The lovers come across as carnal embodiments of a desire which traverses and exceeds them while remaining utterly themselves. Hence the candid corporality of recurring references to limbs, mouths, breasts, hands and navels, etc. Not to mention the sense of deep inner yearning and the sheer naturalism of description which brings *eros* to vivid life: the woman is a lily, garden, mare, vineyard, dove, sun, moon; while the lover is a gazelle, king, fawn, bag of myrrh and cluster of blossoming henna. The powerfully erotic charge of many of the amorous verses and metaphors defies any purely allegorical interpretation: "his left arm is under my head and his right makes love to me" (2.6 and 8.2); he "pastures his flock" among the lilies (6.3); his "fountain makes the garden fertile" (4.15); or "my beloved thrust his hand/through the hole in the door;/I trembled to the core of my being"(5.4).

This kind of language was, according to André LaCoque, almost unprecedented in the Bible. And it was to prove so controversial in the later rabbinical and Christian traditions as to be frequently chastened or censored. And as a certain ascetic and puritanical mind-set took hold, the Song was often explained away in terms of a Platonizing dualism which contrived to take the harm out of its sensual content by attributing its *real* meaning to some supra-sensible metaphysical message—a reading typified, for example, in the refrain "wisdom, *not love*, is divine."[17] In such censorious readings, the suspicion that desire is basically an evil inclination returns.

Equally unique in the biblical Song is the fact that divine desire finds privileged expression in the voice of a young woman. It is the Shulamite who takes most of the initiative and does most of the talking in the Song of Songs. And if the lover-king, Solomon, speaks at some length in his own voice, his discourse often quotes the Shulamite and harks back to her as its source of reference. It is a "woman's song" from first to last and it keeps the heroine centre-stage.[18]

Moreover, since this freedom and centrality of the woman's point of view suggests an Egyptian influence, one might even see the Song as an extension of God's exodic "flame"; that is, an amplification of the voice of the burning bush, which pitted Israel *against* Egypt, to a more inclusive voice which brings them together again in some kind of actual, or promised, nuptial bond (8.6).[19] The Shulamite's passion represents "free love"—she is faithful to her lover "outside matrimonial bonds and social demands" (e.g., demands to remain a servant, wife, child-bearer, mother or commercial family exchange), and this corroborates the view that the Song puts the entire societal orthodoxy into question.[20] The Israelite poetess is not just seeking to entertain her public but also, deep down, to shock them. "The family and familiar guardians of women's chastity, namely the 'brothers' and the night watchmen in the Song, are largely outdone by events over which they have lost control. Those who consider the future marriage of their son or daughter as a commercial transaction are derided. The institution in general is swept aside and the event of love is glorified."[21]

The Canticle of Canticles offers an erotic poetics which sings the unsayable and unnamable by means of an innovative and insubordinate language. Here we encounter a language resistant to both allegorist abstraction and metaphysical dualism. By intimating a similarity of relations between dissimilar things (divinity and carnality), this canticle of *eros* creates a *surplus* of meaning. It twists and turns accredited words and thoughts so as to bring about a mutation within language itself (*catachresis*). And it is this very semantic innovation and excess which transfigures our understanding of both divinity and desire. So that engaging in the Song we can, in Paul Ricoeur's words, think *more* about desire and *more* about God.[22] We can think each of them otherwise.

All of this indicates that burning, integrated, faithful, untiring desire—freed from social or inherited repressions—is the most adequate way for saying a) how humans desire God, b) how God desires humans, and c) how humans, in this light, desire each other. It suggests that human and divine desire may reflect and transfigure one another. A radical suggestion, to be sure, and one which confirms the controversial claim of Rabbi Aqiba that if "all the Scriptures are holy, the Song of Songs is the Holy of Holies."[23]

The eschatological symbolism of nuptial love, witnessed in this text, is enmeshed in an erotics of the body without ever being reducible to it. This elusive effect is accompanied by what Paul Ricoeur calls "a phenomenon of indetermination," evident in the fact that many readers have difficulty identifying the lover and the beloved of the poem.[24] (The lovers never clearly identify themselves or go by proper names: for example, the term Shulamite is not a proper name). So we find ourselves forced to admit that we are never really sure who exactly is speaking, or to whom, or where. We can even imagine that there are up to *three* different characters involved—a shepherdess, a shepherd and a king (Solomon).[25] This puts us on a constant state of alert, like the amorous fiancée herself, as we keep vigil for the arrival of the divine lover. "Who is coming up from the desert?" we too find ourselves asking (3.6). Or to frame our question in more eschatological terms: "Is it not from the end of the world and the depth of time that love arises?"[26] Moreover, we might add that it is precisely the primacy of the indeterminately fluid "movements of love" (Origen's phrase in his famous Homily on the Song), over the specific identities of the lover and the beloved, which guards the door open. We are kept guessing. This guarding of the Song as an open text of multiple readings and double entendres—divine and erotic, eschatological and carnal—provokes a hermeneutic play of constant "demetaphorizing and remetaphorizing" which never allows the song to end.[27]

In sum, what we have here is a story of *eros* that considers the impossible possible, the Word made flesh. Here is a poetic genre set off from other kinds of erotic expression: e.g., romantic infatuation, mystical ecstasy or courtly *fine amour*, not to mention the more extremist genres of matrimonial moralism or libertine pornography.[28] The Song, informed as it is by Egyptian influences, extends the range of Western erotic literature and amplifies the scope of religious expression. The Song marks an opening of religion—understood by Julia Kristeva as "the celebration of the secret of reproduction, the secret of pleasure, of life and death"—to an aesthetics of the ultimate.[29] It adumbrates what we have called elsewhere a poetics of divine epiphany. And the Shulamite herself may be seen, in this context, as a figure who promises the coupling, without final consummation, of desire. Here is a narrative of passion at once "sensuous and deferred."[30]

In short, the Song of Songs confronts us with a desire that desires beyond desire while remaining desire. And it is good. Not evil but good. Perhaps even, in the final analysis, the highest good we have.

Conclusion

Let me conclude, finally, by comparing this biblical hermeneutic of eschatological desire with a certain Greek affirmation of *eros* as good rather than evil. Given the limits of this essay, I will confine myself to a few remarks. Looking to Plato, we could usefully contrast the metaphysical account of desire as lack in the *Symposium* or as disordered passion in the *Republic*, to the more positive appraisal of *eros* in Book XIII of the *Phaedrus*.[31] Here *eros* is described less in terms of ontological privation than in terms of eschatological surplus, namely, as an outflowing from a prior mystical experience of plentitude and nourishment. It is praised as (1) a recollection of Beauty itself; (2) a healing of pain; (3) a power that renews the plumage of the soul (*eros* as *Pteros* or "the winged one"); (4) a source of nutrition and bliss. Here is a select sample of phrases used by Plato to describe the erotically mobilized psyche:

> When one who is fresh from the mystery, and saw much of the vision, beholds a godlike face or bodily form that truly expresses beauty, first there comes upon him a shuddering and a measure of awe which the vision inspired, and then reverence as at the sight of a god . . ... Next, a strange sweating and fever seizes one: for by reason of the stream of beauty entering in through the eyes there comes a warmth, whereby the soul's plumage is fostered . . . as she gazes upon the boy's beauty, (the soul) admits a flood of particles streaming therefrom—that is why we speak of a "flood of passion". . . she is filled with joy . . . then has she refreshment and respite from her stings and sufferings, and at that moment tastes a pleasure that is sweet beyond compare. (*Phaedrus* 251a–52)

Here, as in the Song of Songs, we witness a celebration of desire as flourishing abundance and excess. And as the passage develops we find optical images and metaphors giving way to idioms of the other senses, in particular the tactile, gustatory and olfactory. For here, as in the Shulamite's song, divine *eros* seems to go all the way down. Indeed Plato's recourse in this mystical-erotic text to poetic figures and citations, supposedly derived from Homeric, Orphic and mythic sources, is analogous in some respects to the use of poetical and lyrical language in the Song of Songs. And here, as there, celebration trumps condemnation.

We need not be too surprised then to find a Patristic author like Dionysus the Areopagite bringing both Biblical and neo-Platonic idioms together to celebrate Christ as a divine *eros* that spills out into the entire universe, nurturing and transfiguring all before him. In chapter 4 of his *Divine Names and Mystical Theology*, for instance, Dionysius declares that *eros* is redemptive, empathically resisting the conventional opposition between good "*agape*" and evil "*eros*."[32] *Eros*, he insists, "is eminently a power of unifying, binding and joining. Before subsisting, it is in the beautiful and good on account of the beautiful and good; it is given forth from out of the beautiful and good on account of the beautiful and good . . . ." Dionysus cites approvingly the claim in Kings that "[y]our eros came upon us as the eros of women" and concludes with this rousing liturgical flourish:

Before being, in the good,
flowing forth out of the good to beings,
returning again into the good;
in this the divine eros is excellently
manifested to be without beginning and without end.
The divine eros is like an everlasting circle—

When James Joyce comes to affirm the recreative powers of *eros* in Molly Bloom's soliloquy in *Ulysses*, he does so, like Dionysius before him, by combining the poetic idioms of both biblical and Hellenic ecstasy. "Jewgreek is greekjew. Extremes meet. Women's reason."[33] Imagining Molly's last words as a confluence of the Attic Penelope and Semitic Shulamite, might we not hear her voice as a contemporary conversion of evil desire into good desire, of scatology into eschatology, of perversion into a paradise-to-come?

What else were we given all those desires for I'd like to know I can't help it if I'm young still . . . of course a woman wants to be embraced 20 times a day almost to make her look young no matter by who so long as to be in love or loved by somebody if the fellow you want isn't there sometimes by the Lord God I was thinking . . . and I thought well as well him as another and then I asked him with my eyes to ask again yes and then he asked me would I yes to say yes my mountain flower and first I put my arms around him yes and drew him down to me so he could feel my breasts all perfume yes and his heart was going like mad and yes I said yes I will yes.

Notes

1 *The New Jerusalem Bible*, ed. Henry Wansbrough (New York: Doubleday, 1985).
2 See S. Schecter, "The Evil Yetser: The Source of Rebellion," in *Aspects of Rabbinic Theology*, (New York: Schocken Books, 1961), 242 ff. See also *Encyclopaedia Judaica*, vol. 8 (New York: MacMillan, 1971), 1318.
3 Quoted in Schecter, "The Evil Yetser," 258.
4 St. Augustine, *Confessions* (New York: Penguin, 1961), 174f.
5 John Van Buren, *The Young Heidegger* (Bloomington: Indiana University Press, 1994), 189 f.
6 Thomas Moore, *Dark Eros* (Putnam, CT: Spring Publications, 1990), 22.
7 *Ibid.*, 22.
8 *Ibid.*, 23.
9 Plato, *Republic*, trans. Desmond Lee (New York: Penguin Classics, 2003).
10 Plato, *The Symposium*, trans. Christopher Gill (New York: Penguin, 2003).
11 Martin Buber, *Good and Evil* (New York: Scribner, 1952), 80.
12 Schecter, "The Evil Yetser," 250–51.
13 Frank Porter, "The Yetzer Hara," in *Biblical and Semitic Studies* (New York: Scribner, 1981), 122–23.
14 Martin Buber, *Good and Evil*, 93–97.
15 See André LaCocque's argument that the Song is a subversion of the social, legal and matrimonial establishment: "The Shulamite," in *Thinking Biblically: Exegetical and Hermeneutical Studies*, trans. D. Pellauer (Chicago: Chicago University Press, 1998), 236 f. See also Paul Ricoeur and Karl Barth's eschatological reading of the song in Paul Ricoeur, "The Nuptial Metaphor," in *Thinking Biblically* (Chicago: University of Chicago Press, 2003), 298 f.
16 See Paul Ricoeur's account of certain allegorical readings of the Song in "The Nuptial Metaphor," 287–90. The allegorist interpretation sees the beloved either as the people of Israel returning to YHWH or, in the Christian tradition, as the bride of Christ returning to Christ. Several Talmudic commentaries tend to see the Song as an allegory for the Shepherd leading his lost flock back from Exile to Palestine. According to this reading, the breasts of the beloved symbolize the tribes of the North and South, the "bed of green" symbolizes Palestine covered with olive and fig trees, and the "bed at night" is the bed of Jerusalem.
17 Brevard Childs, *Introduction to the Old Testament as Scripture* (Philadelphia: Fortress Press, 1979), 575. Quoted in LaCocque, "The Shulamite," 238. By contrast, LaCocque claims that the "entire Song strums on the chord of 'free love,' neither recognized, nor institutionalized" (238).
18 LaCocque, "The Shulamite," 243. See also Michael Fox, *The Song of Songs and the Ancient Egyptian Songs* (Madison: University of Wisconsin Press, 1985), 309: "All events are narrated from her point of view, though not always in her voice, whereas from the boy's angle of vision we know little besides how he sees her."

[19] See Michael Fox, *The Song of Songs and the Egyptian Songs* and André LaCocque, *Thinking Biblically*, 243 f. Neither Fox nor LaCocque read this passage, as we do, in the eschatological light of an ultimate nuptial reconciliation between traditional enemies, Israel and Egypt, Jew and Gentile, and other adversarial brothers. For us this is, of course, only one of many readings possible within the semantic surplus of this text as hermeneutically re-read and "re-used" throughout the history of its constant reinterpretation and re-enactment. See Ricoeur, *Thinking Biblically*, 291 f.

[20] La Cocque, "The Shulamite," 245.

[21] *Ibid.*, 253.

[22] See Paul Ricoeur, "From 'I am who I am' to 'God is love'—An Essay in Biblical Hermeneutics" (cited in LaCocque, "The Shulamite," 263). Here Ricoeur suggests that the claim in 1 John that "God is love" provokes a "surplus of meaning" in both the terms God and love. By virtue of this statement "we think more about God and about love." In "The Nuptial Metaphor," Ricoeur makes much of the hermeneutic-linguistic-semantic role of the Song as a poetic reworking and augmentation of meaning, opening the poem up to multiple intertextual possibilities of recital and indeed re-enactment (in liturgy, baptismal rites and sexual acts). "The poetic sublimation at the very heart of the erotic removes the need for contortions meant to desexualize the reference. That it should be poetically displaced is sufficient. And it is this way that the same metaphorical network, once freed of every realist attachment through the unique virtue of the song, is made available for other investments and disinvestments" (274). And so Ricoeur goes on to ask why what is "demetaphorized" cannot be "remetaphorized" on the basis of a "general metaphorization of the nuptial," for example, in terms of an intertexual interpretation of the Song in dialogue with other texts of the biblical and scriptural traditions (276)? This is precisely what Ricoeur himself proposes in the third part of his essay (295–303). Rabbi Volozhyn appears to propose something rather similar when he suggests that the metaphors of fecundity, fruition and flourishing in the Song refer not only to the richness of human-divine love but also to the multiple levels of meaning which flourish and proliferate within the sacred texts themselves, especially when read intertextually or rabbinically, in terms of one another. See Rabbi Hayyhim de Volozhyn, *Nefesh Hahayyim*, translated into French as *L'Ame de la Vie* (Paris: Verdier, 1986), 191–96.

[23] Rabbi Aqiba, Tosephta Sanhedrin 12.10, cited in LaCocque, "The Shulamite," 263.

[24] See Paul Ricoeur on the indetermination and proliferation of metaphorical meaning in the Song, "The Nuptial Metaphor," 268–70.

[25] Paul Ricoeur, "The Nuptial Metaphor," 269: "Is it a question, for example, in 1.6–8 of shepherd and a shepherdess, or in 1.4 and 3.2 and 11 of a king and a woman who might be a townswoman, or of a peasant in 1.12–14 and 7.6 and 13? What is more, the dialogue is rendered even more complex by internal explicit and implicit quotations. Nor is it sure that certain scenes are not dreamed or that they might consist of dreams. . . . These features of indetermination are incontestably favorable to the freeing of the nuptial held in reserve within the erotic."

[26] *Ibid.*, 270.

[27] *Ibid.*, 271 and 274–75.

[28] *Ibid.*, 274.

[29] Julia Kristeva, *Tales of Love*, trans. L. Roudiez (New York: Columbia University Press, 1987), 97.

[30] *Ibid.*, 96. For a more detailed and elaborate reading of the eschatological significance of the Song of Songs see our "Desiring God" in *The God Who May Be* (Bloomington, IN: Indiana University Press, 2001) and "The Shulammite's Song: Divine Eros, Ascending and Descending" in *Toward a Theology of Eros: Transfiguring Passion at the Limits of Discipline,* ed. Catherine Keller and Virginia Burrus (New York: Fordham University Press, 2006).

[31] Plato, *Phaedrus and The Seventh and Eighth Letters*, trans. Walter Hamilton (New York: Penguin, 1973).

[32] Dionysus, *Divine Names and Mystical Theology,* trans. John Jones (Milwaukee, WI: Marquette University Press, 1980).

[33] James Joyce, *Ulysses* (New York: Penguin, 1992).

Evil: Reflections of a Psychoanalyst

Ana-María Rizzuto

The Psychoanalytic Institute of New England

Introduction

The concept of evil subsumes in an abstract name a multiplicity of happenings, events, and human actions that are "physically or morally harmful"[1] to human beings. The harm caused by the natural forces of nature has lost for most modern minds its connotation of evil. Nonetheless, natural disasters causing the suffering of the innocent (in-nocent, those who cause no harm) confront both believers and philosophers with the issue of God's participation in human misery. Theodicies attempt to justify God, but, in the end, the tension between God's justice and mercy remains unresolved.

There is another evil that also claims the effort to justify God. Through the ages, human beings, God's creation, have been the continual source of ordinary everyday evil and also of unspeakable and horrifying deeds. The evil that finds its source in human motivations can be examined not as a concept, but as the result of the psychodynamic disposition of concrete individuals and groups in relation to their own inner reality and their relationships with others. When people, groups, or existing realities are experienced as offensive to the self, as an impediment to compelling personal desires or as enemies, we respond with the desire to eliminate what disturbs us.

The Gospel of Luke offers an excellent example, when Jesus was on his way to Jerusalem: "They entered a Samaritan village to prepare for his reception there, but they would not welcome him because the destination of his journey was Jerusalem. When the disciples James and John saw this they asked, 'Lord, do you want us to call down fire from heaven to consume them?' Jesus turned and rebuked them, and they journeyed to another village" (Luke 9.52–56). James and John wished to destroy the Samaritan town simply because they were not wanted there. If Jesus had not stopped them, it truly would have been a terrorist act! There was no devil pushing them to invoke heaven to destroy the village. They simply wanted to compensate themselves for their humiliation. We all have a very hard time accepting that we want to harm others as James and John did. We prefer to resort to explanations external to ourselves, such as the existence of "a cosmic evil force"[2] that is presumed to be the final source and origin of our harmful actions and the suffering they bring.

As a broad concept, evil belongs to the realms of philosophy, moral disciplines, and religion. But psychoanalysis does not concern itself with the general concept of evil. Instead, it focuses its attention on evil as the adjective that qualifies particular human actions, thoughts, and feelings which may eventuate in physical or moral harm to others. Psychoanalysts, as keen observers of human motivations and the psychodynamic processes that can bring about deleterious behaviors, are interested in unveiling the mental, interpersonal, and circumstantial processes that bring a person to cause or to desire to cause harm to another.

Psychoanalysis is an empirical discipline that obtains its knowledge from the clinical observation of the patient's communications with the analyst and from the theoretical formulations created to interpret the functioning of the human mind. As a result of its source of knowledge, psychoanalysis does not have the conceptual tools to deal with philosophical ideas (such as evil) that belong to the area of abstract concepts. Yet we, analysts, have the adequate authority to assert that the evil behaviors, actions, thoughts, and desires carried out by the people we see in treatment find their source in unconscious and conscious motivations and psychodynamic process. As psychoanalysts we do not need to postulate "a cosmic evil force" acting upon our analysands and influencing them to harm others intentionally or unintentionally. As an analyst, I must agree with philosopher Susan Neiman's assertion that evil has no essence.[3] I have no philosophical authority for my agreement, but my competence as a psychoanalyst allows me to conclude that evil actions and behaviors that harm others can be traced to complex human motivations that may or may not in themselves intend evil results or be malicious. The word "evil" must therefore be restricted to its adjectival function as a descriptor of the harmful result of behaviors, actions, events, thoughts, or even feelings that have brought a person to negatively affect others. Such qualification says nothing about a deep essence that causes a person to harbor evil feelings and thoughts or converts them into actions injurious to others. When people resort to an "evil force" or "the evil one" as the causative explanation for their harmful actions, we analysts must describe such psychic maneuvering as a defensive projection to avoid assuming responsibility for the objective hurt inflicted on others or even oneself.

In this chapter, I will briefly review Freud's use of the term "evil." Then, I will illustrate my points by presenting the treatment and transformation of feelings of a man who said, "I always hurt the one I love—and I like it." Next, I will examine the ideas presented by Emilie M. Townes in her masterful presentation of the cultural production of evil as illustrated by the commercial creation of the Aunt Jemima persona and its destructive effects.[4] Finally, I will reflect on the crucial significance of human relatedness in the developmental formation of the mind as a condition for either considerate or evil behaviors.

Freud and the concept of evil

The examination of the Freud's concordance[5] indicates that he used the word "evil" as a descriptive noun or as a qualifier in the ordinary sense of something being bad or disagreeable. Freud refers in different works to evil sexual desires, wishes to cause harm to others, pleasure in the evil others suffer, evil dream wishes, egoistic evil, and a multitude of evil passions, impulses, and wishes. At the level of individual psychodynamic processes, Freud connects the individual's evil actions and dispositions to the notion of repression:

> Repression invariably proceeded from the sick person's conscious personality (his ego) and took its stand on aesthetic and ethical motives; the impulses that were subjected to repression were those of selfishness and cruelty, which can be summed up in general as evil, but above all sexual wishful impulses, often of the crudest and most forbidden kind. Thus the symptoms were a substitute from forbidden satisfactions and the illness seemed to correspond to an incomplete subjugation of the immoral side of human beings"[6]

Freud developed a grim view of the human capacity for psychic honesty: "We lay a stronger emphasis on what is evil in men only because other people disavow it and thereby make the human mind, not better, but incomprehensible."[7] Freud is pointing out the human ego's disposition not to accept the evil that the ego itself recognizes as present in its actions and wishes. We opt to repress, to project, to displace, to deny, or to disavow any hint or evidence that we harbor evil intentions and wishes that we do not like as part of ourselves. These psychic maneuvers amount only to self deception, as Freud repeatedly demonstrated.

Repression of conscious evil wishes and other psychic defenses, however, do not solve the problem of being responsible for them. Freud assures us that normal people cannot "disregard the evil in the [repressed] id. . . . Experience shows me that I nevertheless do take that responsibility, that I am somehow compelled to do so."[8] We do feel responsible for repressed evil wishes, ignored deeds, and dreams. They become clinically manifest in actions and symptoms motivated by an unconscious sense of guilt. This understanding of repression allows us to say that a significant portion of psychopathology results from the ego's efforts not to confront directly the evil that it desires or has already carried out.

It is clear that Freud locates evil in human desires and intentions at the level of psychodynamic and interpersonal processes. He did not concern himself with the question of evil as an abstract concept because it is located outside the sphere of conscious or unconscious human intentionality. Freud traced in great detail the motivational sources of his patient's evil actions and thoughts. He did not need philosophical concepts to make sense of the evil actions and wishes his patients were describing to him.

The phenomenology of the psychic circumstances that bring individuals and groups to harm others

Human development is an extremely delicate process: during the first few years of life it requires that the young person is provided with the physical and emotional nutrients that are indispensable for the formation of a healthy psychic structure. Each moment of development has its own indispensable needs that must be satisfied for psychic development to continue. Each development stage is organized around significant people capable of offering relatedness and emotional involvement adequate to that particular moment. The self at any stage of development, including mature life, needs other people to acknowledge and reflect its worth and to offer enough feedback to make self esteem and self respect possible. The child invests profound feelings in the persons that provide such indispensable feedback. They are cherished not only as the real people they are but also as idealized beings. The self becomes deeply attached to such persons and experiences the need to preserve the relationship with them at all costs. That relationship becomes the measure for self assessment at each particular moment of development.

Early in life, until development is completed, there is a need for the physical presence of the individual or individuals that sustain the self. Progressively, internal representations of the beloved and sustaining object can provide, through internalization and identification, a sustenance similar to the one offered by actual people. The emergence of symbolic processes make it possible that groups, institutions, shared convictions, ideals, and their symbols become sources of self esteem and emotional support. In summary, self esteem, available loving and loved people, and their symbolic substitutes are the basic regulators of emotional human functioning and of healthy relationship with others. The key component that links self esteem to loving and loved people is the belief and experience that one is seen and known as oneself and, as a natural result, is respected and accepted. This situation obtains universally in all countries and regions of the world.

The conditions described above make us all vulnerable. Frequently, self esteem and respect become entangled in repressed desires and fantasies arising from developmental moments in which either life circumstances or early primary care persons fail to offer the developing child what it needs to satisfy the emotional needs of a particular moment. As a result, the psychic structure becomes vulnerable to situations in which the frustration is repeated or the injury renewed.

In those situations, the individual may unwillingly and unknowingly regress and experience in the present the pain of past. Such regression may lead to the perception that the individual who is causing the suffering in the present is identical to the frustrating caretaker or parent. The individual may be unable to tell those two people apart. The person in the present becomes the frustrating or injurious object of the past. In short, under these circumstances, the other ceases to be him or herself in the eyes of the injured beholder. There is little that person can do to retrieve his or her actual identity. This basic psychic process becomes linked to ideologies, beliefs, institutions, group identity, and other collective sources of self recognition. In that case, prejudiced beliefs may effect the same result. The feared person or group cannot be seen for what it is but evokes the collective prejudice and becomes the generic representative of an enemy that must be avoided, overcome, or destroyed.

To summarize: our developmental vulnerabilities make us all prone, when some repetition of trauma seems imminent, to lose our empathy for real human beings and perceive them as damaging to us, as people we must defend against, stop, force, overpower, push aside, destroy, or confront with other defensive maneuvers. This dynamic process is present not only in individuals but also in instances in which a group, a nation, or an ideal appears to be under attack, vulnerable to the power of others. The first line of defense is to change proper names into the generic name of the offender. We talk no longer about people but about the caricature we make of them as a generic opponent or enemy. We change vocabularies. We no longer say "Lucy" or "Peter"; we say "women" or "men." We do not say our neighbor nation but our "enemy." We do not say a believer of another faith but the "infidel," the "evil doer." We lose respect for others whenever we fear them or think that we are no longer respectable in their eyes. Then, we have to prove, frequently by our overpowering actions or military might, that if they do not respect us they will have at least to respect our power over them. In our conviction of having lost respectability or safety, we lose the capacity to see the other person, group, or nation as themselves. We only see, through the wound we feel has been inflicted on us, a demonized version of them.

"I always hurt the one I love—and I like it": ego-syntonic hurtfulness and its infantile motivations[9]

The treatment of the man who spoke these words throws light on two issues. First, it demonstrates that the persistence of an unresolved relation with an internalized and frustrating mother motivated the patient to torture woman sexually, simply because they were "women." The case unveils an internal psychic obstacle, the pathological involvement with his mother, as the motive for his harmful behavior. Second, it shows that his disposition to hurt women was not the result of a fixed evil tendency that made him act sadistically. The transformation the patient underwent during treatment depended upon the experiential changes he went through with the analyst to become able to recognize and value himself, and to change his hurtful behavior. He was not inhabited by an evil principle. He carried out evil deeds in a desperate effort to obtain a minimum of recognition, a feeling of being seen and responded to.

Mr. T., a 43-year-old man, came to analysis because of his relationship with women. He prided himself in being able to seduce women but lamented he could never find the right one. Most women enraged him and led him to torture them. He felt acutely the "stupidity" of others and their inability to recognize his value and superiority over them. He was always ready to humiliate people or to pick a fight if he felt the slightest offense. He was overtly grandiose in his wishes for power. This grandiosity, conscious, explicit, and greatly satisfying, alternated with fits of rage and fury. The slightest contradiction or event that did not fit his wishes, provoked him to dangerous actions and entanglements.

Mr. T. described his father as a good man of few words, physically very strong, who worked long hours. His mother died during his late teens. He described her as intrusive, meddling with his school work, and dragging him from teacher to teacher. They fought constantly, particularly during adolescence, verbally and even physically. Once, in his adolescence, he shook his mother so hard that he feared that he would kill her if he had continued.

During the first analytic hour, Mr. T. presented a dream: "I am in the Army with others. I am wearing a captain's uniform but it has no insignia. I am marginal, always marginal. I am never in the mainstream of things. I never make a full commitment." From the beginning, he indicated a desire for recognition and felt he could not obtain it. He could only force people to acknowledge him by humiliating them. The analyst did not escape from his manipulations. He made every effort to humiliate the analyst and force her to give him what he wanted. Hours were spent listening to his disparagement of women and his wishes to "fuck their brains out." The analysis was always tense. Every word that displeased him, or suggested to him some limitation in the analyst's understanding, prompted him to ridicule and to devalue her. He demanded absolute attention to his words and perfect remembering of each one of them. Frequently, in moments of intense rage for feeling disregarded, he threatened the analyst with graphic descriptions of his raping her, to convince her that he could make her a plaything for his sadistic and murderous penetration of her.

The analysis uncovered that, as a young boy, Mr. T. had spent many hours a day with his sickly mother as helper and companion. He massaged her, rubbed medicines on her back, attended to her sore feet, and brought her the medications she was to take. He was also very taken with her attractive looks. He desperately wanted to get her attention and approval, hoping she would show she loved him. The mother, instead, was focused on the great dreams she had for her son's professional future and became persistently enraged with his poor performance in school. The boy could not concentrate in his studies because he was taken over by sexual fantasies and constant masturbation. The father remained aloof and uninvolved in the household drama between mother and son.

Post-World War II events (the patient was about 5 years old) deeply affected the household. The father's family had left their East European country of origin much before the arrival of Hitler. The mother had left on her own, leaving her relatives behind. When Hitler came, the entire family was sent to concentration camps. After the war, her life centered on the radio broadcasts reading the names of the people who were still alive. Her tragedy became entangled in the endless fights with her son when she repeated that he was like Hitler. During their intense fighting, the mother humiliated Mr. T. with words and actions, to the point of contemptuously spitting on him. The patient felt torn between an extreme attachment to his mother and a great hatred of her. He felt that she was not there for him, that she was like an impenetrable wall.

The analysis became a constant invitation for the analyst to be involved in a sadistic fight, a replica of his relationship with his mother, centered around Mr. T.'s persistent efforts to seduce the analyst while he continued berating her for her incompetence and stupidity. The analyst needed all of her professional integrity and commitment to sustain the effort to understand the meaning of his hostile and contemptuous displays.

After a period of time, Mr. T. began to concede that the analyst was trying to help him, that she remembered most of what he had said, and that some of her remarks were not as stupid as they had seemed. That recognition prompted Mr. T. to explore his life and behavior in more detail. He described his relationships with his girlfriends and his wish to penetrate them forcefully, to force them to be for him what he wanted them to be. His "forcing" involved sadistic pinching of their breasts or "fucking" them with such destructive desire that the women would implore him to stop. He came to recognize that he wanted to kill them. In a couple of situations he was not far from doing so. The motive for the wish to kill was always the same: the woman's inability to respond to him exactly as he wanted. Frequently, he exploded with insults and hurtful remarks. If the woman cried, he felt satisfaction for reducing her to nothing. He felt contempt for her weakness. Yet, her pain would force her to deal with him. It was during his talking about a situation of this type that he said, "I always hurt the one I love—and like it." What he liked was the feeling of power, of overwhelming the woman and "forcing" her to recognize him. If she was hurting, she had no choice but to take notice of him and to beg him to stop. The power was in his hands.

The progressive analysis of these repeated events and the unswerving respect of the analyst led Mr. T. to recognize that the analyst did not have to be "forced" to listen to him. His analytic regression brought out childhood longings for maternal love and memories of isolation when he experienced his mother as an unresponsive wall. He acknowledged that all his provocation had not distracted the analyst from listening to him. He confessed that at some moments he felt understood and attended to. He had tears of painful recognition in his eyes when he felt that something he tried to express all his life had finally been understood. It was through repeated experiences of this type that he began to feel "fond" of the analyst. After some time, Mr. T. came to believe that he was in love with her. The feeling of being in love with the analyst made him realize that he had never loved anybody in his life. Love was a new feeling he had not known before.

Enticed by his new feelings, Mr. T. wished to understand what had happened to him because he was developing a wish to love without being compelled to hurt. He acknowledged that his failure to seduce the analyst and to engage her in a sadomasochistic relationship without losing her respect had helped him to see that there were other ways of relating to people. Nonetheless, childhood wishes returned with full force. Hours were spent listening to his desire and demand to have perfect sex with his mother and with the analyst, together with the memories of endless verbal and physical fights with his mother.

The dynamic components of their sadomasochistic relationship included Mr. T.'s intense pre-Oedipal and Oedipal frustration with her. Pre-Oedipally, he wanted "fusion" with his mother. He wanted her to attend to him exclusively, to hear him and see him. The mother's illness and her depression about the loss of her family in the Holocaust combined to make her personally remote and unable to respond. Earlier, she seemed to have been able to show him some tender, if limited, affection. In the midst of his transference, Mr. T. overtly expressed his wishes for tenderness, "softness," and mirroring. He came to see that his mother had not been able to respect him but recognized that the analyst had always respected him. He realized that his relationship with himself was a continuation of his relationship with his mother. He said, "I insulted myself. I don't hear me . . . It is ME that is missing. I feel love and affection for you but a 'me' is missing." He also reflected, "In analysis I am getting back something that is really mine. I have to have a sense of security about myself. There is goodness in you. Myself, my 'I.' I have to find what is behind the 'I' behind 'me' . . . If I trust you I can trust myself."

The Oedipal components were equally strong in the second part of the analysis. The fantasies about perfect sex with his mother returned in full force together with tremendous sadistic and revengeful wishes for not obtaining it. When the analyst interpreted that his persistent masturbation showed that his penis was his mother between his legs, he agreed that it was 110% correct. He felt the pain of his empty struggle: "When I am revenging myself on a woman I feel like a piece of meat, completely humiliated." He realized that sex alone could not satisfy him and that he had spent his life between "fighting and fucking." He concluded, "It is the soul that I want to touch."

The sequence of events just described illustrates the progressive evolution of Mr. T.'s psychic change. First, he found his "I," one that he could call "really mine," emerging from the trusting relationship with the analyst. In the context of regression with a maternal analyst he was able to separate his penis from his desire for his mother and to claim it for himself. The separation from the maternal object, the renunciation of the compelling sexual desire for her, and the sense of ownership over himself facilitated the emergence of a wish for meaningful relationships, a wish to "touch" the soul.

Finally, Mr. T. reconstructed his Oedipal struggle: "My mother did not belong to me. . . . We had no language between us . . . I had no right to speak . . . Mother's rejection was compounded by my and her disrespect. My capacity to kill the people I love scares me. I did wish to murder her." He concluded, "My relationship with my mother was a lie. I was not able to be the perfect child. I chose to put myself between my parents. I lied. I was inferior. I felt superior. I want to cry for ages." In a sober mood he concluded that he had to grow up and put his parents together as a couple in his mind.

Mr. T. had extended his relationship with his mother to all encounters with women. He could not talk to women without feeling humiliated, ignored, unheard, and disrespected. Finally, he uncovered the key unconscious conviction that prompted him to "force" women to respond to him. He said, "If I couldn't conquer my mother, how could I conquer anybody else?"

Mr. T. recognized he had to accept his losses. He said, "If I accept that I lost my mother and she lost me, I can be free. Then, I can love a woman." He reviewed his past behaviors:

"I am understanding my narcissism. I'll never be the same after I leave this office . . . I feel shame. I spent a life sexualizing rejection to undo a rejection . . . I kept myself safe by not having relationships . . . I am realizing how bad and corrupt I am. I feel ashamed . . . I can tolerate the shame. I have tears in my eyes. The problem was that we had dishonest communication, corrupt messages with my parents." The relationship with the analyst also evolved in new directions: "How wonderful is to feel connected [to you], to have psychic space . . . In growing up the more I showed respect for my mother the angrier she got with me." Finally he declared, "If I trust you, then, I can trust myself . . . I am changing my perception of women. There is respect here. I have respect for you . . . I am opening the door for affection in me."

The statement indicted the termination of analysis by signaling the transformation of his sadism into the recognition that he had been understood and that he did not need to hurt anyone to "force" them to recognize him. He could see now, after experiencing it in the analysis that he was able to love. That capacity alone was the main contributor to his feeling lovable. His core conviction had been reversed.

Reflections

What were the cultural and dynamic conditions that contributed to Mr. T.'s evil behavior and feelings? First, he had not received from his mother the recognition, mirroring, and respect he needed during his development. Nor had his father helped him to deal with his problems. Second, intrapsychically, he had several responses. He transformed his suffering into a conviction that if he could not get his mother to respond to him, then no other woman would; he could not mourn not having his mother's response; he compensated for it with grandiose, defensive fantasies and behaviors with which he forced a response from hurt women. He felt entitled to that response. It was that entitlement that made his sadistic behaviors ego-syntonic.

On his mother's part, besides her personal pathology and narcissistic wishes for her child's achievements, there was the major trauma of the Holocaust and her grief and guilt over it. Without it, perhaps she could have been more responsive to her child. His father's emotional limitations and Mr. T's rage and envy at watching his parent's affectionate relationship made it impossible for him to ask for his father's help.

What we see in this case is the domino effect of everyday harmful and neglectful actions, i.e., evil actions in the life of a family. When a child has not been responded to during the critical period of psychic structure formation, he may be compelled to do to others what was done to him. We also see the domestic effect of the Holocaust in the relationship between mother and child. The mother's grief and guilt consumed and confused her even to the point of calling her own son Hitler. That name added confusion and disorientation to Mr. T. as a child who barely knew who he was and where he stood in relation to a mother he needed so desperately.

This brief examination of Mr. T.'s domestic and sexual life leads me to a major conclusion: evil is psychically contagious. No hurtful action stops at the moment of its completion: it becomes embedded in the psyche of its victims and perpetrators and that of all people affected by it. Feeling unloved, humiliated, neglected, unnoticed, and impotent to change the situation calls for compensatory moves to make up for the suffering. Frequently, the individual forms grandiose fantasies involving restoration and compensation in which others pay for what the person feels is due to him or her. The feelings and the actions they lead to can also become unconsciously motivated convictions rationalized under the rubric of politics, religion, or even morality.

The case also suggests that evil actions can be transformed by a commitment to offer the individual unswerving respect and analytic focus. Such attention is, in the end, experienced as love and, if accepted, provides the individual with the feeling of being acceptable and lovable. To help an individual in his or her inclination to do harm to others we must offer an experience of recognizable respect and illustrate with actions our capacity to acknowledge the reality of his or her being as valuable in itself. That condition permits the emergence of empathy for the other, when one imagines his or her pain and consciously decides not to inflict pain on someone else.

As a psychoanalyst I draw two conclusions from the case of Mr. T.:

1. Human development is so complex that no measure of good parental intentions will protect a child from pain, suffering, and a measure of humiliation and rejection. Such reality creates the foundation for the tendency to do to others the evils we have experienced. I agree with Freud that honesty demands that we recognize that evil is always latent and alive within us, even in the absolutely best among us, secretly waiting for the right purported injury to feel entitled to harm others, even if it is only in the private reality of the fantasies of our mind.

2. Evil, hurtful behavior is self-perpetuating and trans-generational because of its effect on the injured person's psyche and its embedment in repressed thoughts and wishes that never cease to call for some restitution. Resistance to the transitive effect of having been the subject of evil harm requires profound psychic work and a conscious effort not to surrender to wishes for retaliation. The offended person needs to be able to mourn the injury and accept its consequences to be able to move forward. The task is not easy, either for individuals or for communities.

In the end, we need to see that in the great complexity of interactions in everyday life, none of us can fully escape our unintentional psychic participation in the transmission of evil. Even our best loving intentions may harbor seeds of evil. Only constant self-awareness of our motives and of what we are doing can minimize the evil we transmit. The banality of evil at the psychic level rests upon complacency about our goodness and lack of awareness of others, who deserve our respect.

Evil as part of everyday culture

In her article "The Cultural Production of Evil,"[10] Emilie Townes paraphrases James Baldwin who described being "tired of black folk being treated as mere social agendas rather than as flesh and blood . . . the loss of identity be it stolen, borrowed, denied, or annihilated has consequences far beyond those who are the immediate victims" (31). Townes helps us see that, culturally, blacks have been looked at as a social project and not as living people. As an example, she examines the commercially created image of Aunt Jemima, so ubiquitously present in pancake boxes, as "the commodification of identities in U.S. culture" (32). Townes tells us, "I find that exploring evil as a cultural production highlights the systemic construction of truncated narratives or stories designed to perpetuate structural inequalities and forms of social oppression. I look at the interior material life of evil through these narratives" (34).

Townes informs us that Aunt Jemima was created for commercial purposes by a white man's imagination. She "became a part of minstrel tradition of the 1800's and 1900's," appearing as though she was a real slave although "she came to life from the pens of advertising copy editors and illustrators to 'grace' the pages of ladies' magazines" (38). She was a mythical creature created by the dominant cultural imagination who presented her as a woman who was believed had given her recipes to "a northern milling representative" (39). It was the myth about a black woman, a slave from Mississippi, who revived southern soldiers with her pancakes, and who was supposedly freed after the civil war. In fact she was and is a caricature, a being that never existed. Her continuous presence in supermarkets is due to the fact that "she is profitable and identifiable" because "image matters when it is making money" (41). In short: "Aunt Jemima is a lie modeled after the old black mammies of the south and these mammies never existed in the ways the white southern imagination has presented them to us" (42). The smiling, well-fed, pancake-bestowing Aunt Jemima catering to gluttonous white people never existed: she is an apparently innocent image which has the power to humiliate all the people of her race.

Townes calls us to "dismantle the fantastic hegemonic imagination" even when she knows that Aunt Jemima is not going away. She calls for African-Americans to "name [themselves] with precise righteousness and ornery love blending justice and truth " (42). What is the social and personal harmed caused by the invention and cultural persistence of the image? Townes answers that: "this imagination . . . helps to hold systematic, structural evil in place and spawns generation after generation" (38). This evil permits the dominant groups to obtain the consent of those it subordinates to its rule (37).

What is this "structural evil" when we look at it from the psychoanalytic point of view? It coincides with the core predicament of Mr. T. when he could not get his mother to see him as himself. Each stereotyped person has to wrestle with a cultural pattern that hides his or her reality as a flesh and blood human being. The real person is not seen and there is nothing the individual can do to emerge. The structure of evil in the stereotype is to blur our individual faces to the point that we can neither recognize ourselves nor demand that people look at each of us as we actually are, individuals with a history that must be known if we are to be treated as a person with legal, social, commercial, and psychological rights.

Each person must have the opportunity to become (like Mr. T.) the "I" he or she can call "really mine." There are social and relational conditions for the emergence of such "I." Socially, Townes calls for the right of each individual and the group to be named by means of an "ornery love, blending justice and truth." When we look at an African American woman and we see in her a replica of Aunt Jemima, however modulated it may be, we are not looking at the real person. We are only looking at our image of her. We do violence to her identity, her personal history and story, her need to be recognized as the exquisitely unique individual she is. In short, our mode of looking at her is evil because it causes her relational and moral harm. She cannot be in our eyes the person she actually is.

My description is not far removed from the common dynamics of widespread, violent evil. For Hitler, the Jews were not individuals but a collective and destructive "parasite" in the body of the German nation.[11] Hitler believed that the Jews wanted to "to subjugate the German people and make of it its slave."[12] Their complete elimination in gas chambers was Hitler's "final solution" against such perceived danger. All wars, just or not (if there are just wars!) are based on blurring the face of actual individuals, groups, and nations and transforming them into a collective: the enemy. People who have studied present-day terrorism[13] converge on asserting that the impotent experience of being humiliated lies at the foundation of the motivation to harm others. Mr. T.'s wish to kill his mother and his women lovers originated in his desperate efforts to force her and them to attend to him as himself. He could not tolerate his mother seeing him as a person to spit on or as Hitler.

Psychoanalytic understanding of human relatedness and the potential for evil in each of us

Freud said clearly that evil human behavior is incomprehensible unless we accept that its source lies in our hearts, hidden in our repressed thoughts, desires, and actions.[14] Where do such repressed sources of evil come from? They come from feelings and intentions that our conscious self deems unacceptable because we find ourselves unable and unwilling to confront them as our own. We may ask with Freud: What is the impediment to looking at ourselves as we are, people with good and evil desires? The correct although highly simplified answer is that we want to do anything we can to believe that we remain lovable and acceptable to ourselves and to those we need for psychic sustenance. The same idea can be presented from another angle: we cannot survive psychically without a modicum of love and appreciation, real or imaginary, hoped for or actual.

This absolutely basic psychic law of human functioning is, paradoxically enough, the foundation of all evils harbored in the human heart. The paradox is profound. Nonetheless, that is the way it is, at least for a psychoanalyst such as myself. Why should love and the need for love be the foundation of our evil disposition? The answer is brief: it has to do with childhood development and our absolute dependence on nurturing caretakers: maternal, paternal, physical, and cultural environments. Wexler[15] demonstrates the profound interpenetration between environment and the brain, to the point that the brain and the physical and cultural environment cannot be teased apart. Our brain organization represents the encounter with our milieu. From the psychoanalytic point of view, the relation with parents and the family is the critical factor in the formation of a personal and affective identity, as well as the organizer for all later dispositions for relational and social life.

This being the case, we must ask: What do developing children need to become adults capable of loving themselves and others? For the purposes of this essay I offer a very condensed answer. Children need to be seen and heard as themselves. This seeing and hearing must mirror back to them an image of themselves as who they are at the moment. The emotional response in that seeing and hearing must be complementary (smile–smile; giving–receiving) and have a similar level of affect.[16] The absence of these two features may generate profound shame and humiliation, as illustrated when a person extends a greeting hand and the other person refuses the gesture. Respect for the inner experience and intentions of the child are essential for the young person to feel worthwhile and accepted.

But it is impossible to grow up without having felt at least to a minimal degree rejected, unloved, humiliated, shamed, unworthy, in need of compensation and reparation for some experienced wrongs. We cannot avoid having at least some wishes to harm others as a belated compensation for having felt harmed. This is the potential for evil we all harbor in our beings: a wish to retaliate, to practice the revenge that demands an eye for an eye and a tooth for a tooth. Is there something we can do to ameliorate this condition?

Freud says (and I with him) that our best protection against committing evil deeds rests on our awareness that we want to commit them. That is the first step. The next step consists in finding in ourselves or in our surroundings the psychic nutrients we need to contain our wishes for compensation and retaliation. We need ideals, moral values, and religious convictions to guide our disposition not to surrender to our evil wishes. Some may say that this is the territory of moral education, but moral education cannot have any lasting effect unless it is offered to a developing child or an adult who has experienced a measure of personal love and empathy. Without such psychic conditions, morality or religion remain a set or rules, beliefs, and rituals that do not affect interaction with others, in particular the interaction with others that may be defined as "enemies." When the enemy does not qualify as a full-psychic being, the conditions are given for cruelty, torture, and the compelling need to humiliate in the enemy that aspect of ourselves that has been humiliated by others. Any moral person who intends to remain moral must examine the history of his or her own personal humiliations and rejections in order to avoid inflicting them on others. He or she also needs a commitment to confront the implicit prejudices present in his manner of thinking about others. Such a simple act as buying pancakes may represent participation in a social prejudice capable of erasing the true human face of person next to us in line at the cashier.

In the end, the containment of our evil dispositions rests upon the experience and internalization of genuine loving exchanges in the context of socially shared ideals and convictions that insist on respecting others as they are.

The psychic experience of having been recognized and respected conditions the commitment to respect others. Mr. T., at the end of his analysis, could say: "If I trust you I can trust myself." He could feel that he no longer was compelled to force others to recognize him. He wanted a true relation with the emotional depth of another person: "It is the soul that I want to touch." He could wish for it only after he had taken possession of his own being, the "I" he could call "really mine," emerging from the trusting relationship with his analyst. Such new development allowed him to own his faults and his wishes to kill and harm.

The best protection against unrelenting evil in the world, then, is the effort to offer children and one another, be it individuals, groups, nations or cultures, the profound respect and recognition that each deserves. The task is overwhelming because diversity and difference breed prejudice and contempt. Yet I truly believe it is the best we can do.

Notes

[1]   *Shorter Oxford English Dictionary* on CD-ROM, Version 2.0 (Oxford and New York: Oxford University Press, 2002).

[2]   *Merriam-Webster's Collegiate Dictionary*, 11th ed. (Springfield, MA: Merriam-Webster, Inc., 2003).

[3]   Susan Neiman, *Evil in Modern Thought* (Princeton: Princeton University Press, 2004), xiii.

[4]   Emilie M. Townes, "The Cultural Production of Evil: Some Notes on Aunt Jemima and the Imagination," Harvard Divinity Bulletin 34, no.1 (2006): 30–42.

[5]   Samuel A Guttman, Randall L. Jones, and Stephen M. Parrish, eds., *The Concordance of the Standard Edition of the Complete Psychological Works of Sigmund Freud* (Boston, MA: G. K. Hall & Co., 1980).

[6]   Sigmund Freud, "A Short Account of Psychoanalysis," in *The Standard Edition of the Complete Psychological Works of Sigmund Freud*, vol. 19 (London: The Hogarth Press, 1924), 191–212.

[7]   Freud, "Introductory Lectures on Psycho-Analysis," in *Complete Psychological Works*, vol. 15 (London: The Hogarth Press), 147.

[8]   Sigmund Freud, "Some Additional Notes on Dream-Interpretation as a Whole," in *Complete Psychological Works*, vol. 19 (London: The Hogarth Press, 1925), 133–34.

[9]   This case was published as "'I Always Hurt the One I Love—and Like It': Sadism and a Revised Theory of Aggression," *Canadian Journal of Psychoanalysis* 7 (1991): 219–44. A similar version of this case was published in *The Dynamics of Human Aggression. Theoretical Foundations, Clinical Applications*, ed. A-M. Rizzuto, W. W. Meissner, and D. H. Buie (New York and Hove: Brunner-Routledge, 2004).

[10]   Emilie M. Townes, "The Cultural Production of Evil: Some Notes on Aunt Jemima and the Imagination," *Harvard Divinity Bulletin* 34, no. 1 (2006): 30–42.

[11]   Richard Koeningsberg, *Hitler's Ideology: A Study in Psychoanalytic Sociology* (New York: Library of Social Science, 1975).

[12]   *Ibid.*, 33.

¹³ See Mark Juergensmeyer, *Terror in the Mind of God: The Global Rise of Religious Violence* (Berkeley, CA: University of California Press, 2000).

¹⁴ See Freud, "Introductory Lectures on Psycho-Analysis."

¹⁵ Bruce E. Wexler, *Brain and Culture: Neurobiology, Ideology and Social Change* (Cambridge, MA: MIT Press, 2006).

¹⁶ Ana-María Rizzuto, "Shame in Psychoanalysis: The Function of Unconscious Fantasy," *International Journal of Psychoanalysis* 72 (1991): 297–312.

Index

Lightning Source UK Ltd.
Milton Keynes UK
UKOW04f1046181013

219232UK00008B/62/P